THE
CHANGE
CHEAT
CODE

A LEADER'S GUIDE TO EFFECTIVE CHANGE MANAGEMENT

Suzanne Rudnitzki & Liz Lance, Ed.D

The authors can be reached at thechangecheatcode.com

The Change Cheat Code / Suzanne Rudnitzki and Liz Lance, Ed.D. -- 1st ed.

ISBN:
978-1-990830-84-6 (Paperback)
978-1-990830-92-1 (Hardcover)
978-1-990830-95-2 (Hardcover)
978-1-990830-93-8 (Kindle)
978-1-990830-94-5 (Audiobook)

TABLE OF CONTENTS

FOREWORD

This book belongs on the desk of every leader managing change.

This is a vital book for leaders ready to embrace the messy, iterative and ultimately reinforcing reasons why humans in groups actually do change.

So many organizations today are grappling with the forces driving linearization and automation of change. With Big Data and AI, it is more than tempting to think that humans in groups can work with routines and APIs for change that make it habitual, continual, and perhaps not even painful. But we're not machines yet, and it's much more realistic to recognize change as episodic, uneven, and anxiety-producing.

The organizational change framework proposed by Rudnitzki and Lance has four cornerstones that are not routines as much as they are uniquely human abilities. We are able to deeply listen and communicate motivational nuances (I have yet to see a machine do this, and while I suspect there are generative AI devotees who have plenty of examples, human empathy still stands alone). We feel, acknowledge and embrace the anxieties (fears) that go along with doing something in a new way that is better than the old way. We recognize how important adaptations and iterations are in an active learning process, because without the ability to fine-tune and correct small errors, we too often find ourselves paralyzed into doing nothing. And we find ways to recognize, celebrate and reward forward progress so that even if incomplete, we come back tomorrow and keep at it.

The Change Cheat Code introduces a practical change framework. The four cornerstones are mnemonic and memorable. The underlying philosophy is modern and humanistic: humble inquiry and psychological safety truly make a difference in innovation and organizational transformation. And the expectations set by Rudnitzki and Lance are intrinsically practical—clarity is achievable (by hearing what others are really saying), and even small changes are laudable, especially if you as a leader—or you and your leaders—embrace an adaptive spirit to improve day by day.

There is an old line from a T.S. Eliot poem (*The Rock*, 1934) that refers to humans facing challenges "dreaming of systems so perfect that no one will need to be good". Rudnitzki and Lance's work invites us to flip that idea: to focus on being good (clear, curious, action-oriented) as a way to move our systems closer to better. *The Change Cheat Code* encourages the journey of change regardless of where your specific destination may be.

The last thing a change book should do is give you any reason to think you have failed to change. This book does the opposite—it gives you a simple and practical model to get you started and keep going, so at worst, you might wonder why you did not start the journey sooner!

Peter A. Schein
Bestselling Author of *The Humble Leadership Series*

INTRODUCTION

**Change doesn't have to be hard
—when you know the cheat code.**

Change is happening faster and more frequently than ever before. Advances in technology, global connectivity, and the rapid exchange of ideas are accelerating innovation, constantly bringing new products, processes, and challenges that require us to adapt.

Yet, despite this constant stream of change, managing it remains one of the most challenging tasks in both our personal and professional lives. Whether at work or at home, change takes many forms—shifts in market conditions, technological advances, career transitions, or even adjustments in personal relationships. How we manage these changes can profoundly impact the outcomes. When handled poorly, change disrupts daily routines, lowers morale, and can even result in financial setbacks. But when managed well, it propels us forward, opening up new opportunities for growth and success.

The ability to adapt and lead through change isn't just a nice-to-have anymore—it is essential. We must all equip ourselves with the tools to move and lead others through change. Organizations that can move quickly and process change efficiently gain a competitive advantage. Looking back on history, we can see the gravestones of past organizations that could not change fast enough. Unfortunately, these failures will be more prevalent in our future. Names like Kodak, Blockbuster, Polaroid, Sears, and RadioShack serve as cautionary tales of how important it is for businesses to continuously change and innovate to remain competitive.

Why, then, is change so often mismanaged? The answer often lies in common pitfalls: underestimating the scope and time required for adaptation, miscommunicating key messages, turning away from feedback, or failing to engage the right people in meaningful ways. These mistakes can turn what should be a positive transformation into a stressful ordeal, leading to missed opportunities and unnecessary setbacks.

But here's the good news: all hope is not lost. From the failures and missteps of those who came before us, we've learned that change, though challenging, is also predictable. It follows a certain pattern or formula, and once you understand this formula, you can apply it to almost any situation or challenge you encounter. This book will show you that repeatable formula, empowering you to not only navigate change but to lead it with confidence and success. That's what *The Change Cheat Code* is all about.

Now, we didn't just learn this from research—we've lived it. We—Suzanne and Liz—have spent years leading organizations, teams, and individuals through high-stakes transformations. We've worked through mergers, acquisitions, cultural shifts, leadership transitions, downsizing, and business overhauls in companies ranging from fast-moving startups to global enterprises. Sometimes we got it right. Other times, we learned the hard way. But through it all, one thing became crystal clear: most organizations don't struggle because change itself is hard. They struggle because they don't have a clear, repeatable way to manage it.

That's why we created *The Change Cheat Code*.

The idea for *The Change Cheat Code* started when Suzanne was leading a company through yet another transformation and saw just how much people struggled—not because they weren't capable, but because they lacked a simple, practical framework for navigating change. At the time, the Tuckman Model (Forming, Storming, Norming, Performing) was circulating in the organization, and she admired how simple yet powerful it was. It made her wonder: Why don't we have something this intuitive for managing change? So she built it.

That's when she started developing *The Change Cheat Code*. As the model took shape, Liz joined the journey, bringing expertise in project management, organizational change and people leadership. Together, we put this framework to the test in real-world situations, refining it as we led teams through uncertainty, applied it in high-growth environments, and proved its effectiveness in both large-scale business transformations and personal life transitions.

Along the way, we studied dozens of change models—Kubler-Ross, Satir, Kotter, Bridges, and more—but we saw the same gaps over and over again. Some models focus only on process, emphasizing urgency and execution but overlooking the human side of change. Others focus on people, offering guidance on emotional buy-in but little structure on what to actually do. And almost none of them give leaders a simple, repeatable way to manage both execution and emotional resistance at the same time. Too often, leaders are told to just "push through resistance" rather than being given the tools to help people move through it effectively.

This is exactly where *The Change Cheat Code* stands apart.

This book gives you a practical, easy-to-remember framework for navigating change successfully—whether you're leading a major transformation at work or adjusting to a shift in your personal life.

The Change Cheat Code is designed to make navigating change easier—no matter the context. Our goal is to equip you with the insights and tools needed not just to manage change, but to lead it successfully. By mastering the fundamental principles of change, you can become a more effective leader and a true change champion. The strategies in this book will help you turn uncertainty into structure, resistance into momentum, and potential chaos into a clear path forward.

At the heart of *The Change Cheat Code* are four distinct stages:

1. Hear – Recognizing the need for change and ensuring people understand it.

2. Fear – Addressing resistance, uncertainty, and emotional reactions to change.

3. Near – Moving from uncertainty to action, ensuring the change gains traction.

4. Cheer – Reinforcing and sustaining the change so it becomes the new normal.

These four stages follow the way people naturally process change, making them easy to apply in any situation.

As you move through this book, you'll see how these stages play out in real life. Many of the stories we share come directly from our own experiences leading change—names and details have been adjusted, of course, but the lessons remain the same.

Part 1 will walk you through each stage, helping you decode the psychology behind change and why people resist it both at the individual and organizational level. Part 2 is your playbook, packed with step-by-step strategies, real-world examples, and practical tools to help you apply *The Change Cheat Code* in any situation.

By the time you finish this book, you won't just be surviving change—you'll be leading it and using it as a strategic advantage. You'll know how to turn uncertainty into opportunity, resistance into momentum, and disruption into innovation.

Change doesn't have to feel unpredictable or overwhelming. It can be done well, repeatedly—when you know the cheat code.

Let's dive in.

PART 1: UNDERSTANDING THE CHANGE CHEAT CODE MODEL

Welcome to Part 1, where we begin learning to navigate and lead change effectively. This book is organized into two specific parts. Part 1 is the theoretical understanding of change and navigating change. Part 2 contains practical applications of change management advice and practices.

Part 1 is foundational, crafted to introduce you to the sequential stages of change that make up the change cheat code: Hear, Fear, Near, and Cheer, which each serve as a building block for mastering the dynamics of change. By understanding this model, you'll gain insights into the psychological, behavioral, and logistical aspects of managing transitions, whether in a corporate or personal setting.

In the following chapters, we'll explore each stage in detail. We will uncover the typical reactions individuals and organizations experience as they traverse these stages. From initial awareness to final acceptance, we aim to equip you with a comprehensive understanding of the natural progression through these stages. This knowledge is not just theoretical but immensely practical, providing you with the tools to anticipate challenges, leverage opportunities, and mitigate potential setbacks before they arise.

Each chapter in Part 1 of this book will conclude with key takeaways, practical tips, dos and don'ts, and a short quiz to test your understanding of the stage. We'll take this same approach for each stage: Hear, Fear,

Near, and Cheer, ensuring you have a thorough grasp of every stage of the change process.

With this structure, we ensure you have a solid grasp of the theoretical underpinnings before moving on to the practical applications in Part 2, the playbook. This approach is designed to inform and empower you, offering a lens through which you can effectively view and manage change. Now, as we embark together, prepare to transform how you perceive and lead change, making it a less daunting and more rewarding journey.

CHAPTER 1

THE CHANGE CHEAT CODE MODEL

Our sales team had been barely holding things together for months. We were hitting numbers, but only because our reps were hustling hard and working around our tools, not with them. Our Customer Relationship Management system (CRM) was clunky, outdated, and filled with years of inconsistent data entry and one-off workflows that only half the team understood. Notes were missing. Deals were miscategorized. Forecasts were off.

Leadership was pushing for better data and more predictability. Our Sales Professionals were asking for less administrative work, more support, and AI tools. I thought I had a solution that could serve both: a new CRM platform that promised automation, clean dashboards, and smarter sales motion. I made the case, got the budget, everyone nodded, and there was not a single objection or comment.

But what I missed was this: no one had asked for a CRM change. It wasn't their priority. It was mine. I only learned this lesson after it was too late.

Here is how the CRM rollout saga went…

It was two weeks into the second quarter of the year and an ideal time to make the CRM change. Our contract with the legacy CRM was up for renewal and I didn't want to commit to another year of the same problems. With the blessing of the whole executive team, I did not renew our existing agreement. That decision gave us a tight, non-negotiable timeline. We had just six weeks to prepare, migrate, and go live. All leaders, particularly the CFO, were on board.

We had reviewed all our options, received budget approval, and hired a project manager, so we were more than ready for the change. Let the change begin!

Two weeks before launch, I gave the team sandbox access. I posted links to tutorials, dropped a checklist in Slack, and hosted a quick walkthrough over Zoom. I figured we'd learn by doing, because who likes training classes anyway?

Fast forward to implementation day, we flipped the switch on a Monday morning. Everything was to now be happening in the new CRM. By Tuesday, utter chaos had set in.

Key accounts were missing contact histories. Opportunities had been split across duplicate records. Notes hadn't been transferred. Quotes couldn't be located. New opportunities and contact records couldn't be saved correctly. No one knew what was up to date, or where to find anything. Reps stopped trusting the system and started rebuilding their own files, spreadsheets and tracking systems.

One rep joked she was "going full analog" and went back to handwritten notes. Another privately created a duplicate pipeline in a word doc "just in case." People started texting managers instead of logging activity, because it felt safer. Communication broke down. Tension climbed.

Then the real consequences hit.

We missed a client renewal—because no one knew who was following up or what had happened. We had not configured renewals correctly in the system. The next, a major opportunity stalled when a contract version disappeared. Our most tenured rep resigned, citing system fatigue and lack of support. Others started quietly updating their résumés and I could see their LinkedIn profiles being changed.

The rollout of the new CRM didn't just slow us down. It shattered confidence, fractured communication, lost us revenue and exposed the cracks in our culture.

One night, I stayed late, staring at a whiteboard filled with deal names, timelines, and crossed-out fixes. I finally admitted what I hadn't wanted to say out loud: this wasn't just a system failure. It was a leadership failure.

I had rolled out a change without earning trust. I skipped the hard work of building understanding, listening to concerns, and preparing people for what the transition would actually feel like. I had confused a new tool for a strategy.

The next morning, I called Brian, a longtime friend and advisor who'd seen more change efforts than I could count.

"It's fixable," he said. "But you can't just fix the tool. You have to fix how you're leading through the change."

So we hit pause and I pivoted to a better way to lead change.

We didn't just relaunch the software—we reintroduced the change itself. We walked the team through why the change was necessary and where we went wrong. We solicited fears and frustrations. We rebuilt the rollout plan together, this time with their input and their timing. We invested in data cleanup, created a shared vocabulary, recruited change champions, and documented clear paths for support and feedback. We slowed down to go faster.

It took weeks. Maybe longer than anyone wanted. But slowly, things turned around.

Finally, people started using the system again. Questions shifted from "Where is my deal?" to "How do I optimize this step?" Skepticism gave way to momentum. Performance stabilized. The team didn't just adapt—they began to lead the change forward.

That experience reshaped how I lead. I learned that change doesn't fail because people resist it; it fails when leaders don't guide people through it intentionally. With Brian's help, I realized and lived the experience of using a change process not only as a critical leadership skill, but a strategic advantage.

We have all been through change in our lives; therefore, we all have personal experiences with change. Whether you've relocated, transitioned through relationships, changed schools, or started a new job, each of these experiences has introduced shifts in your life that required you to adapt. Change is a universal experience, and it's something we all share, even if the specifics differ from person to person.

If you're a parent, you've likely experienced hundreds, if not thousands, of change cycles with each of your children. From the sleepless nights of infancy to the unexpected challenges of adolescence, you've navigated countless shifts. You've watched your children transform from curious and obedient youngsters, wide-eyed in awe of the world, to independent and sometimes rebellious teens, confident in their understanding of the world around them.

But it's not just your children who have changed, so have you. As you've matured through different stages of life, you've encountered a multitude of changes, each shaping who you are today.

Imagine all the changes we've gone through in our adult lives—from new technology like smartphones, streaming services, and shifts in how we work. Every day, we are facing new tools to use, hit with changes to absorb, use, and adapt to. When you compare the amount of change we've experienced with that of our parents or grandparents, it's clear that the pace of change today is far more intense, requiring us to adapt faster than ever.

You have also experienced change within your organization, either as a participant or as a leader. We've all seen examples of change being mismanaged, as well as change that was handled smoothly. While change management is not new, being intentional about how we approach and implement change can make a huge difference in the outcomes. It can determine how quickly people adapt and how successful the change will be.

For example, think about moving to a new home. If you take the time to plan ahead—sorting out your packing, arranging movers, and setting up utilities before you arrive—the transition will be much smoother. You'll settle in quickly and feel comfortable in your new space sooner. On the other hand, if you move without much planning, you might find yourself surrounded by boxes, with no idea where anything is, and struggling to get things done. The stress builds up, and it takes much longer to feel settled. Being intentional about how you approach the move ensures a faster, more successful transition.

Working with many organizations, we've seen that most leaders have a clear vision for where they want to go. However, their success often depends on how well they manage the change process. Leaders who ignore proper change management often leave their organizations in a state of fear, stagnation, or even chaos. On the other hand, leaders who embrace thoughtful, well-planned change management (which doesn't mean slowing down) create organizations that move together, gain momentum, and achieve incredible results. These leaders clearly have a strategic advantage.

Starting a change with a clear plan and process will help you organize your thoughts and prepare for what's ahead. You will also feel more confident when the chaos of change begins, knowing you have a solid plan. While no one has all the answers when they begin planning for change, starting with a model or formula gives you a framework to follow. Having a repeatable model for change gives both leaders and teams confidence in the steps needed to succeed.

This chapter aims to introduce a formula for change management that will serve as the jumping-off point for the rest of the book. This formula provides the framework for change, which is designed to be understandable, applicable, and repeatable. While the primary focus of this book is on leadership and leading change at work, these lessons can easily be applied to personal situations as well.

The Hear, Fear, Near, Cheer change cheat code model is intentionally simple and easy to remember. While there are untold numbers of studies, books, and methods to describe change, the most effective model is easy to understand, relayed to others, and repeatable. You have the best chance of remembering and using something that is easy to understand, just like you learned your ABCs to a melody or use a rhyme to determine which months have 31 days. The simplification of this model is not to be elementary but rather to drive rapid understanding and relatability.

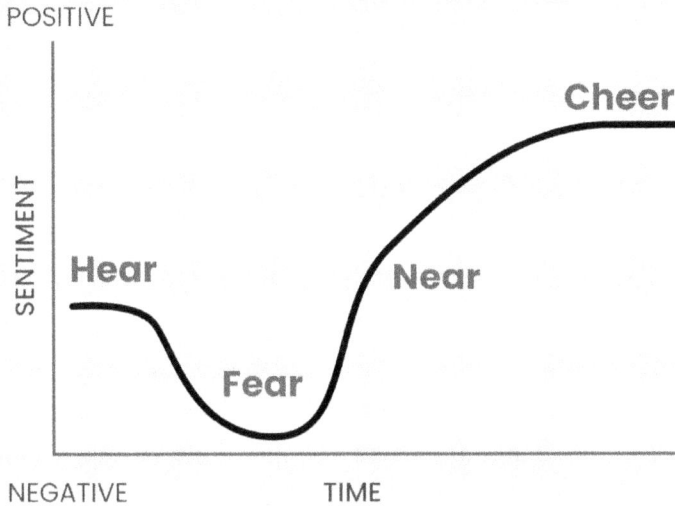

Figure 1.1: The Change Cheat Code Model

This curve illustrates what is sometimes described as a roller coaster of emotions, not because it's fun to go through, but rather because of its ups and downs, twists and turns, and sometimes bottom-dropping emotions that come with riding a roller coaster. Take note that the reason for showing these stages on a curve is to indicate that change is not linear. People ride this unfortunate change roller coaster frontwards and backwards. They get jerked around a lot. Sometimes, they feel like they are going to throw up, and sometimes they scream for fun.

While the change roller coaster can be daunting, those who learn when to grab on, when the drop is coming, and what the loops feel like will become more proficient riders and experience less pain throughout the process. They will also become role models for the next change and will likely move through it faster.

The four stages of change described in this book are:

1. Hear
2. Fear
3. Near
4. Cheer

It is convenient that the stages rhyme and it is intentional that they are easy to remember. Change is most easily described in four stages. There are different emotions and reactions that can be predicted at each stage of change. People hear about a change. They will fear the change. They will get nearer to the change and cheer when it's done. At that point, it may all start over again. When you reflect on change in your life, you realize you have ridden this roller coaster many times.

My friend Sarah and her family had lived in their cozy downtown apartment for years, but with a growing family, they needed more space. Sarah had heard about a charming house in a nearby suburb with a spacious yard and excellent schools. The idea of moving excited her and her family, promising more room for her children to play and a quieter environment. However, fear soon set in. Sarah worried about leaving behind the familiarity of their current neighborhood, the convenience of being close to her workplace, and the disruption to her children's routines, not to mention the additional cost and maintenance work.

Sarah and her family resolved their initial worries and decided to move. As moving day approached, Sarah got to work preparing for and actively participating in the change. She started packing, making lists of things to do, and visiting the new house more frequently to measure rooms and plan furniture arrangements. She also reached out to new neighbors and learned more about the community. Her children expressed concerns about changing schools and leaving friends behind, so Sarah arranged a visit to their new school and scheduled playdates with kids in the new neighborhood.

Finally, the moving day arrived, and Sarah and her family settled into their new home. They began to believe in the positive aspects of the change as they experienced the benefits firsthand. The kids loved their new, bigger rooms and quickly made new friends. Sarah enjoyed the peacefulness of the suburb and the extra space for family gatherings. The initial fears faded away as the family adapted to their new environment. Sarah threw a housewarming party, inviting old and new friends, celebrating the successful move and their new beginning.

Sarah's journey through the change model illustrated how hearing about the opportunity, facing and overcoming fear, getting nearer to the new reality, and finally cheering for the successful adaptation are all part of embracing significant changes within their lives. As the family grew more comfortable in their new home, they remained open to future changes, ready to cycle through hearing, fearing, nearing, and cheering once again.

While there are four stages of change, not everyone makes it through the entire curve. Some people starting a change will give up, opt out, be forced out, etc. They may pursue a degree, start a health journey, restore a car, or launch a new business, but they will never complete the journey.

The very real experience most of us have is of rolling up and down on this curve like the roller coaster referenced earlier. Some stages go faster or slower for us based on how we react to a change and the change itself. You may ride through change quickly upon receiving a new office chair but slowly with a new boss. We all go through these four stages to make it through a change. Thankfully, the journey through change is predictable; what is not predictable and can be influenced is the velocity, the curve and the depth of the "dip."

Recognizing the predictability of these stages is crucial for effective change leadership in your personal and professional life. By planning for change, informed change leaders can make each stage more efficient, accelerating the journey through the curve with intentional strategies and support. To drive change effectively, you must understand the stages, identify which stage you're in, and know how to address each stage's specific needs. When you can provide what people need at each stage, you help them move through the process faster. Conversely, failing to meet these needs can cause a change to get stuck, slow down, or be abandoned altogether.

In the Hear stage, we start to experience a shift from our status quo to "something will be different." This stage is often characterized by sharing information and gathering information.

Let's look at the change curve through the lens of starting a new job. What happens as you move through the change curve of starting a new position? Imagine these steps:

Hear

You hear about the job and read the job description. You hear the offer. You get it in writing. You hear about the people you will work with and get a copy of the handbook. You might receive a T-shirt and a notebook. You change your LinkedIn profile and do a practice drive to the office or test your computer. You are excited to start the position and very prepared. This is going to be GREAT!

Then, at some point, you move to the Fear stage. You might move to this stage before you start the job, after you walk in the door, or two weeks into the position. You will feel yourself move into Fear and notice that it doesn't feel right. Maybe your responsibilities are different than you thought they would be, there's a member of your new team whom you've already clashed with, or you find out on your first day that the manager you were going to report to has left the company. These changes or uncertainties may lead you to question whether you made the right decision, causing fear. You may even wonder if you should have taken the other offer or stayed at your former employer.

These feelings of hesitation and questioning indicate you have moved from the Hear to the Fear stage.

Fear

What each person experiences in the Fear stage will vary. In our example of starting a new job, Fear might manifest as difficulty remembering people's names, discovering the coffee tastes bad, finding the job is not what you expected, noticing your manager is more absent than you hoped, or having to use unfamiliar work tools. Fear can be minor or significant, but it's always present in some form.

Everyone experiences Fear when navigating the change curve. Everyone reading this book has had that moment where Fear sets in when starting a new job. That moment might have lasted 30 seconds or until you left the position. Your self-talk might have started with, "Oh my, what did I sign up for? This isn't exactly what I thought. Why did I leave my last job? Can I get my old position back?" We all experience change differently. Some people experience deep Fear, while others have a brief moment of doubt or second thought and move on to the next stage.

If you can resolve or rationalize more fears, you can move forward. If you successfully navigate the Fear stage, you'll arrive at the next stage: Near.

Near

In the Near stage, you start to feel more confident, thinking, "I've got this. It was a little harder than I planned, but I get it now. I'm on it." You begin to understand who to contact within the organization to get what you need, and you know how to set up meetings. In the Near stage, you are figuring out "how" and are starting to reduce or eliminate your worries and fears.

The key change as you move from Fear to Near is an increased feeling of positive sentiment. Your internal dialogue shifts from "Why did I do this?" to "How can I do this?" Your perspective changes from questioning and looking backward to focusing forward.

Once you are comfortable in the Near stage, you will move to the final stage: Cheer.

Cheer

Continuing with the new job example, you will reach the Cheer stage when you know how to navigate the organization, complete your work, identify who to call for help, and understand your regular responsibilities. In the Cheer stage, you will know what success looks like and how to achieve it. Your daily tasks will feel more automatic rather than intentional. In this stage, competence is the key sentiment.

Influencing the Difficulty of Change

To understand how to make change easier or harder for individuals, consider the following scenarios.

Imagine if the company had not updated its job description, so the role you accepted is different from what was described or advertised. This mismatch can cause you to stay in the Fear stage longer, reducing your trust in the organization and lowering your overall contribution. Companies that ensure job descriptions accurately reflect the actual role help new hires transition more smoothly, leading to faster productivity. Additionally, a well-designed orientation program can ease the "dip" of Fear by introducing new hires to the organization's processes and moving them more quickly to the Near stage.

The larger the career move, the deeper the Fear can be. For example, hiring executives such as CXOs or Vice Presidents involves significant career changes. These individuals likely discuss the move extensively with advisors and family and research the organization thoroughly. Despite this preparation, they will still experience the dip of Fear. One effective practice is to send a welcome gift, like flowers, to the executive's home a few days after they accept the job offer. The accompanying note might acknowledge their decision and provide reassurance, such as, "You made the right choice" or "The team is excited to have you for these reasons..."

While this gesture alone won't eliminate Fear, it helps the new executive feel supported and understood, which can ease their transition. Recognizing and addressing the Fear stage is crucial. Ignoring this stage or dismissing concerns can hinder progress. For instance, telling new hires not to worry about forgetting names or reassuring them they'll be fine without addressing their specific fears does not help. It would be more helpful to provide aids such as organizational charts with photos to help overcome the Fear vs. minimize it.

By acknowledging and addressing fears, you help individuals move through the Fear stage more efficiently, ultimately guiding them through Near and towards the Cheer stage, where they feel confident and competent in their new role.

Fear is a real stage, and the way to help people get through it quickly is through acknowledgment. Reflect on how fellow employees and managers often mismanage change by telling new hires to "not worry about it" using phrases like:

- "You'll get it soon."

- "Don't worry about it."

- "You'll remember everyone's names soon."

- "None of the job descriptions are accurate."

- "It's not a big deal."

- "There's nothing to be afraid of."

- "Everyone goes through this; you'll be fine."

- "You don't need to worry about that right now."

Do any of these statements alleviate Fear? No. Telling someone not to worry doesn't relieve their worry and can be minimizing and demoralizing. Instead, try these phrases:

- "We expect it to take time to learn."

- "We know you have concerns and questions as you onboard, and we will provide a conduit to get your questions answered."

- "We use the features in Zoom to put everyone's name on their video tile to help you learn them faster, but if you forget a name, we expect you to ask. It's okay to do that."

- "Let's review and update your job description so we are on the same page."

- "We're here to support you through this transition."

- "Your learning curve is expected, and we've built in time for you to get comfortable."

- "Let's set up regular check-ins to address any questions or concerns you might have."

- "Remember, it's okay to make mistakes as you learn."

By using these approaches, you can help individuals navigate the Fear stage more effectively, paving the way for smoother transitions and successful change implementation.

THE CHANGE CHEAT CODE MODEL · 23

Can you skip the Fear stage?

No, you cannot skip the Fear stage. However, you can mitigate its impact and move through it more quickly. Everyone experiences the Fear stage, and it's common to oscillate between stages before progressing through the change curve.

Even if the change is a "good" thing, will we still go through the Fear stage?

Yes, even universally acknowledged "good" changes will go through the Fear stage. Everyone has a different perception of what constitutes a good change. What one leader sees as a positive shift, others might perceive as disruptive or challenging. Therefore, it's essential to recognize that Fear is a natural part of any change process.

Let's imagine this example: It is Wednesday morning. You just received a call from the local Chamber of Commerce informing you that you won the raffle you entered last week. You and a guest will be provided a trip to Las Vegas from Friday through Monday. You will receive $500 per day to spend, and all your transportation, hotel, and meals will be fully paid. The plane leaves at 7 a.m., and they need to know who you want to take on the trip and your personal information to book the flight and hotel.

What would you feel? Excitement? Of course! But did you think about any fears? What meetings do you have on Friday that need to be canceled? Who are you going to bring? Who will watch the kids/pets? Is $500 enough to gamble? What if you don't gamble? What if you don't like Las Vegas? Will you get a tax bill for this? Do you have to share a room, or does this include two rooms?

The Fear stage is real and present, even with good news. It is important to understand that you will not avoid the Fear stage. You need to recognize it, embrace it, and figure out how to move through it quickly but correctly.

Even a good change can evoke a negative reaction, no matter how well you plan for it. Planning to buy a new house or move to a better office is an "improvement" or "good change," but it will still drive you through the change curve. Now imagine that the change is not perceived as good or positive, such as being forced to use a new operating system you are not familiar with or having one of your projects put on hold. In that case, the Fear stage will be more negative, the dip will be deeper, and people will stay in the Fear stage longer than they would with a perceived positive change. For this reason, it is imperative that you anticipate this stage and plan how to manage it effectively.

Let's imagine you are leading an effort to complete a Salesforce Customer Relationship Management (CRM) integration. The organization has four instances of Salesforce because four companies recently merged from acquisitions. Additionally, half the companies communicate and have email on Microsoft, and the other half communicate on Google Workspace, meaning they are even more separate in their work processes, preferences, collaboration, and style. The merging of communication systems will be happening simultaneously with the Salesforce integrations, so nearly every aspect of how people currently work will change. These changes will affect everyone, and the changes are not optional.

The first group to enter the change curve will be the top leaders of the organization, who will be informed by technical experts and will decide to combine Salesforce instances and communication methods. These leaders will ask/answer what, why, when, who, and where. They will likely bring in consultants and experts and wring their hands about the costs and disruption. After long debates and multiple iterations, they arrive at the conclusion they need to proceed, spend the money, and initiate the disruption. They rode the entire change curve by looking at the problem, worrying about all the implications, figuring out how to pay for it, and finally ending with a decision. The leaders then arrive at the cheer stage. They are tired from the long and exhausting decision process but are highly confident it is the right thing to do.

As great leaders, they bring in their next-level leaders (those who report to them) to talk about the decision. The executives will be appalled at the negativity of these next-level leaders who only complain and bring up issues (which have already been considered by the top leadership team). In fact, these leaders are thinking, "What is wrong with these people?" The executives will fail to realize that the executive leaders had reached the Cheer stage, but the next-level leaders were in the Fear stage. If the top leaders are not careful, they can easily diminish input and perhaps delay the absorption of the information by not managing this Fear stage. Keep in mind that you will always go through the Fear stage. Just because you went through the Fear stage does not mean others can skip the stage. Avoid the common disparaging comments such as, "It will be fine." This change does not feel "fine" to your audience at this point.

It is imperative to recognize where the people hearing the information are on the Change curve and give them what they need at their stage. The next-level leaders should have heard the Five Ws (who, what, when, where, and why) and should be provided the opportunity to react and process just like the executives had the chance to do. Managing this reaction allows you to help people move through the Fear stage. Some techniques in leading people through this stage include asking, "What's on your mind as you hear this?" or "What could go wrong with this plan?"

Imagine if these top leaders viewed their next-level leaders' negativity with anticipation vs. irritation. These next-level leaders would likely make it through the Fear stage of the change curve with only two more stages to go. It is far worse to announce a change and have no one move to Fear. Imagine the disaster of people just listening to the change and waiting to see what everyone else does. This reaction would stall the change at the beginning of the process, and you would have much more work to do.

If you find yourself thinking these things regarding people's reactions to change:

- Why are you so negative?

- Why don't you just play ball?

- What's wrong with you people?

- Don't you trust us/me?

You need to change your mindset. You need to lean into the Fear stage, not avoid it. If you minimize the Fear stage or act like people should not feel as they do, you will have trouble helping people move forward. You will also contribute to a lack of trust.

Remember that in the Hear stage, people need to know the basic information. What is happening, and most importantly, why is it happening? When is it happening? To whom is it going to happen? We don't need to tell people HOW in the Hear stage. There are exceptions, of course, for immediate changes, but for large changes, we want to move people through the curve and discuss the HOW in the Near stage.

Imagine you hear about a change for the first time, and the next sentence from the speaker dives straight into the details. You would not have been able to process the Ws, and now the HOW is being added. Can you recall a change where someone was digging deep into the details of how it would work, and you were still trying to absorb what was changing? The concept of providing people with what they need at each stage is designed to focus on progress and accomplishing the change rather than having all information outlined at the outset.

Change is more of an art than an exact formula. Your job is to do your best to give people impacted by the change what they need at the right time, but different people will move through the curve at a different pace, so adjustments and exceptions will happen. If you have a person who rapidly assimilates change, has experience making the change you are discussing, or has been part of the planning process, they may Hear about the change and, in the blink of an eye, pass through Fear and start asking HOW.

In the Near stage, leaders should focus on providing resources as they discover their approach or learn the How. Leaders or the instigators of the change should back off because people have accepted the change and are starting to move toward completing it. Don't disrupt change by getting too involved or continuing to "sell the change." If a team is running an agile sprint, leave them alone at this stage. Let them work.

Leaders in the Near stage may also take their teams on field trips at other organizations to see where similar changes have been made successfully. The leader hopes the team will see something applicable, learn something valuable, and experience a model of success related to the change at hand. For example, a manufacturing team considering the adoption of lean practices might visit a facility that has already implemented those techniques effectively, or a store adopting a new checkout technology might tour or spend a couple of days working at a store already using the new process. Many changes have been accomplished by others before, often in different industries—so look to these examples for ideas and inspiration. It's easy to imagine you're brilliantly inventive, but aside from splitting atoms, most of us haven't created anything truly unique. Someone has likely done what you're attempting before. If you can show people a successful example at the Near stage, it will propel them to move faster.

In the Near stage, people are figuring out what they need to do and how they need to do it. During this time, they will experience micro-wins—small but significant victories that indicate progress. These might include successfully navigating a new system for the first time, mastering a new process, or receiving positive feedback on their initial efforts. It's important to recognize and acknowledge these micro-wins, as they build confidence and momentum, helping to reinforce the change without interrupting their progress.

As a leader, you may notice that while some individuals have entered the Near stage, others are still in Fear, hesitant and uncertain about the change. When you observe that at least 25 to 35 percent of the people have moved into the Near stage, it's a signal to shift your change leadership focus to meet the needs of those progressing. It can be tempting to keep circling back to those still in Fear, trying to bring them along, but your attention should now pivot to supporting those moving forward. This doesn't mean abandoning those in Fear; rather, it's about balancing your efforts to maintain the overall momentum of the group.

Sometimes, this transition is challenging because you don't want to leave anyone behind. However, there is strength in numbers—when people in Fear see others successfully moving into the Near stage and achieving micro-wins, it can encourage them to follow suit. In some cases, a few individuals may be left behind in Fear. They might gradually move to the Near stage with the rest of the team, but some may choose to check out, deepen their resistance, or even leave the organization. It's important to recognize these dynamics and continue fostering an environment where those ready to move forward can do so while providing the necessary support for those still struggling.

Utilizing learning Loops is another technique that helps people move through the change curve. Learning Loops are an iterative process of continuous feedback and adaptation throughout the change process. The goal of Learning Loops is to enable stakeholders to try or pilot an idea and learn from their experiences, continuously improve their performance, and adapt to changing circumstances to make change more bearable for those impacted.

Once a change is nearing completion or a decision is shaping up, you will move to the Cheer stage. The Cheer stage ranges in feeling from the elation of completion to relief that the journey is over. People like to celebrate when they finish something or get comfortable with it. It's beneficial to acknowledge people or teams at this stage. By acknowledging or celebrating a win, you emotionally cement that feeling with individuals who will want to achieve that emotion with the next change. In essence, you are developing the change muscle.

The Tale of An Acquisition

Imagine you are advising a company completing an acquisition and integrating two competing companies. Much work was done to get the deal across the line, and the announcements have been in the works for weeks. Finally, the acquisition was completed on Friday. On Monday, the organizations held separate all-company meetings to announce the acquisition. By Tuesday, they held a combined all-staff meeting for both organizations, followed by FAQs being distributed, department meetings, press releases, and new logos of the combined company. Weeks of planning had finally come together. There were daily stand-ups with the planning team to manage all the details and nail the necessary announcements and next steps. You arrive at the Wednesday standup with all announcements complete and no major issues. You are in the Cheer stage for the announcement and communication! It is time to celebrate, acknowledge, and enjoy your accomplishments. Your contribution in the next stand-up should sound something like this:

"John, how you organized the run of show and handled the production quality kept the announcement very professional and calm. Janice, your meticulous pouring over every detail of the announcement, FAQs, and press releases made sure we were on message the entire time. Elizabeth, I am so glad you suggested that 'dry run' on Friday. It helped calm all our nerves, and we got great feedback to incorporate. Now, I know the next six months will have even more changes to work, but given how you handled the communications, I have great faith in this team."

It is common for a group of people who survived and even thrived through a change together to move more quickly to the next change and tackle it with excitement. You are creating a change routine or muscle and providing a repeatable process that people will recognize. You are also building trust and predictability across the team. Change is disorienting enough; you can help the whole process by using the same steps each time. Most people will not run toward change but may be less hesitant when introduced to the next change, knowing you have a solid process to manage it.

So what did we learn? The change process is predictable, and predictable things can be made repeatable. You can't avoid these stages, but you can manage them. And that's the important part.

You now have a basic understanding of the change curve. Once you fully grasp this curve, you can plan more effectively through each stage of change. Whether the change involves your child going to school for the first time, managing a project, or leading a major organizational shift, leveraging the change curve as a repeatable process will ensure you have all the ingredients and steps necessary for success. By doing so, you can navigate changes more smoothly, minimize disruption, and build confidence and trust within your team.

The Language You Use

Another benefit of the four-stage change cheat code model is that it enables an organization to develop its own rhythm and languages using the same framework or four easy-to-remember words. Many organizations consider change management training necessary for all employees to ensure everyone can participate and name the stages they are in during change, thus building it into the company's language. Imagine if you trained all individuals and leaders in a company on change management. When you roll out a change, all you can hear in a meeting is, "Wait a minute. You're talking about how we're going to do this, but I'm still in the Fear stage. I am still worried about X or Y." If you have employees who can name the stage they are in and express what they need, there is a higher probability of bringing everyone together and providing what is needed. You can also provide people assurance that the emotion they are feeling is part of the journey and, in fact, it is normal. If what people are experiencing and feeling is normal, we can talk about it and find ways to support each other through each stage.

You'll know you are successful in implementing a solid change process when someone in a meeting says, "Hey, I'm not able to move out of the Hear stage because these questions aren't answered yet." When this happens, that person is advocating for their needs and helping you understand what is needed to help them and others move forward. When someone can do that, it is like being able to go to a doctor and explain their own diagnosis.

The Cabinet Company

Let's consider a change that affected the employees and customers of one organization.

A person from another industry purchased a custom cabinet manufacturing and sales organization. After running the company of craftspersons and talented designers for a few months, it was clear that to increase sales, the sales process itself needed to change. The current, tried-and-true method of selling cabinetry and kitchen remodels relied on showing a customer cabinet door samples with paint/stain colors and discussing cabinetry needs (silverware drawers, pull-out pantries, etc.). After multiple meetings to nail down the details, the designers would summarize their notes and send them to engineers who prepared a drawing and provided a price. The buyer often needed quite a bit of time to review the drawings to understand if all their needs were met.

The new owner decided that providing some basic sketches up front in the sales process would help customers visualize the cabinetry and be able to make a faster decision. Salespeople and designers were instructed to hand-sketch the layouts to gain alignment with the customer and speed up the decision process. This method did indeed shorten the sales cycle, and customers were more confident with their decisions along the way instead of waiting until the end to make final changes and sign off on the production of the cabinets.

With that success underway, the new owner had the idea to further develop the cabinet buying process. "What if we make cabinets in standard sizes out of whiteboard material and put them on wheels? That way, when a customer comes in the showroom, we can assemble their cabinets, draw on the doors and drawers, and show where special features are included, like silverware drawers." As the owner explained this to the sales and design team, there was initial speculation about how customers would react. One designer said she did not have time to assemble a whole kitchen and get all their design choices. When the engineering team heard the idea, they laughed out loud and said their professional drawings were far better.

"Let's just try it," said the new owner, who proceeded to order the whiteboard material and assembled a list of what cabinets needed to be produced. Within a few weeks, the showroom had 30-plus cabinets on wheels that could be moved together and provide a "living" example of what a new kitchen may feel like to a customer. The first few meetings with customers were a bit clunky. Customers remarked that they had never seen anything like this, but most were willing to give it a try. Designers became good at setting up the "moveable" kitchen, and customers were finding it easier to visualize the space between the island and the kitchen's perimeter. Through continued use, the sales cycle time started decreasing, and the design and engineering teams began making improvements to the process such that new customers stepped into the amazing moveable kitchen showroom and were actively assisted in designing the kitchen of their dreams.

To start building a kitchen design, the designers would ask the customers for pictures and dimensions of their space before the first meeting, and when the customers came into the showroom, they were walked over to their new kitchen where they could see the designers' initial ideas. Customers could be seen erasing doors and adding drawers, moving islands farther from perimeters, and stating how they would store their coffee cups close to the coffee maker as the designer used the dry-erase markers to draw a coffee maker in the exact spot the customer planned to place it.

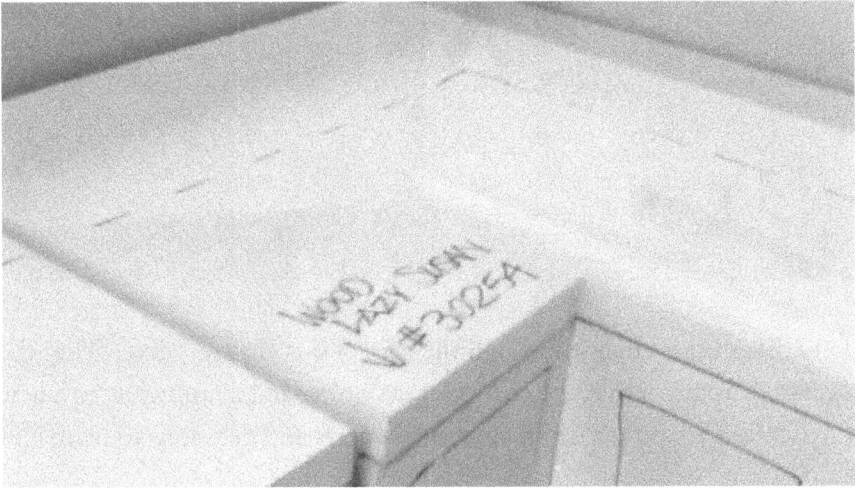

Engineers started to enjoy the concept when the designers would write the part numbers of the exact Lazy Susan part on the cabinet and send pictures of the design to the engineering team who no longer had to guess or look up what part the designer might want.

The change was so successful that customers brought their friends in to see their "new" kitchen before it was built. One customer asked why other cabinet companies were not doing this, which delighted the owner.

Let's dissect this change through the eyes of our change curve. From the customer's perspective, the change of designing and committing to a new kitchen is a big one, with many moving parts and decisions to be made.

Hear Stage

The refrigerator in the customer's house stopped working and could not be repaired. The model was no longer made, and no refrigerator would fit in their cabinet space. This customer had desired a new kitchen for a long time. They decided it was time to get new cabinetry, appliances, counters, a sink, and a backsplash. The customer started gathering information.

Fear Stage

The customer started making a list and budget for the kitchen remodel. Their estimate for the cabinets, appliances, counters, backsplash, and sink was based on research they had done and the average prices their friend had paid. Now that all the figures were in, the total was more than they planned. To add to the cost worry, they also heard from friends that a kitchen remodel meant they would not have a functioning kitchen for possibly months and probably longer than they initially estimated.

The couple started asking themselves if it was worth the time, money, and hassle. After weeks of discussion, they decided they could shorten their vacation to save enough money to pay for the kitchen, project manage the remodel themselves to keep the tightest possible timeline, and buy a portable microwave and two-burner cooktop to serve as a makeshift kitchen while theirs was out of commission. They even decided to buy the refrigerator in advance and put it in the garage until the remodel was ready for the appliance.

Near Stage

With excitement and somewhat of a plan, the couple decided to go to a custom cabinet shop that their friends had used in the past. Their friends had raved about the team's design and project management skills and were very happy with the quality of the cabinets. Upon entering the showroom, the couple was delighted to be greeted by the designer, who immediately walked them over to a group of white cabinets with doors, drawers, sinks, and other features drawn on them in an erasable marker.

The designer had called the couple in advance, received the dimensions of their current space and pictures of their current style, and asked some questions on the phone about what they were looking for. When the couple was led over to their mocked-up kitchen at their first meeting, they immediately started changing the cabinets and making decisions. One said, "I think I want the dishwasher to the right of the sink so I can put the garbage to the left when I clear the dishes, rinse them, and put them in the dishwasher in a row." Another remarked that pull-out drawers would be better next to the stove so large pots and pans could be stored close to the cooking area.

In a matter of a few hours, the customers had made most of their buying decisions, including the layout of their kitchen, the color and finish of other cabinetry, the countertop and backsplash, and even left with recommendations of what appliances would best match and fit into the space perfectly. The designer promised to follow up within two days with pricing and ask them to stop back in with details about their selected appliances so they can discuss the entire package.

When the couple returned in two days, they had already picked the appliances and sent them to the designer. The designer had an engineering drawing, pricing, and a final sign-off contract for the couple. They chatted about the timeline and said that the speed of installation would be important. They also agreed on the best time in the month to do the installation based on their scheduled visitors.

Cheer Stage

When the couple left the showroom and got into their vehicle, they were excited that they were able to make their own decisions and get started on their project. They had a couple of brief discussions on the way home, asking each other and themselves, "Are we really doing this? It's a lot of money." But they were able to respond to their fears by visualizing their finished new kitchen.

This example illustrates how the cabinetry company was able to make a change easier for their customer. As the customer completed the change curve for deciding to proceed with the project, they realized they would enter the next change curve of starting the project and have a whole new roller coaster to ride.

From the Employee Perspective

Now, let's look at the change at the cabinetry company when they were establishing this new process.

Hear Stage

The designers and engineers were surprised when the new owner shared their idea about using a moveable kitchen to aid in the decision-making process. The new owner didn't come from the cabinetry industry, and there was a general feeling that they might not know what they were doing. The new owner meticulously explained why this change was important and why it would speed up the decision-making process while reducing planning work for both the designers and the engineers.

Fear Stage

The designers and engineers freely voiced their concerns about this idea. The designer started with the fact that they'd never seen this done before and weren't sure it would work. The engineers were convinced that professional drawings were far more professional than whiteboard cabinets on wheels. Other concerns surfaced, such as taking up such a large amount of space within the showroom, not to mention the amount of time it would add to setting up a moveable kitchen.

The new owner listened and took these fears seriously, noting each one on a flip chart as they discussed the idea. Next, designers and engineers were invited to look at each concern they named and brainstorm a way to relieve or eliminate them. Some of the concerns could not be eliminated until they tested the idea, but by the end of this meeting, they all agreed that they would try the new idea and produce the whiteboard cabinets on wheels.

Near Stage

In the next meeting, the designers and engineers agreed on the number of cabinets and the sizes that would be easiest to move around on the showroom floor. They selected the wheels that were easiest to glide on the floor, and the engineers optimized the materials used to make the cabinetry. Within a few weeks, the new whiteboard cabinets on wheels were delivered to the showroom. To the owner's surprise, the designers were actually excited to do a first design with their new tools. The cabinets arrived in the morning, and one of the designers met with customers to test the new moveable kitchen that afternoon.

Working together, all of the designers set up the first moveable kitchen. They drew on the sink, the dishwasher, and where the stove would go and used a measuring tape to space the island from the perimeter. They looked at their design and made a few changes to their original plan.

The customers came in in the afternoon for their appointment and were surprised to see their potential new kitchen in real life. They remarked that they'd never seen anything like this. It made them feel so much more confident about what they had decided for island size and where to place the refrigerator. In the next few weeks, the designers got better and better at the moveable kitchen setups. They started to iterate on what they would need to know prior to the next customer appointment to support the best possible outcome.

Cheer Stage

Within months, the cabinetry company was the talk of the town. People brought their friends into the showroom to see their new kitchen even though it hadn't been produced yet. One potential customer even asked for all the moveable cabinets to be loaded in the truck and brought to their house under construction so they could see the kitchen in the actual space. Sales increased dramatically, and cycle times for decision-making decreased. This was a clear win for the organization, and both the designers and engineers were happy with the time savings.

Questions You May Have

Just with this small basis of understanding of the change process, you probably already have questions. Let's tackle a few of the more common ones:

When you announce a change, should you also work to implement that change immediately, even if you don't have a detailed plan on how to do so?

Change actually starts when you're thinking about it. Having all of it worked out is an impossibility because you will never think of everything. The recommended approach is to lead with all the Ws because that's the most helpful. While you'll likely still have to work with people to get answers, just be honest and say, "I don't know when yet, I'm going to come back and tell you when I do know." You don't have to have the answers to address the question; you just have to acknowledge what you know and what you don't know as you lead yourself and others toward the change.

Is there any value in explaining or reinforcing the message to employees that we are experiencing change and that change is inevitable, good, and means growth?

The value in discussing how change feels is to normalize it, not minimize it. To say that change happens is the same as saying, "Don't worry about it." It's not effective to just tell somebody to stop worrying. Leaders often introduce the change by telling people how they should feel about it, which has the opposite effect of inspiring people to embrace it. When a leader gets in front of a group of people and states, "You will love this change," many people become more suspicious.

Pro tip: As a leader, never tell people the emotion they should experience. If you tell them what they should feel, they will channel their energy into fighting that emotion instead of spending it on the change. Phrases to avoid include:

- Change is constant, so get used to it.

- You will be happy with this new…

- This will feel hard, but it is the best thing for our future.

Why do we resist change?

We are resistant to change for a very good reason: to survive. When you drive your car, you are constantly looking for changes in your environment. It is a defense mechanism. Who's not going to stop at that light? Who is going too fast and just crossed the line? You are looking out for these changes to stay alive. Think back to a time when you drove for a long stretch and felt exhausted afterward. It's not because you were physically exerting yourself. Rather, it's because you were mentally exerting yourself the entire time. We are predisposed as humans to resist change for survival. We are programmed to look for what can go wrong in a change.

You will never fight upstream against a survival mechanism. So don't even try. However, you can swim with the survival mechanism and roll through change the right way. If you build up this change muscle and put all change through the same pattern, it gets less alarming to people. For example, if every Monday morning meeting has the same agenda, that's less of a change for people, even though there is a new topic every Monday. Meeting attendees know how things are going to happen. If your team has a change methodology, you make change easier because people will reflexively move through the curve.

What happens if you discover the change is wrong after it's been announced? How do you differentiate between normal resistance and signs that a change should be stopped based on new information?

Sometimes, despite the best intentions, a change initiative turns out to be a bad idea. The concept of "failing fast" is essential here. The key is to be open-minded and willing to reassess and, if necessary, stop the change when new evidence suggests it's the right move.

Recognizing when to halt a change is challenging. Leaders often become deeply invested in their ideas, making it hard to abandon them without clear, compelling evidence—typically financial or strategic data highlighting the change's shortcomings. While it's rare for employee complaints alone to derail a change, overwhelming feedback can sometimes signal the need for reconsideration.

If you feel a change you are working on might be a terrible idea, do your best to adopt a mindset of continual learning and openness to feedback. Not all resistance means failure; some is a natural part of the change process. However, being willing to make tough decisions based on solid evidence sets you apart as an effective change leader.

If you are not the one leading the change, remember that leaders seldom change direction based solely on feedback from below. While your input is valuable, it's one factor among many. Focus on providing well-grounded insights that can influence decision-making, but understand that leaders must consider the bigger picture. Still, do your best to be proactive and realistic in these cases, as you can contribute meaningfully and potentially even influence a course correction.

Does everyone eventually make it through the change curve?

All organizations will pull some people through that Fear stage kicking and screaming. There are always people who will not change or participate. You do lose people in change. Some people decide not to come along with the change, and others do not agree or, for some reason, cannot move through the curve. Let's look at some of the profiles of people who don't move through the change curve:

The Smiling Non-changer

There is danger in not addressing the non-changer. One quality they exhibit is mentally quitting and physically staying at an organization. They continue to attend the meetings but fail to embrace or even participate in the change. They are like dead wood dragging down the organization. These people need to be addressed as soon as the behavior becomes apparent. Some organizations will offer a package to move them out or certainly away from the group making the change.

The Slow but Loud Changers

Some people are going to be lagging behind others in the curve. Not everyone will travel at the same pace, but you do not want the people who are lagging to dig such a hole for themselves that they're too embarrassed to jump on the curve later. You must provide space for them to join. And in doing so, you'll hope to bring more people along. For that reason, you do not berate publicly those who have not progressed. Rather, you try to provide private counsel or even ignore them.

The Leaders of the Revolt

These people take it upon themselves to speak for others on why this change will not work. Bring these people close to the change leader and give them a role in making the change successful. If they continue their disruptive behavior, consider discussing what behaviors and actions are acceptable.

The "Need More Information" Stallers

These people seem reasonable at first and ask for additional information to understand the change. However, once provided a fair amount of information, they ask for more. This can cause a group to stall out. If you continue to provide for every one of their requests, you will be on a slippery slope of catering to and reinforcing this behavior. Once a reasonable amount of information has been provided, you must signal that the group does not need to be at 100 percent consensus on every feature to make the change. Communicate that the group can still iterate on the approach or add more processes if needed.

Does a leader or CEO with a proven track record of getting it right proceed through the cycle faster than somebody new and untested?

If you can say I've done it before, I've seen it before, it certainly calms fears, but it doesn't allay them. First-time leaders can be just as brilliant at leading change if they've been part of good change processes before earning their current title. And long-term leaders sometimes make the same mistakes, even after decades. Someone who is "new" may be more open to feedback than someone who's led a significant amount of change.

Why do people get comfortable after a change and then resist the next one?

Once we reach the Cheer stage, most people are reluctant to revisit the Fear stage. That stage represents discomfort and uncertainty, which naturally makes people hesitant to go through it again. This is why people often avoid changing jobs: because starting over is difficult. They don't change banks, because it's inconvenient. And they resist switching technologies, like moving from Android to iPhone, because they want to avoid the challenge of learning something new. People resist change because they want to avoid the discomfort of the Fear stage.

Think about the COVID-19 situation. At first, when we were forced to isolate at home, everything was new and uncertain. The advice was constantly changing, and the shift to working from home was a major adjustment for many. In the beginning, most people hated the isolation and being stuck in one environment. But after a few months, people adapted, and by the time a year had passed, it became difficult to get them back to the office. Now, companies are split—some promote an in-office culture, while others embrace remote work as their advantage. This shows how people grow comfortable with change once they've moved past the Fear stage.

This reluctance to return to the Fear stage creates resistance to future changes. Even when you know the next solution or idea is better, how do you convince your team that it's worth the temporary discomfort of change?

The truth is that we are all in the business of change management, whether we realize it or not. If you're in sales, your role is essentially to guide people through the change process—helping them adopt a new technology, product, or service as smoothly as possible. This same principle applies to customer support, human resources, and marketing. Marketing is about convincing people to embrace new ideas or change their behavior. The HR team often supports people through transitions like changing jobs or joining a new organization. Even the finance team is involved, pushing for changes that require doing more with fewer resources. No matter your role, we are all navigating the change curve, so let's work together to move through it successfully.

Now that you have a clear understanding of the change cheat code model and its stages (Hear, Fear, Near, and Cheer) it's time to take a closer look at each one. In the next chapter, we'll dive into the Hear stage, the critical first stage of any change process. Together, we will explore how to enter the Hear stage, the goals you should aim to achieve, and the responsibilities you hold as a change leader or participant during this pivotal time. You'll also read real-world stories and case studies that illustrate successful and not-so-successful change efforts, offering valuable lessons on what works and what doesn't.

Now, let's explore how to lay the foundation for a smooth and effective change process, beginning with Hear.

CHAPTER 2

HEAR

As I settled into my seat for the unexpected all-staff meeting, the room buzzed with tense anticipation. The CEO took the stage and, without preamble, dropped the bombshell—our company had been acquired. Murmurs turned into a low roar as the implications began to sink in. The CEO spoke of "synergies" and "enhanced opportunities," but my mind swirled with immediate, pressing concerns. How would this affect my job, my benefits, or the projects I have worked so hard on?

Leaving the meeting, I felt a mix of betrayal and anxiety. The decision had been made far above me. Nobody had asked for our input or even hinted that our work was about to change dramatically. I decided to touch base with several colleagues to gauge their reactions. Discontent was brewing, not just about the acquisition itself but about how it had been unveiled—with more questions raised than answered. Were our jobs secure? What about the company culture we had all worked so hard to build? In the meeting, we were promised transparency and a smooth transition, but with few specifics—they said more information would be forthcoming in the weeks ahead. Yeah right…

The array of emotions and questions stirred by this announcement highlights an unavoidable and highly impactful aspect of organizational change. The initial impact of how news is delivered can set the tone for everything that follows. This employee's anxiety and uncertainty could have been mitigated with a more thoughtful approach to this critical communication.

In this chapter, we'll explore the Hear stage—the initial stage of any change process where information is first introduced and initial reactions are formed. We will delve into effective strategies for introducing change that can help minimize shock and foster a more receptive atmosphere. By understanding the key components of effective communication at this stage, leaders can avoid the pitfalls of poorly managed announcements and prepare the ground for a smoother transition, addressing concerns proactively and clearing the way for the change to occur.

Entering the Hear Stage

The Hear stage is the first step on every change journey, as it is during this initial stage that the groundwork for understanding, acceptance, and eventual adaptation to change is laid. As individuals and teams first encounter information about upcoming changes, their reactions can range from curiosity and openness to apprehension and resistance. The key to navigating this stage successfully lies in how the change is communicated and the environment created for this communication to unfold.

Effective entry into the Hear stage requires leaders to approach the announcement of change with clarity, empathy, and a comprehensive high-level strategy. Clear communication means not only outlining the specifics of what will change but also providing context—why this change is occurring, what the anticipated outcomes are, and how it aligns with the organization's broader goals. This clarity helps to minimize misunderstandings and mitigate the initial shock or confusion that can accompany change announcements.

Equally important is the empathy with which the change is communicated. Recognizing and validating the emotional responses of team members underscores the leadership's understanding and care for the human aspect of organizational change. This empathetic approach encourages a more open and trusting dialogue about the change, allowing individuals to express concerns and ask questions freely.

Furthermore, the Hear stage is about setting expectations for the journey ahead. It's crucial to communicate that while the announcement marks the beginning of the change process, it is just the first step in a series of actions and discussions that will take place. Normalizing a wide range of reactions to the change helps to foster an inclusive environment where all team members feel their perspectives are valid and valued.

By effectively entering the Hear stage, leaders set the tone for the change process, building a foundation of trust and openness that will support the organization through the subsequent stages of change. It's an opportunity to unite the team with a shared understanding and readiness to engage with the challenges and opportunities that lie ahead.

Here's a quick reference of what you will experience entering the Hear stage:

Indicator	What You Will See	What People Will Be Doing
Initial Reactions	Diverse reactions ranging from curiosity and openness to apprehension and resistance.	Reacting to the change announcement, either with interest or skepticism.

Indicator	What You Will See	What People Will Be Doing
Communication of Change	The initial communication about the change will be repeated by the audience (accurately and inaccurately)	Listening to the change announcement, seeking clarity from any place they can find information (even if it is not a good source of information)
Emotional Responses	Visible emotional reactions that may include confusion, worry, or excitement.	Expressing their feelings and concerns about the change, possibly asking questions and sometimes just being shocked into silence.
Setting Expectations	People trying to establish expectations	Absorbing the information and beginning to adjust their expectations for future involvement.

This table reflects the key aspects and behaviors typical of groups entering the Hear stage of change. At this point, change leaders should focus on the critical role of communication and the initial reactions to the change. It's a stage where leaders must be particularly attentive to how information is presented and received, being repetitive to establish accurate communication and setting the stage for all subsequent stages of the change process.

The Goals of the Hear Stage

The goal of the first stage, Hear, is to ensure all impacted participants are informed about the change and understand what will come next as the change progresses. The Hear stage is often the most shocking, as some may feel surprised or blindsided by just hearing that a change is coming. In these moments, allow people to react, but repeat and reiterate the information about the change, setting the course for what is to come. This stage is crucial for establishing a clear understanding and setting the right expectations. Here's how to approach it:

- **Comprehensive Communication**: The primary goal in the Hear stage is to ensure all stakeholders receive clear, detailed information about the change. This involves explaining not only the "what," "who," and "when" but also the "why" behind the change, including potential impacts and anticipated benefits. Utilizing a checklist can ensure that no essential details—such as the scope of the change, the expected timeline, and the roles individuals will play—are overlooked. It is also sometimes helpful to include what is not changing.

- **Set Clear Expectations for Future Processes**: It's important to show that the initial announcement is just the beginning of a dynamic and iterative change process. Transparency about what to expect in subsequent steps, decisions, and adaptations is crucial. This setting of expectations encourages ongoing engagement and outlines how stakeholders can contribute and what milestones or checkpoints they should anticipate.

- **Normalize Emotional Reactions**: Acknowledging the diverse emotional responses to change is essential. Leaders create an atmosphere of trust and openness by validating feelings of excitement, curiosity, anxiety, or resistance as normal. This supportive approach encourages stakeholders to express their thoughts and concerns, fostering a culture where these can be addressed constructively and support is readily available.

- **Build a Foundation for Future Engagement**: The goal of the Hear stage is not to ensure universal happiness or immediate agreement, the Hear stage should begin to build a foundation for understanding and acceptance. This involves preparing stakeholders for what lies ahead and providing them with the opportunities to process and react to the information shared, setting the stage for a smoother progression through the change curve.

In short, the goal of the Hear stage is to ensure everyone affected by the change is well-informed, prepared for what lies ahead, knows the next steps, and feels supported throughout the process. By focusing on clear communication, openness, and early engagement, leaders can lay a strong foundation for the change initiative, making subsequent stages more effective and less stressful.

Again, it is important to note that the goal of the Hear stage is NOT to make everyone happy, minimize the impact of the change, or force compliance or agreement. This may be what you want as an outcome of announcing change, but you will be wildly disappointed if you expect any of these reactions. People will react and need time to process the information they receive.

When executed effectively, the Hear stage begins to build the foundation for the change itself, working to ensure stakeholders are well informed, prepared for what lies ahead, and have a space to express their reactions to the change.

Hear Stage Responsibilities

In the Hear stage of change management, setting the foundation for successful communication is paramount. This stage's primary focus is ensuring that the initial announcement of change is effectively communicated, understood, and accepted across all levels of an organization. Here's a detailed look at the responsibilities of individuals, leaders, and the company during the Hear stage.

Individuals:

- **Hear Actively**: Try to actively listen and engage with the information being presented about the change. This is the time to be present, open, and attentive to what is being shared.

- **Seek to Understand**: Try to understand the depth and breadth of the change. Focus on the details of the announcement, striving to grasp the "what" and "why" behind the change.

- **Ask Questions**: If aspects of the change are unclear, don't hesitate to ask questions. Seeking clarification at this stage is required to build a solid understanding of the change and its implications. Try to ask questions to seek information and avoid asking questions that provide opinions. "Help me understand" or "tell me more about" is a good start to information seeking questions. Questions that start with "why would anyone want to change that" or "what's wrong with what we are currently doing" will not be taken as information seeking.

Leaders:

- **Communicate Effectively**: Present the change in a clear, concise manner, ensuring that the message is understandable to all members of the organization. Use the Hear stage checklist in Part 2 as a guide to cover all necessary aspects of the change.

- **Address Emotional Reactions**: Be prepared to address and normalize emotional reactions. Acknowledge that changes can evoke a range of feelings and that having questions or concerns is natural and acceptable.

- **Provide Support**: Offer support and resources for individuals to process the information. Make yourself available to answer questions and engage in discussions about the change.

Company:

- **Reinforce the Message**: Support communication efforts by consistently reiterating change messaging across various channels. Ensure the information is accessible and consistent to all employees through emails, chat channels, meetings, and internal communications platforms.

- **Offer Comprehensive Information**: Provide detailed information about the change, including the reasons behind it, the expected outcomes, and how it will be implemented. The more information available, the easier it is for individuals to understand and accept the change.

- **Create an Open Environment**: Foster an environment where individuals feel comfortable voicing their thoughts, questions, and concerns about the change. Encourage open dialogue and feedback to ensure that everyone feels heard and valued.

When adhering to these responsibilities during the Hear stage, organizations can create a solid foundation for the change process. Effective communication at this stage not only informs but also begins to build the trust and understanding necessary for navigating and accelerating the subsequent stages of change.

Navigating the Hear Stage

The Hear stage serves as the entry point into the change process, where people who will be impacted by the change are first introduced to new information. Successful navigation of the Hear stage involves meticulous attention to the foundational elements of communication. This approach helps people along the path to understanding by addressing all critical aspects of the change, ensuring no important information is omitted.

In this section, we will delve into effective strategies for communicating during the Hear stage. We'll discuss how to craft messages that resonate, techniques for reinforcing messages through repetition, leveraging retrospectives to gauge and improve communication effectiveness, and setting the groundwork for subsequent stages of the change.

Hearing and Being Heard

Hear is the first step in the change process, when people are initially exposed to a change. Oftentimes, this stage comes as a shock because new information must always be new at one point. Once that moment is over, then you can move through the other stages. The Hear stage is unavoidable. People must always be informed of the change; they must hear of it and receive enough information to understand what is going on and build a mental model of the future. Thoughtful execution of the Hear stage is the best way to ensure the change process is managed as efficiently and effectively as possible. Get started on the right foot!

To truly hear, people need information that will allow them to build awareness and gain context for the change, and they need to hear this information repeatedly. Specifically, people need to know who is driving the change, who it impacts, what is happening, what is not happening, when it is happening, where it is happening, what will be different as a result, how we will know we are successful, and most importantly, why the change is happening. At the basic level, people need answers to the questions: who, what, when, where, and why. These elements in a more abbreviated form are often talked about as the Five Ws, the "who, what, when, where, and why."

What People Need to Hear in The Hear Stage (The Hear Stage Checklist)

The Hear stage checklist is designed to ensure that every stakeholder receives a comprehensive overview of the change. This includes understanding the reasons behind the change, the expected outcomes, and how it aligns with the organization's broader goals. Furthermore, it aims to provide clarity on the process that will unfold, setting expectations for future involvement and the steps that will be taken to facilitate the transition.

Here, we delve into what people need to hear during the Hear stage, guided by a checklist that ensures no important information is left unaddressed. This introductory framework is key to building trust, managing expectations, and fostering an environment conducive to open dialogue and constructive feedback.

The basics:

- Who is involved in the change, who is aware of the change, who made the decision to change?
- What is the change?
- When will the change start and end? When will updates be provided?
- Where will the change be?
- Why are we making the change? Why is this change happening now?
- What is not changing? What will remain the same, and what is not affected?

The best change leaders also include:

- What will be different as a result of the change.
- How to know when we are successful.

Your sixth-grade writing teacher might have told you never to write a story without all the Ws, leading to many of us being trained to include answers to the Five Ws for context. However, if you examine change communication, you will be amazed at how often information is missing.

> Take this example: A leadership consultant was at a manufacturing plant where they had been consulting for a year. They observed someone from the communications team approach the company bulletin board, a primary form of internal communication in this company. The employee diligently tacked up a memo with an announcement that read, "As of Monday, this facility and the parking lot, including in your car, will be non-smoking. This non-smoking area also includes the side of the plant and the sidewalk next to the plant. Thank you for complying."
>
> The consultant's first thought was, well, this will be interesting. They got the what (no smoking), and they got the when (as of Monday), the where (plant, parking lot, sidewalk, and car), and who (everyone), but they completely missed the why! This was puzzling, so the consultant decided to walk around and talk to people about the change. She approached a woman working at her desk, started chatting, and asked the key question: "Hey, why did you go non-smoking?"
>
> The answers she got were key to understanding the message. The first person said, "Oh, you know, the maintenance crew was tired of picking up cigarette butts. They have been complaining about it for years…" Then, the consultant went to the next person, asking the same question, to which they replied, "The Vice President's wife has lung cancer, and to honor her, we're all going to give up smoking." The third person said, "This is just another management tool to break the union." The consultant continued searching across different people at the company and got different answers every time!

Finally, the consultant approached the person who initiated the change with the same question, "Why did you go non-smoking?" Yet again, the response differed from any of the other responses. The change initiator said, "Oh my gosh, someone filled out our property insurance form last week and said our facility was non-smoking. We had an audit for insurance purposes, and the auditor saw someone smoking in the parking lot! They responded by telling us that if we don't make the facility non-smoking by Monday, they were going to significantly increase our insurance rates just because people smoke here!"

This is an example of people not knowing the real driver for the change initiator. Yet, everyone had a very clear interpretation of the "why" and was happy to share it proudly. The problem is that people's stories about why something is happening are typically significantly more far-fetched than the reality. In this scenario, each person had a different understanding of the "why" driving the change. In the best case, the fabricated "why" was positive and logical. In the worst case, it was negative and conniving, implying larger systemic issues were at play. Just think of how much time was wasted discussing it among the employees or the emotion expended on the wrong cause.

Had the change leader included the "why" and provided context for the change, the people impacted by the change would have a clearer view of the need and would be more likely to adapt. Someone who has made a habit of smoking in the parking lot is much more likely to cross the street to smoke if they understand the why behind the change.

The Five Ws—who, what, when, where, and most importantly, why—are essential to helping people get into and through the Hear stage. If you've heard this pattern before, you might think we are leaving an important piece out, as "how" often comes after the Five Ws. But in the Hear stage, "how" is not included. The exclusion of "how" is intentional. This stage aims to focus on absorbing the change and allowing for other potential "how" ideas after you involve others. "How" will be vital in the Near stage (Chapter 4). In Hear, people need to know who is impacted, what is happening, when it is happening, where it is happening, and why it is happening. They don't need to focus on the how just yet.

When you lead with the why, you lead with context. When you give context for the change, you help those impacted understand the conditions and scenario that led to the decision driving the change. Giving people enough information and context about the change helps people understand the change drivers, and in the base case scenario, they see the change in a way that leads them to support the decision, sometimes as if it were their own. If people understand the context, they can add value with more ideas.

Getting People to Actually Hear You

Humans reject new information at first as a protection mechanism, especially when that new information threatens the status quo. Some of us, especially kids, even cover our faces or ears when we attempt to reject new information. We are not built to hear and accept something new, especially at the outset. We are programmed to hear something new as danger.

Research and marketing best practices reveal that humans must receive seven impressions of a message before it sticks or drives an action or behavior change. That doesn't mean hearing or reading the same message seven times to remember it. Instead, it means having a total of seven different types of impressions of the information such that the message is retained and influences behavior. These impressions are best made multi-modally. For example, seven impressions can be made during an in-person meeting, a follow-up FAQ, an open session for Q&A, a department meeting, a progress report, a discussion at a one-on-one meeting, and again at an all-hands virtual meeting.

The rule of seven is an age-old marketing rule that dates back to the late 1920s, stating that it takes a prospective customer seven impressions or touches to "hear" the advertiser's message before making an action toward buying that product or service. One popular example of this rule in effect was within the American movie industry, where marketing plans targeted individuals so they would have seven impressions about a particular film to inspire them to take action to see it. Impressions were from advertisements on the radio, in the newspaper, and on billboards or signs. Seeing and hearing something everywhere provides the impression of stability and trust.

It's not just entertainment and for-profit marketing that leverages this trick. In 2017, the University of Oregon was working to improve its ability to reach and influence graduate students in high-level professional programs such as business, journalism, architecture, and law; the problem was that these students were not on campus all the time and did not experience education in the same way as typical undergraduate students.

The University of Oregon, Portland Library, and Learning Commons wanted to break through this challenge and adopted a "seven touches" communications model for their most important communications. They set a goal of having at least seven impressions of key information with graduate students. The idea behind the change in process was driven by the rule of seven and the psychological principle of exposure effects, where frequent exposure to something builds awareness, familiarity, and understanding. Through adopting this new methodology, library staff saw more than three times increase in engagement from these hard-to-reach graduate students, all because they intentionally adapted their communications and outreach strategies.

Today, this rule has expanded as the opportunities for advertising impressions have changed dramatically with different mediums, and social media has become a staple in most consumer's daily lives. With these ever-expanding communication opportunities, advertisers across the globe can engineer experiences to create seven impressions, all without needing anyone to leave their homes. That also means you are competing for attention and must use all your resources to make impressions, including speaking, video, email, and meetings.

An example of this can be seen in your local community. If you live near restaurants, you will probably walk by a new restaurant under construction from time to time. In this case, you walk by and see a sign that says, "Coming soon, a great new sushi and sake spot." You live in the neighborhood, and this new restaurant will be within walking distance of your home. This is great news for you! For the new restaurant, this was one impression—only six to go.

Next, the restaurant reaches its opening day and starts operation. The next time you walk by, you notice people eating outside. You see the amazing sushi tray on the table and a bottle of sake served with tiny cups. You get to smell some of the hot dishes that are also available. People are sitting on the patio enjoying their meals, drinking, eating, and having a great time. This is impression number two or three, depending on how tasty the food smells and looks. In-person impressions count the most since they provide signals from sight, smell, taste, and hearing. The same is true for an in-person meeting, which provides more impressions than an email. With an in-person meeting, you can see the person, ask questions, see body language, etc.

A few days later, you get a postcard in the mail with a coupon with no expiration date; it has full-color pictures of some of the food, including a few specials that look tasty. You file the postcard away next to your takeout menus. You haven't yet made a specific action to go to the restaurant; you still have a few more impressions to go.

Next, you see a social media ad for the restaurant or a friend posts about how good their happy hour drinks are. You're even closer. In fact, the chances of you being curious and familiar enough to check out the new restaurant are high. You have now reached seven or more impressions, and you're likely to ask someone you know about their experience or even try it out yourself.

Social media marketing works in this same way. Have you ever purchased something you didn't know you needed but decided you needed it because you saw it enough times and became familiar with it? Social media marketing has an incredibly sneaky way of getting people to buy things they didn't necessarily need or want by showing people problems, products, and solutions enough times that they become familiar with them and can't imagine their lives without them.

The rule of seven is real. It is a secret weapon to get people to hear, understand, and remember the change is coming. However, when mapping your path to reach seven impressions, it's important to remember that not all communication mediums count as one impression. Some have a larger impact, and some have a smaller impact. For example, consider the difference in impact between videos and text.

Utilizing multimedia such as videos can significantly enhance information retention by engaging viewers both visually and audibly. The human brain processes visual information much faster than text, and integrating audiovisual elements such as music, dialogue, and visual metaphors engages emotional responses, which are crucial for memory. Emotions stirred by these multimedia presentations help embed the details of the change deeper into memory, making the initial introduction of new information more impactful and memorable.

Additionally, videos and films employ storytelling that helps clarify the narrative of change, making complex information more relatable and easier to digest. By presenting change through a story with clear beginnings, middles, and ends, multimedia can offer practical contexts and visualize scenarios that text alone might fail to convey effectively. This storytelling approach helps stakeholders visualize the practical implications of change and provides a richer, more detailed understanding of the processes involved. For instance, a video explaining a new company policy shows real-life applications that written memos cannot capture, thereby supporting diverse learning styles and ensuring that stakeholders not only hear but truly understand the aspects of the change.

When planning to facilitate the hear stage, consider how to mix and match different communication methods to reach seven impressions. By using a formula to ensure you reach seven impressions, you allow change participants to understand what you are trying to convey and, better yet, a solid opportunity to remember what you said after you're done saying it.

As we transition to exploring communication methods, remember it's not about repeating the same message but creating multifaceted impressions that engage and inform. Next, we'll dive into a guide to communication methods ordered by their impact and frequency needed to truly resonate with the audience. This guide aims to equip you with strategies not just to reach but meaningfully connect with your audience, ensuring the message of change is heard and embraced.

Guide to Communication Methods, Ordered by Number of Impressions

Not every communication type or method is created equally when it comes to the number of impressions they create. Impactful mediums like face-to-face communication are more memorable, counting for up to three or four impressions. These types of communications will inform people impacted by the change with the goal of helping them move forward in the change process. This practice isn't only applicable to change; it can and should be applied to anything you need people to adapt to, learn, do, or understand.

The list below categorizes communication techniques from the most impactful, such as face-to-face interactions and video conferencing, to less direct methods like bulk emails and public signage. Understanding each method's varying degrees of influence allows you to craft a communication strategy that maximizes both reach and effectiveness. By judiciously mixing these methods, you can ensure that your messages are heard and resonate deeply, laying the groundwork for successful navigation through the Hear stage and beyond.

More effective, more impressions; Less effective, less impressions:

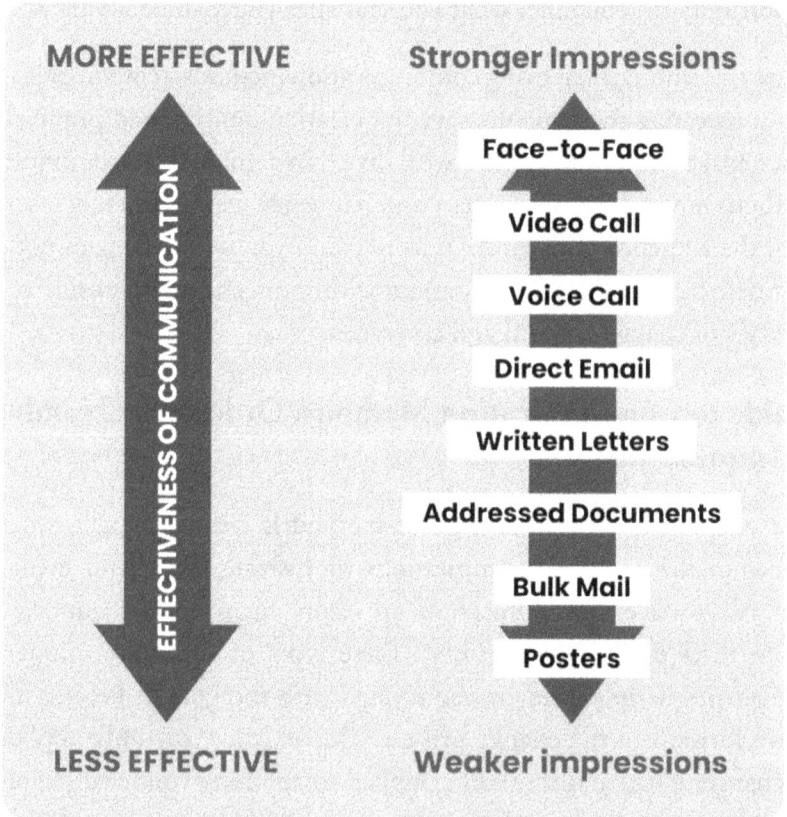

Figure 2.1: Communication Types by Impressions, ordered by Strength

The more personal the media is, the greater its effectiveness. This is because more impressions are gained with more senses involved.

When we lead change or projects that create change, the majority of our job is oriented specifically around communication. It is our job to repeat ourselves over and over again without becoming irritated or tired. The "I already told you when this is happening" line must be struck from change leaders' repertoire because unless you have given that person seven impressions of the information and the change in question, you have not yet done your part to aid people in understanding the change.

While we try to be planful and hope that will lead us to change success, not all impressions are planful, formal, official, or organized. Sometimes, the most influential impressions are received through rumors, especially when the change hasn't been formally announced yet. You can actually use rumors to your advantage to get early adopters to join in. You might be quick to think, "A rumor, that's bad; why would we encourage rumors?" but strategic rumors can be very powerful when working to ensure everyone hears of an upcoming change. Strategically placed rumors must be factually correct to be valuable and still require all of the details and Five Ws to minimize the stories people make up about the rumor itself.

A compliment to rumors, when driving change in organizations, you might consider leveraging a Change Champion Network (CCN) to help identify, clarify, and drive change socially. A CCN is a group intended to get a preview into upcoming changes, give feedback, and assist in the execution of strategic rumors or information sharing where appropriate. In our experience of driving change in organizations, CCNs have been very helpful in refining messaging, determining how to best reach the people impacted by the change, and executing information sharing through social networks. We have lots more to share about CCNs, including how to set one up, which is included in the playbook for the Hear stage later in this book.

As you lead in the Hear stage, a great way to monitor the success and effectiveness of your communication is listening for when people begin to ask questions or about specific considerations or impacts that are important to them. A person asking questions indicates that they have heard enough to inquire about the content of the change. Questions are a great indicator of progress in the Hear stage and are in themselves an additional impression. When someone brings you questions, comments, or criticisms of your change, welcome them! These items are excellent feedback that should not be taken lightly; questions also indicate progress in the Hear stage and movement towards the next stage, Fear.

When Extra Support is Needed

Some people are more resistant to hearing new information about upcoming changes than others, often because they don't like surprises, especially when the surprise is a change that impacts them, and they feel they have no say in the matter.

One effective method to help these folks through the Hear stage is to deliver the news early and personally, if possible. Having a personal conversation with a highly impacted person can relieve angst and provide more impressions. Some call this the "pre-read" approach, where you read someone in early or personally. This means taking time to communicate with these individuals intentionally, often before a large change announcement. In the discussion where you facilitate the Hear stage for this individual, you can get it right by covering the Five Ws and repeating what is happening.

Utilizing this method has multiple benefits, including:

- The person hearing about the change can react in a private setting.

- The person hearing about the change can ask questions specific to them.

- The person hearing about the change can voice any concerns immediately.

- The person hearing about the change can support others in the future as the change is announced more broadly.

We have used this practice consistently across significant changes, especially those involving people shifts: leadership changes, organizational restructuring, and mergers and acquisitions. In each case, we have found great success in investing the time to let specific individuals hear about a change in a way that fits their style so they can then help others through the Hear stage when it is their turn. By facilitating the Hear stage personally, you prepare people to progress in the change process to the Fear stage (this is a good thing).

This pre-read method also works exceptionally well with leadership teams to the point where it is a standard practice in our change methodology. Rather than announcing big changes all at once to all people, consider cascading information and, therefore, the Hear stage, from the decision-makers to the next most influential group. For example, when a CEO makes a decision, they should take the change associated with the decision to their closest peer group. After that group is informed and has a chance to weigh in on the change so they can stand behind it, it is time to move to the next most influential group, and so on.

Figure 2.2: Cascading Communication Throughout Levels

Informing different groups about a change in the order of influence kicks off the Hear stage for each group independently and supports trust-building among teams and leaders. In addition, leveraging this practice in Hear helps prepare people and teams for the Fear stage and minimizes later cleanup.

For example, let's say that a CEO plans to create two separate divisions in their organization. This person announces some basic information at the all-staff meeting on April 5th. The information includes:

- The timeline for the change (end of the year).

- The people involved in planning.

- The departments that will merge and those that will be divided.

- That the next update will be in the June all-staff meeting.

Because only the CxOs have been involved in these discussions, this comes as new information to all other leaders and employees. People are shocked! Wild panic and anxiety set in as people start talking to each other, trying to understand the change and making up some interesting reasons that are nothing close to accurate.

If you have experienced something similar to this, that's completely understandable because it is not in our nature to "trust and wait." Given the new information, we need to protect ourselves. To do that, we need to go out and fill in the rest of our impressions. We will also ask others who do not know additional information. These people will, of course, offer their opinions, and these opinions will translate to non-fact-based rumors that will spread in the organization. The result is that these rumors receive seven impressions, not the true message.

Let's replay this scenario with more attention to how people process change.

After making the decision, the CEO and the CXO team should communicate to the next leadership layer in the organization to have a similar conversation, covering all of the required elements in the Hear stage, gathering feedback from the team, and making any needed iterations to the message. The CEO and CXO team should also give extra support to those who may need it at this stage by having personal conversations with people who need additional understanding and reassurance. At this point, both the CXO and the top leadership teams are well on their way through the change process, making them better equipped to support the following layers of the organization through this change as they begin their journey through the curve.

When the re-organization announcement reaches the staff, the entire top leadership team will already be informed and given an opportunity to see some FAQs about the change (even in draft form), as well as ask questions and provide feedback about the change itself. Once the all-staff meeting occurs, the informed leaders should meet with their teams to discuss the change, listen to reactions, gather feedback, and provide additional information. An internal FAQ should be posted and updated throughout the implementation of the change to ensure people have as much information as they can. When members of the organization ask good questions, the FAQ can become an even richer tool.

By taking time at the outset to socialize the change, get feedback, iterate, socialize, and update with more folks, the change will be a smoother process and can likely be executed more efficiently. Changes that are well planned, well socialized, iterated on, and communicated appropriately are most likely to be successful and cause less disruption. By working through each layer of the organization, the general employee base (who hear about the change as a surprise) receives significantly more support, encouragement, and guidance than if the CEO were to announce a change without going through these steps.

Acknowledge Your Position and That of Others

When leaders announce significant changes with great enthusiasm, saying, "This is going to be so great; you are going to love it!" they may inadvertently set the stage for misunderstanding and resistance. Leaders must recognize that they are typically further along in the change process than their teams.

By the time a leader is ready to communicate the change, they have likely moved into the Near stage, having internally processed and accepted the change themselves. However, their team, just being introduced to the concept, is not yet on the same page. Simply announcing the change with expectations for immediate acceptance overlooks the need to assess where team members are in their own journey through the change curve. Leaders must provide not just information but also context and support, recognizing that their team needs time to adjust to and understand the new direction.

The people they are informing are in Hear, and they just got there because you told them something new! It should be no surprise that people hearing about a change for the first time might pause or reject the new information. They might have a lot of questions about the proposed change. When a leader is in Near, and their people are in Hear, the leader must pause and realize their role in facilitating the transition from Hear to Fear and then to Near, where folks can catch up with the leader on the curve. Only after most people are aligned and executing in Near is it time to consider acceptance of the change and entry into the Cheer stage. Remember the words "This is going to be so great; you are going to love it!" used at the beginning of this example? Those words should come into the Cheer stage but not from the leader. The leader should look to hear these statements from the team as they have accepted the change.

The second big mistake we see leaders make in announcing change is telling people how to feel about the change. As an overarching rule, you should never tell people how to feel, especially when introducing change. This tip is not specific to change but is universal across all interactions and all people. By telling someone how to feel, you suppress or diminish the opportunity for a person to have a natural reaction, to share their true feelings, and to give feedback that is not aligned with how you told them to feel.

This crime is especially damaging when committed by managers, as the power dynamics of many organizational hierarchies will further minimize employee perceptions of their ability to be their authentic selves and feel anything other than what they were told to feel. Also, telling people how to feel plainly doesn't work. We reflect on any time we have been told to "calm down" and ended up even more upset! You know better now.

Common Tricky Scenarios in Hear

Navigating the Hear stage effectively hinges on managing first impressions, which shape people's initial responses to change. In Hear, you may encounter complex scenarios where standard communication strategies are challenged, such as dealing with confidential information, implementing immediate changes, or handling incomplete details. Here, we explore how to craft these crucial first interactions to ensure they build understanding and trust, setting a positive tone for the entire change journey.

Change Involving Confidential Information

When leading changes such as layoffs, competitive acquisitions, or involuntary leader changes, you typically do not have the luxury of cascading the information about the change. In these cases, you should acknowledge that you would have liked to inform everyone with more time and preparation, but it was not possible. After this explanation, you can then work to cascade the information and provide the same amount of diligence for the Hear stage; it just might be a tad later than you would have liked.

Change That "Must Happen"

When changes are non-negotiable or driven by urgent needs—such as legal requirements, safety regulations, or critical policy shifts—the traditional pace of the change management process may need to be accelerated. For instance, in scenarios like mandating a non-smoking policy within a facility, the immediacy of the change does not allow for a gradual introduction or lengthy deliberation among employees.

In such cases, you should also look to integrate the "how" directly into the initial communication phase, or the Hear stage. This means that along with announcing the change, you must simultaneously provide clear, actionable steps on how the change will be implemented and who people should go to for support. This approach helps to reduce uncertainty and resistance by immediately addressing how the change affects daily routines and what specific actions are required from everyone involved.

Change Where Not All the Important Information Is Known

In some cases, you will need to announce a change before all of the details (Five Ws) are fully known. When this happens, be sure to communicate transparently about what is known and, just as importantly, what is not yet clear, as well as when you anticipate knowing.

While announcing a change without all the important details might seem risky, there are moments when this is absolutely necessary. Being transparent about what you know, what you don't know, and when you will find out gets people into the Hear stage of change and works to build a foundation of trust and credibility with change leadership. By clearly stating what you don't know and when you will find out and sharing the currently unknown information, you actively reduce the potential for rumors and misinformation to spread.

Handling incomplete information requires a delicate balance. It involves sharing enough to ensure people are informed and prepared for upcoming changes without overwhelming them with uncertainties that might lead to anxiety or resistance. This means focusing on the available facts, the objectives of the change, and how it aligns with the broader goals of the organization while also being upfront about the unknowns.

The Hear stage applies universally to all types of change and is a required stage in the change process. If you learn to facilitate the Hear stage well by providing information and resources and ensuring seven or more impressions, you can effectively drive change through the Hear stage to the next step, Fear.

Stories From the Field

To illustrate some of the concepts we've discussed so far, we will turn our attention to some examples of changes.

Restructuring Failure

An ambitious restructuring was initiated at a longstanding nonprofit organization to realign with new strategic objectives. Spearheaded by Executive Director Sarah Jensen, the plan aimed to streamline departments to enhance efficiency and increase impact. However, the critical missteps during the initial Hear stage would soon unravel into chaos, underscoring the need for careful and clear communication in organizational change.

Sarah began the restructuring process with a brief, ambiguous email distributed to all staff, hinting at "exciting changes ahead" and "strategic realignment." However, this email was notably light on details, lacking information about which positions would be affected, how roles would be reshaped, or any clear timeline for these changes. This vagueness brought uncertainty and fear among the employees, who were left to fill in the blanks with their worst fears.

As days turned into weeks without further clarification, the office became a hotbed of rumors and speculation. Anxiety surged as employees whispered about potential job cuts, abrupt department changes, and unmanageable increases in workload. The lack of transparency from Sarah's initial announcement had inadvertently set the stage for mistrust and speculation, which began to erode the fabric of the organization's culture.

Attempting to salvage the situation, Sarah organized a series of last-minute meetings to explain the restructuring process and address staff concerns. However, her efforts were met with skepticism and low turnout—many employees felt that these reactive attempts were insincere and too late to be genuinely reassuring. Meetings that were attended spiraled into heated confrontations, with staff openly challenging the lack of foresight and questioning Sarah's leadership. The atmosphere grew increasingly toxic; collaboration was replaced by conflict, and productivity plummeted as the focus shifted from organizational missions to personal job security.

The situation reached a boiling point when a group of influential staff members petitioned the board for intervention. The mounting unrest and chaotic leadership prompted the board to act decisively. Sarah was removed from her position at the dramatic culmination of the failed change initiative. Her departure was seen as a necessary step to prevent further damage to the nonprofit's morale and operational stability. This chaotic episode left the organization in disarray, with the restructuring process halted mid-course and the staff grappling with the fallout of a poorly managed Hear stage. The entire ordeal underscored the catastrophic impact of neglecting transparent and timely communication in times of critical organizational change.

We feel for Sarah. She tried to lead change effectively but completely lost her footing in the Hear stage. Sarah's initial approach to communicating the restructuring was fundamentally flawed due to its lack of clarity and detail. While she communicated her excitement, Sarah's vague and brief emails left too much room for interpretation, causing employees to speculate about the impacts of the restructuring on their jobs and the organization's overall direction. This speculation was then fueled by the absence of follow-up communication, which should have been timely and informative. If Sarah had noted the issue with the first announcement, she could have engaged with the staff, offering reassurances and a clear roadmap of the planned changes. Instead, Sarah's delay in providing detailed information allowed rumors to take root, undermining trust and morale across the organization, which eventually led to her removal.

College Curriculum Overhaul

At a large university, a significant challenge awaited: updating the school's curriculum to keep pace with fast-moving global industry and technological advances. Under the leadership of Provost Dr. Emily Tran, the university embarked on a bold plan to revamp its academic offerings and ensure wide acceptance within the university community. Faculty knew this change was being worked on. Still, they were quite happy teaching the courses they had developed already, with little regard for the changing skills and labor markets their students were entering post-graduation.

Dr. Tran was on a mission to modernize the university curriculum, and she knew she had to get the Hear stage right if the changes were to be adopted. After some preliminary design and testing of new curriculum content, it was time to inform the faculty and students about the upcoming changes being considered. Dr. Tran pulled people into the Hear stage by sending an email with a video describing the change. She also attended multiple small-group faculty meetings to describe the upcoming changes. Next, Dr. Tran facilitated a series of town hall meetings, both on campus and online. These weren't just informational sessions; they were designed as interactive discussions where faculty and students could share their thoughts, interact with the curriculum developers, and see how the changes could benefit them.

Before these meetings, the university sent out detailed information packets across campus. These packets contained FAQs, schedules, and stories from classes that had tested the new courses. Additionally, Dr. Tran's team made good use of the university's online platforms, posting articles and interviews that showcased the positive experiences of those who participated in the pilot courses. At this point, the faculty was squarely in the Hear stage and getting into the Fear stage, thanks to the work of Dr. Tran and her team.

The town hall meetings turned into lively centers for debate and learning. Dr. Tran and her team listened to concerns, answered questions, and took real-time feedback seriously, adjusting the curriculum as needed. For example, when the elimination of some traditional courses caused an uproar, the curriculum design team cleverly incorporated these subjects as elective options within the new curriculum framework. Also, in response to faculty concerns about adopting and leveraging new technology in their classrooms, the university held workshops for faculty that demonstrated new teaching methods and technologies.

Thanks to Dr. Tran's strategic approach in Hear and facilitating through the Fear and Near stages, the curriculum launch was successful, with students noting higher job placement rates and feeling better prepared for their post-graduation work. Dr. Tran's handling of the Hear stage built a culture of openness and readiness for change, showing that even some of the most complex and contentious changes can be successful with effective communication and leadership.

Exiting the Hear Stage

Exiting the Hear stage marks the first threshold in the change management process, moving from Hear to Fear. It is the point where initial information has been disseminated and understood, setting the stage for the emotional and psychological reactions that characterize the Fear stage. Recognizing the signs that your team is transitioning from initial awareness to emotional engagement is key to navigating this stage effectively.

Identifying the Transition

The transition from the Hear to the Fear stage is marked by a shift from factual understanding to emotional reaction. Team members begin to internalize the change, moving from "What is this change?" to "What does this change mean for me and my role?" This shift is a natural progression and indicates a readiness to engage more deeply with the implications of the change.

Encouraging Open Expression of Concerns

At this juncture, it is common for concerns and apprehensions to surface. The Hear stage and transition to Fear is characterized by a need for reassurance and further clarification as team members begin to process the change on a personal level. Leaders should foster an environment where expressing concerns is encouraged and supported.

Recognizing and Addressing Anxieties

While moving towards the Fear stage, it's vital to be open to hearing the anxieties that inevitably arise. Ensuring ample feedback mechanisms and responsive leadership can help solicit fears and encourage people to move forward in the change process. Leaders should be approachable and ready to address any issues that surface during discussions, providing reassurances and adjustments to plans as necessary.

Preparing for Emotional Engagement

As you prepare to leave the Hear stage, it's important to acknowledge the shift from informational reception to emotional reaction. This preparation involves reinforcing the support available and setting the stage for the more intensive emotional processing that occurs in the Fear stage.

Exiting the Hear stage effectively means that stakeholders are informed about the change and are beginning to emotionally engage with it. This sets the foundation for addressing fears directly and constructively in the subsequent stages of the change process. By managing this transition thoughtfully, leaders can ensure that the groundwork laid during the Hear stage supports a more resilient and responsive journey through the entire change management cycle.

📌 Key Takeaways

- In the Hear stage, people learn about the change; they hear it for the first time. Early and comprehensive communication will help set a positive tone for the change process.

- In Hear, people need answers to the Five Ws: who, what, when, where, and why. Clear details about what is changing, why it is necessary, and how it aligns with broader organizational goals are crucial to minimizing misunderstandings and building a foundation of trust.

- In Hear, people need to hear the message repeatedly. Up to seven impressions are needed for someone to really hear what is intended to change. Diversifying communication formats— such as meetings, emails, videos, and Q&A sessions—supports understanding across varying types of listeners.

- In Hear, it is your job as a leader to inform people about the upcoming journey through the change curve, including the next steps. Let them know the information that is available now and when they can expect more communication.

Tips for the Hear Stage

Leading change in the Hear stage is all about helping people acknowledge and understand the upcoming change while preparing for the Fear stage. It is here that people first encounter information indicating elements in their world will shift. Actively manage this stage to help build a solid foundation for the stages to come. Try out these tips:

- **Tailor Communications to Audience Segments**: Recognize the diversity within your audience and customize your messages accordingly. Segment your audience by department, role, or even sentiment towards the change. Tailored messages ensure that the information resonates more deeply and is relevant to each group's specific concerns and contexts.

- **Establish a Feedback Loop**: Create structured opportunities for feedback to flow back to the change leaders. This can be through digital forums, anonymous surveys, or scheduled focus groups. A feedback loop not only helps identify areas of confusion or resistance but also demonstrates that leadership values and acts upon input from the team.

- **Leverage Storytelling Techniques**: Instead of just presenting facts, weave the change narrative into a story that outlines the journey, the challenges overcome, and the envisioned future. Storytelling can make the change more relatable and memorable, increasing emotional engagement and support.

- **Promote Transparency with Regular Updates**: Even if no new information is available, maintain a rhythm of communication that keeps everyone informed about the progress of the change process. This can prevent the rumor mill from filling voids with misinformation.

- **Develop a Resource Hub**: Create a central repository for all change-related materials, including FAQs, schedules, contact information for change leaders, and links to additional resources. This hub should be easily accessible and regularly updated to serve as a reliable source of truth throughout the Hear stage.

- **Integrate Change Advocates**: Identify and empower enthusiastic supporters within various teams to act as change advocates. These individuals can help disseminate information, model positive behaviors, and provide peer support, thereby amplifying official communications. Know someone at work that many people look up to? Partner with them to start the change off on the right foot

Dos in the Hear Stage

- **Do Provide a Comprehensive Overview**: Offer clear, complete information about the change, addressing the Five Ws, who, what, when, where, and why, to ensure thorough understanding and minimize misconceptions.

- **Do Use Multiple Communication Methods**: Deliver key messages through various channels like emails, meetings, video messages, and visual presentations to reinforce the information, accommodate different learning styles, and reach seven impressions!

- **Do Foster Interactive Communication**: Encourage two-way communication by organizing forums and Q&A sessions, making individuals feel valued and heard, and allowing for clarification of doubts.

- **Do Address and Clarify Misunderstandings Promptly**: Proactively manage misconceptions or incorrect information as soon as they arise to prevent misinformation from derailing the change process.

- **Do Build Trust Through Transparency**: Maintain openness in your communications, showing the genuine intent and the bigger picture behind the change, which is crucial for smoothly transitioning from Hear to Fear.

Don'ts in the Hear Stage

- **Don't Overwhelm with Information**: Avoid bombarding individuals with too much information at once—structure communication to be digestible and phased to prevent information overload.

- **Don't Assume Uniform Understanding**: Recognize that not everyone will grasp the change at the same pace or depth. Regularly check for understanding and readiness to adapt to individual needs.

- **Don't Neglect Emotional Responses**: Do not underestimate the emotional impact of change. Acknowledge and validate the feelings and reactions of team members to foster a supportive environment.

- **Don't Rely Solely on Formal Announcements**: Incorporate informal interactions as part of the communication strategy. Casual conversations can sometimes address concerns and reinforce the change message more effectively.

- **Don't Rush the Process**: Allow sufficient time for the information to be absorbed and understood. Rushing through the Hear stage can lead to resistance and a lack of preparedness for subsequent stages.

- **Don't Try to Make the Change Sound Easy**: Avoid over-simplifying the change process. Acknowledge the challenges and the effort required, setting realistic expectations about the journey ahead.

- **Don't Tell People the Emotions They Should Have**: Avoid dictating how individuals should feel about the change, e.g., "You will love this; this will be great." Allow people to experience and express their genuine emotions.

- **Don't Forget to Acknowledge Your Place in the Change Curve**: Be mindful of where you are in the change process compared to others. Recognize that you might be further along and more comfortable with the change, which can affect how you communicate and relate to those just starting their journey.

Quiz

There are many concepts and tools described in this book. To ensure you can apply them to real-life situations, consider taking the following quiz.

Question 1:

The HR department is introducing a new performance appraisal system. What is the best strategy to introduce this system to the company during the Hear stage to ensure understanding, multiple impressions, and responsiveness?

A)   Develop a multimedia presentation that includes an FAQ section, followed by interactive Q&A sessions across different departments, as well as regular email updates.

B)   Send out a brief email announcing the introduction of the new system with a link to the policy document.

C)   Arrange for a mandatory training session that all employees must attend to learn about the new system.

D)   Release a video from the CEO explaining the new system without follow-up discussions.

Correct Answer: A) Develop a multimedia presentation that includes a FAQ section, followed by interactive Q&A sessions across different departments, and regular email updates.

When the HR department implements its multimedia presentation with a FAQ and Q&A along with additional communications, this not only aims to provide clear and comprehensive information but also ensures repeated impressions through interactive sessions and regular updates. This multi-touch approach helps solidify understanding and allows HR to be responsive to employee reactions which will be very important for them in the Hear stage.

Question 2:

Mr. Anderson, a high school principal, is introducing a new digital learning platform. He aims to ensure a smooth transition and sustained use in future educational activities. What comprehensive strategy should he employ during the Hear stage to involve students, parents, and teachers effectively?

A) Post an announcement on the school's digital bulletin board and consider the job done.

B) Arrange separate, tailored orientation sessions for students, parents, and teachers, supplemented with detailed resource packets and a feedback mechanism on the school's website.

C) Hold a general assembly to announce the platform quickly without follow-up.

D) Send an email blast to all parties and avoid follow-up to reduce workload.

Correct Answer: B) Arrange separate, tailored orientation sessions for students, parents, and teachers, supplemented with detailed resource packets and a feedback mechanism on the school's website.

This approach caters to the specific needs and concerns of each group involved with the platform. By providing tailored orientation sessions and resource packets, Mr. Anderson ensures everyone understands how to use the new platform. The addition of a feedback mechanism encourages ongoing communication, which is crucial for addressing issues promptly and ensuring the platform's effective integration into school activities.

Question 3:

Lane, the CEO of a mid-sized technology firm, is about to announce the acquisition of his company by a larger industry leader. To manage potential uncertainty and maintain trust among employees, he needs to plan the communication strategy carefully. What should Lane do during the Hear stage to ensure the acquisition is communicated effectively and sensitively?

A)   Immediately send a company-wide email with details of the acquisition and an FAQ document, followed by a brief all-hands meeting.

B)   Hold a confidential meeting with the leadership team to discuss the acquisition details, then allow the leaders to conduct an all-staff meeting, coordinate departmental meetings, and schedule ongoing structured feedback sessions.

C)   Post an announcement on the company intranet and hold a general Q&A session afterwards without prior detailed discussions with the leadership team.

D)   Allow the leadership team to find out through the general company communication channels to see how they handle the news without prior coaching.

Correct Answer: B) Hold a confidential meeting with the leadership team to discuss the acquisition details, then allow the leaders to conduct an all-staff meeting, coordinate departmental meetings, and schedule ongoing structured feedback sessions.

Choosing to first engage with the leadership team in a confidential setting allows Lane to ensure that key company leaders are fully informed and understand the strategic vision behind the acquisition before the information is disseminated throughout the organization. This step helps leaders process the Hear stage, prepare to support their employees, and effectively handle questions and concerns from their respective teams. This approach not only facilitates a more controlled and coherent spread of information but also empowers department leaders to tailor their communications to their teams' specific needs and dynamics. Regularly scheduled feedback sessions enhance this communication strategy by creating opportunities for ongoing dialogue, allowing Lane and his team to address emerging concerns, adjust communication strategies as necessary, and maintain engagement throughout the organization during this significant transition.

Question 4:

Susan, the CEO of a medium-sized enterprise, plans to restructure the company to better align with emerging market demands. This restructuring will involve merging several departments and creating new roles. Susan understands the potential anxieties such changes might provoke and wants to ensure the transition is smooth and well-received. What strategy should Susan employ during the Hear stage to effectively communicate this organizational change?

A) Release a detailed report about the restructuring on the company's intranet and assume that all employees will access and understand the information on their own.

B) Schedule a general assembly to announce the changes all at once and then follow up with an email summarizing the new structure.

C) Use the company newsletter to slowly introduce the changes over several issues to gradually get employees accustomed to the idea.

D) First hold confidential meetings with department heads to discuss the upcoming changes, followed by a series of team meetings led by these department heads to explain how the changes will directly affect each team.

Correct Answer: D) First hold confidential meetings with department heads to discuss the upcoming changes, followed by a series of team meetings led by these department heads to explain how the changes will directly affect each team.

By first engaging with department heads in confidential meetings, Susan ensures that key internal leaders are fully informed and prepared for the restructuring before the wider employee base is informed. This step is critical for several reasons: it allows leaders to understand the strategic reasons behind the changes, address any of their concerns, and equip them with the information needed to lead their teams through the transition. Following these initial meetings and introducing the restructuring to teams through their direct leaders allows for tailored communication that considers the specific impacts on each department. This approach facilitates clearer understanding, as employees receive information relevant to their roles from trusted supervisors, which can help mitigate resistance and confusion.

Question 5:

Angela, the Chief Compliance Officer at a multinational corporation, must introduce a significant update to the company's data privacy policy due to new international regulations. This policy change will affect how all employees handle customer data and require compliance across all departments globally. To ensure everyone understands and adheres to the new requirements, what should Angela do during the Hear stage to effectively communicate this change?

A) Send all employees a detailed policy document via email and require electronic receipt acknowledgment.

B) Publish the updated policy on the company intranet and mention it briefly in the monthly newsletter.

C) First conduct a series of webinars for department heads to thoroughly explain the policy changes and their implications, followed by team-specific sessions led by these trained leaders to ensure the message is correctly passed on and understood.

D) Organize a one-time, company-wide virtual meeting where the policy changes are presented, followed by a Q&A session without further follow-up.

Correct Answer: C) First conduct a series of webinars for department heads to thoroughly explain the policy changes and their implications, followed by team-specific sessions led by these trained leaders to ensure the message is correctly passed on and understood.

Angela's strategy of first educating department heads through detailed webinars allows for an initial layer of understanding among leadership, who are crucial for further cascading the information accurately. This method ensures that those responsible for leading their teams are fully aware of the changes, why they are necessary, and how they affect daily operations. These leaders can then tailor the communication to the specific contexts of their teams, making it more relevant and comprehensible.

Following up with team-specific sessions led by these informed department heads helps address the diverse needs and questions that may arise in different areas of the organization. This two-tiered approach facilitates thorough understanding through targeted education and promotes compliance by ensuring that all employees receive consistent information contextualized to their specific roles. The leaders' direct involvement in these sessions reinforces the seriousness of the policy change and the commitment of the organization to ensure everyone is informed, prepared, and compliant.

CHAPTER 3

FEAR

I work in an office every day and really enjoy where I sit, who I sit with, and how my day goes when I'm in the office. Today, I got an email that said that my team was going to be moved to another place in the building. As I read those words, a mixture of curiosity and apprehension washed over me. I couldn't help but wonder how this new arrangement would affect the camaraderie and synergy we had developed.

The email said that we would be staying in the same building but would move one floor up and be on the south side of the building near the windows. I didn't know why this change was happening. It wasn't explained in the email, and I didn't realize that we would be moving desks. I wonder who made this decision.

Glancing around the office, I noticed a range of reactions from my coworkers. Some seemed excited, eager for a fresh start and the opportunity to connect with new faces. Others wore expressions of uncertainty, perhaps fearing the unknown or the potential disruption to their daily routines.

I don't want to move to a new desk. I like where I am now and don't know if I will like the team's new seating arrangement. It is louder on that floor, and I worry I won't be as productive. Will the new seating arrangement bring my team closer or create a divide? Will the dynamics of our team change, for better or worse? It seems impossible to know for sure.

Reflecting on past experiences, I remember times when workplace transformations had brought chaos and disarray. The adjustment to new dynamics and the loss of familiar surroundings had caused tension and unease, not to mention a disruption in productivity.

Sure, my equipment will move, and I'll still have a desk, but I am not supportive of this change. I don't want to move to a new desk. I wonder if I can stop it.... [writes strongly worded email to office manager].

Fear is a natural human reaction to change; we can have fears of any change, big or small. We all fear different things, and these fears can overwhelm a proposed change process even to the point that it is stopped, considered an immediate failure, never spoken about again, or slowed down because it was not planned correctly. In essence, fear is the greatest threat to effective, high-velocity change, and unfortunately, all change creates feelings of fear.

In this chapter, we will explore the Fear stage and learn what should be done at this stage to help you change from falling flat. We will tackle the waves of emotion and blockers surrounding change rooted in fear and share some time-proven strategies for addressing a wide range of fears and keeping your change effort moving forward.

Why are people so afraid of change?

"The world as we have created it is a process of our thinking. It cannot be changed without changing our thinking."
—Albert Einstein

At its core, fear is a natural part of being human, linked to our habits, how our brains work, and how we react to things that scare us. We naturally like things we're used to because they make us feel safe and comfortable, both physically and in our minds. Sticking to routines isn't just about feeling good; it also helps save energy. Since our brains use up about a quarter of our body's energy, they prefer sticking to what they know best.

But when change comes knocking, our brains must leave their comfort zone, using more energy to deal with new information and situations. This can make us feel stressed or tired because our bodies are working harder than usual. So, our love for routines isn't just about what we like; it's also our body's way of not using up too much energy. Understanding this helps explain why we often resist change: it demands more from us mentally and physically.

As we go through life-building habits, these habits shape how we see the world. They help us feel less uncertain about things around us. When we have to migrate from our habits, discomfort sets in until we build new habits. It requires more of us and drains our likely over-taxed reserves.

Our brains don't like change because it means dealing with the unknown. They would rather deal with something familiar, even if it's not great, than face something new. This fear of change comes from our "mental models"—what we expect will happen in certain situations, even if those expectations might be off the mark. Let's review an example that shows us a typical situation as we face change.

Mia manages a mid-size marketing firm that specializes in traditional advertising strategies. The firm has built its reputation on creative print and media campaigns, priding itself on its human touch and intuition in understanding market trends and consumer behavior. The team is a tight-knit group of seasoned professionals, deeply committed to their craft and skeptical of the burgeoning reliance on digital technologies in marketing.

Throughout Mia's experience managing the firm, the shift toward digital marketing had been gradual, but the advent of artificial intelligence (AI) technology in the industry marked a turning point. Mia's competitors began leveraging AI for data analysis, consumer insights, and even content creation, achieving unprecedented levels of personalization and efficiency. Mia recognizes the need for change; to stay competitive, her firm needs to integrate AI technology into its services. However, Mia is extremely concerned about this shift and its impact on the perception of her team's talents and the firm's future success.

The team values creativity and human insight above all, viewing AI as a threat to their jobs and the quality of their work. They fear that relying on AI would make their skills obsolete and erode the personal touch that defined their brand. Mia faces resistance and skepticism as she approaches the idea of adopting AI tools.

When change is outside of our control, it can leave us feeling powerless. And when we feel powerless, we feel wide open to threat. And, of course, that sense of threat leads us to feel fear and infer the worst possible outcomes, causing us to run to one of three responses: fight, flight, or freeze.

When Mia first encountered the sweeping trend of AI integration within the marketing industry, her immediate reaction was a visceral blend of apprehension and denial. The thought of integrating artificial intelligence into her firm's deeply human-centric creative process seemed not just daunting but fundamentally at odds with everything her team valued. This challenge to her established beliefs and business practices triggered the natural biological response to perceived threats: the fight, flight, or freeze reaction.

Initially, Mia found herself oscillating between a "fight" stance, where she considered vehemently opposing the integration of AI as a matter of principle, defending the sanctity of human creativity against the encroachment of machines. Part of her wanted to rally her team to double down on their traditional methods and prove that technology could not replicate or surpass human ingenuity.

Simultaneously, the "flight" response surfaced, tempting Mia with thoughts of sidestepping the issue entirely. She considered focusing the firm's efforts on niche markets where traditional advertising methods still held sway, potentially avoiding the need to confront the AI trend head-on. This path seemed to offer a way to maintain the status quo, preserving the firm's identity in the short term but at the risk of long-term obsolescence.

Underpinning these reactions was the "freeze" response—a sense of paralysis stemming from the uncertainty of how to proceed. Mia experienced moments of indecision, where the magnitude of the shift towards AI in her industry left her feeling stuck, unsure how to adapt or whether adaptation was even possible without losing the essence of her firm's approach to marketing.

This fight, flight, or freeze reaction is a natural biological response to perceived threats rooted in our evolutionary history. For Mia, the threat wasn't physical but existential, challenging the identity of her business and her place within the industry.

Mia was at a crossroads. She needed to change something, but she wasn't yet sure exactly what she needed to do to stay relevant and preserve the current and future opportunities for success for her business. Ultimately, Mia did not want to change but was being forced by external changes to consider her options swiftly. Feeling at a loss, Mia sought guidance from a few trusted people around her who helped her think about the challenge in new ways.

When faced with fear and sent into the fight, flight, or freeze reaction, we need a way to break out of this state. One of the best ways to try to break free is to consider the challenge, change, or cause of fear in a different way. This is often challenging, but when done effectively, it can be a game-changer in how you both react to and lead change. One of the best ways to practice thinking about a change or challenge differently is to do what Mia did and look to others to consider the change through different lenses. The goal here is to become psychologically flexible and learn how to view problems, fears, and challenges from different points of view or through different lenses.

People who are psychologically flexible can use their skills to view a challenge or fear through different perspectives and reframe their response to threats. Knowing what you value and what you're striving for can help you through this. As you face fears, navigate change, and learn about new concepts or begin to embody new behaviors, your brain adapts, changing its chemistry to reflect the new perspectives, habits, attitudes, and values you form. Your view of the world and the mechanisms your brain uses to sort out good from bad are changed as you learn and change your behavior.

In other words, if you can learn to re-frame changes and your reaction to fears, you can train your brain to work through the fight, flight, and freeze response and move towards a much more productive framing of a challenge or change, which can ultimately enable you to be much smarter in working through the fear stage and navigating change successfully.

> Mia, through the help of her trusted friends and colleagues, allowed herself to become more psychologically flexible, move beyond initial impulses, and consider a more strategic approach to change, one that embraced the potential of AI as a tool to augment and enhance her team's creative capabilities, rather than a threat to their relevance and value.

Confronting these challenges, Mia embarked on a strategy to shift the firm's mental models regarding AI. She started with a listening session and then swiftly moved towards AI education, organizing workshops demonstrating AI's capacity to enhance rather than replace human creativity. Mia both re-framed the challenge for herself and then began the journey to lead her firm in embracing AI as a tool rather than an existential threat to its future.

Mia's journey from the initial shock and resistance to the threat of AI to her marketing firm sets the stage for a deeper exploration into the dynamics of change, specifically as we pivot towards understanding the fear stage. Her story, rich with personal and professional dilemmas, illustrates the natural progression from initial resistance to needing to confront her fear. Next, Mia will need to address the fears and needs of her team since she is not alone within her firm. This progression is not unique to Mia; it's a universal experience shared by leaders and teams across the spectrum when faced with significant shifts.

Entering the Fear Stage

As you enter the Fear stage, people may complain loudly about the change. In other words, they are going to identify barriers. They will tell you what is wrong with your idea, why it won't work, and why you shouldn't even continue forward with the idea that change may occur.

The Fear stage is when the hallways and chat channels buzz with conversations, not about the potential of what's coming, but the multitude of ways it could falter and potentially why it is a bad thing. Employees, entrenched in the comfort of the known, begin to voice apprehensions. They'll highlight every flaw in the plan, questioning its feasibility and your rationale for advocating such a shift. It's not just skepticism you'll encounter but a vivid picture of every possible scenario where things could go awry.

Though fraught with challenges, this stage is integral to the change journey. It signals engagement, albeit in the form of resistance. Yes, this can be painful, but here's the silver lining: this resistance is a beacon of progress, an essential milestone on the path to transformation. As daunting as they may seem, articulating fears and identifying barriers are clear indicators that the wheels of change are in motion. Consider the case of Alex, a tech startup founder who decided to pivot his company's focus from consumer apps to B2B software solutions due to shifting market demands and concerns with the future revenue model of the consumer app space.

> Alex's announcement was met with immediate backlash. His team, having poured years into developing consumer products, couldn't see the vision behind the shift. They bombarded Alex with a barrage of concerns: loss of brand identity, the steep learning curve for new technologies, and the risk of alienating their existing user base. Alex was overwhelmed with negative feedback from his team, but he understood this was a step towards successful change and that his job at that time was to listen to and even solicit his team's concerns.

In the Fear stage, your job as a leader is to collect information about the things that people are concerned about, the barriers they have identified. Find out what is causing fear, look for ways to solve or mitigate the elements causing fear, and let everyone know what you are doing about it.

In Alex's case, he understood that genuine concerns lay beneath the cacophony of complaints needing acknowledgment and risk mitigation. His people wanted to be heard, and they came from a place of care for the history and experience of the organization to date. Alex's role morphed from a decision-maker and change communicator to a listener, an investigator seeking to understand the root of each fear. Alex held town hall meetings, one-on-one sessions, and feedback circles, gathering insights into his team's apprehensions.

> After collecting a considerable amount of feedback, Alex worked to provide clarity, offering training resources for technologies, highlighting the research behind the pivot, and drawing a clear roadmap of how each team member fit into the new vision.
>
> Alex took the time to acknowledge and address the fears of his team. This approach did more than just quell fears; it transformed them. The team's apprehensions gave Alex a comprehensive view of potential hurdles, allowing him to strategize effectively and bring his team in on problem-solving and crafting the future strategy. By openly addressing the fears and actively involving his team in crafting realistic solutions, Alex turned the fear stage into a collaborative process of problem-solving and innovation.

Conversely, had Alex chosen a different path, bypassing his team's concerns, the fabric of his company could have unraveled quickly. Ignoring the simmering fears would have cast a shadow of uncertainty and mistrust across the organization. Team members, feeling sidelined and unheard, might have retreated into silence or, worse, become even more openly resistant both in actions and words. Such an atmosphere of doubt could erode the trust in Alex's leadership that had taken years to build.

As morale dips, the once vibrant culture of innovation and collaboration is replaced by a climate of apprehension. Key talented employees, feeling unanchored and unsure of their future within the company, might start to look elsewhere, leaving gaps that cannot easily be filled. This exodus disrupts ongoing projects and dims the spark of innovation that has been the backbone of the company's reputation.

The external repercussions soon follow. With the team's spirit dampened, the company's output and customer engagement suffer, tarnishing its reputation and, potentially, its standing in the market. The missed opportunity for growth and adaptation looms large, with Alex's company lagging behind its competitors as they embrace change and innovation.

In essence, bypassing the Fear stage without addressing the team's concerns would have been a huge misstep, stunting the company's growth and weakening its foundation. Thankfully, Alex did not try to skip the fear stage. He instead embraced it and took time to listen to his team, hear their concerns, and engage in collaborative efforts to address the fears and mitigate risk.

As you navigate the fear stage in your own change, remember Alex's story. It's a testament to the power of facing fears head-on, of transforming resistance into a constructive dialogue. This stage, for all its discomfort, is a crucible for strengthening your change initiative. By embracing the fears, engaging with the barriers, and involving your team in finding solutions, you lay the groundwork for a change that is resilient, well-considered, and can ultimately be accepted by your team.

Here's a quick reference for how to identify if your change is entering the Fear stage:

Indicator	What You Will Observe	What People Will Be Doing
Vocal Resistance	Conversations focus on the negatives; discussions are filled with skepticism and highlight potential failures.	Complaining about the change, identifying all potential barriers, and expressing why the change won't work.

Indicator	What You Will Observe	What People Will Be Doing
Apprehension and Uncertainty	An atmosphere of doubt pervades, with employees appearing anxious about the future.	Voicing concerns about the impact of the change on their roles and the company's direction.
Focus on Barriers	Focus is predominantly on the obstacles rather than the opportunities presented by the change.	Questioning the feasibility of the change and the rationale behind it, often hypothesizing worst-case scenarios.
Seeking Assurance	A need for reassurance about job security, company direction, and personal impact of the change.	Actively seeking information that might allay their fears or confirm their suspicions.

This table reflects the typical behaviors and environmental cues that characterize entry to the Fear stage of change. During this stage, the challenge for leaders is to acknowledge and address these fears constructively, engaging with the concerns raised and working collaboratively to mitigate them, similar to Alex's approach in leading his team.

The Goals of the Fear Stage

The goal of the Fear stage is not to dismiss fear but to identify and analyze the elements or variables of the change that cause fear and work to mitigate or resolve some of the issues that cause fear. Fear itself cannot be removed by force; the only way to reduce or remove fear is to inspire confidence in others that the change in question is well-understood, manageable, and will be handled with care. Here's how to approach it:

- **Identify the Sources of Fear**: The first step is pinpointing exactly what aspects of the change are causing concern. This clarity allows for targeted interventions and reassures your team that their fears are recognized and being addressed.

- **Solicit and Value Feedback**: Encourage open communication by inviting feedback from those affected by the change. This provides insights into specific fears and reinforces to your team that their perspectives are important and valued.

- **Develop and Communicate Mitigation Strategies**: With an understanding of the fears, work with your team to develop solutions. Sharing these plans transparently with everyone involved is crucial; it shows that you're committed to addressing concerns thoughtfully and thoroughly.

- **Foster a Shift from Panic to Curiosity**: By addressing fears directly, you can help steer the team's initial panic towards curiosity about the change. This shift is essential for opening dialogue about the change's potential benefits and opportunities.

- **Inspire Confidence with Empathy and Preparedness**: Finally, showing that you have a well-considered plan to manage the change and are empathetic towards your team's experience can transform apprehension into trust. Demonstrating your commitment to guiding them through the transition with support and understanding is key.

In short, the goal of the Fear stage is to navigate through it with intention, transforming fear into a constructive force that drives the change forward. By understanding, addressing, and communicating about fears, you can build a foundation of curiosity and trust that paves the way for achieving a successful change.

Fear Stage Responsibilities

In the Fear stage of change, the roles and responsibilities of individuals, leaders, and the company are distinct yet interconnected as groups begin navigating through apprehensions and concerns brought on by change. Here's a breakdown of the responsibilities by role.

Individuals:

- **Identify and Articulate Fears**: Encourage individuals to openly identify and articulate their fears regarding the change. This can be through direct communication, feedback mechanisms, or anonymous surveys.

- **Seek Clarification and Support**: Individuals should proactively seek more information and support to better understand the change and mitigate their fears.

- **Participate in Solution-Finding**: Engage in discussions and brainstorming sessions aimed at finding solutions or workarounds for the challenges identified, contributing to a collective approach to overcoming obstacles.

Leaders:

- **Solicit, Accept, and Validate Feedback**: Leaders must create a safe space for feedback, accepting and validating the concerns raised by team members. Acknowledging fears as legitimate concerns is the first step in addressing them.

- **Communicate Transparently**: Maintain an open line of communication, providing clear and consistent information about the change, its rationale, and the expected outcomes. Transparency is key to dispelling rumors and misinformation.

Remember to be honest about any barriers that have been brought up that cannot or will not be removed so the team can move on.

- **Facilitate Problem-Solving Sessions**: Organize sessions where fears and concerns can be discussed openly and potential solutions are explored collaboratively. This fosters a sense of ownership and involvement among team members.

Company:

- **Iterate the Plan Based on Feedback**: The organization should be flexible in iterating its change plan based on the feedback received. Recognizing that initial plans may not be perfect allows for adjustments that can address the concerns raised.

- **Provide Resources for Support and Learning**: Make available resources such as training, counseling, or informational sessions to help individuals and teams better understand the change and reduce their fears.

- **Promote a Culture of Openness and Learning**: Encourage a company-wide culture where expressing fears and concerns is seen as a part of the learning and growth process, not a sign of weakness. This culture shift can make navigating the Fear stage more constructive and less daunting.

In the Fear stage, the collective effort focuses on turning apprehension into understanding and engagement. By addressing fears head-on, facilitating open discussions, and iterating plans based on real feedback, the organization moves closer to successfully implementing change.

Having delineated the roles and responsibilities during the Fear stage of change management, we've laid a roadmap for constructively navigating apprehensions. Yet, understanding the common causes behind the fear of change is crucial for applying these responsibilities effectively. The transition from identifying responsibilities to recognizing these causes is a step deeper into the intricacies of change management, allowing for a nuanced approach to addressing fear.

Navigating the Fear Stage

The Fear stage represents a natural human response to the unknown, where the anticipation of change stirs deep-seated fears and concerns, causing a variety of emotional responses, from apprehension about the future to a nostalgic clinging to the past. This stage is not just about resistance; it is an opportunity for deep engagement and transformation, provided it is navigated with empathy, clarity, and strategic foresight.

As leaders, our task is not merely to quell fears but to transform them into constructive dialogue and action. This requires a thoughtful approach, where we listen actively, communicate transparently, and provide the necessary support to help individuals move through their fears toward a more secure understanding of the change. We must address the root causes of fear, which often stem from concerns about job security, loss of control, or the demands of acquiring new skills. By acknowledging these fears and addressing them head-on, we can begin to dismantle the barriers to change.

In this section, we will explore strategies to effectively navigate the Fear stage. We'll discuss how to identify common fears, engage with them empathetically, and provide practical solutions that help individuals transition from apprehension to acceptance. By understanding the psychological impacts of change and implementing supportive measures, we can lead our teams to adapt to change and embrace it as an opportunity for growth and innovation.

Common Causes of Fear of Change

The apprehension surrounding change is often rooted in a variety of factors, each contributing to the resistance one encounters when driving change. Understanding these can illuminate why the Fear stage elicits strong reactions:

- **Comfort with Status Quo**: The familiar is comfortable, and deviations from this norm can be unsettling.

- **Threat to Security**: Changes may raise concerns about job security or the stability of one's position.

- **Loss of Control**: Change can create a sense that individuals no longer have control over their environment or future.

- **Shifted Expectations**: Adjusting to new goals or benchmarks can be a source of stress.

- **Failure to Convince/Persuade**: When the reasons behind the change are not clearly communicated or understood, resistance can grow.

- **Lack of Trust or Negative History**: Previous experiences of poorly managed change can influence reactions to new initiatives.

- **Concern about Results**: Worry that stakeholders or customers might react negatively to the change.

- **Work Pressure**: The anticipation of increased workload or pressure to adapt quickly.

- **New Skills Required**: The fear that one may not be able to acquire new skills or adapt to new methodologies.

- **Lack of Familiarities**: Uncertainty about new processes or environments can be intimidating.

The list above shows common concerns we face with change. The concerns come from past change experiences, witnessing change failures, and our own personal worries. One key understanding of change is that these concerns are common and natural. They should not be shoved aside; more appropriately, they should be addressed and/or acknowledged as part of the process.

Why do people fear things that don't seem to be real?

Fear is based on emotions coming from past experiences or fears that turn into stories, both the real ones and ones we tell ourselves. When change leaders do not provide sufficient information about the change, people fill in any missing information and begin making up stories! These stories are often quite outlandish as the stories we tell ourselves are always more extreme or malicious than reality. This needs to be kept in check.

Your goal as a change leader is to provide enough information to help people avoid filling the empty space while also avoiding inserting your own fears into the mental model of the change.

Understanding the common causes of fear of change sets the stage for the vital work ahead. Recognizing the roots of apprehension—from the comfort found in the status quo to the anxieties about new expectations and skills—provides us with a map through the tangled forest of fear. With this understanding, we pivot from merely identifying the sources of fear to actively addressing them and dismantling the barriers they erect in our path.

As we transition to addressing fears and removing barriers, we adopt the stance of a seasoned captain navigating stormy seas. This journey requires more than just understanding the waters; it demands active engagement, clear direction, and unwavering support for our crew. The challenges we face, akin to the fierce waves and obscured horizons of a tempest, call for a determined and strategic approach. Armed with the knowledge of what sparks fear, we are better prepared to face these challenges head-on, turning obstacles into opportunities for growth and transformation. Herein lies our next course of action: leading our team with empathy, strategy, and determination to weather the storm and emerge from it stronger and more cohesive than ever before.

Addressing Fears and Removing Barriers

Navigating through the Fear stage of change is akin to steering a ship through stormy seas. The waters are rough, the visibility is low, and the crew is anxious. As a leader, your role transcends mere navigation; it involves instilling confidence, providing direction, and ensuring the well-being of your crew as you chart a course through the tempest.

When Suzanne joined a new organization, she introduced a few changes and, with each one, asked her team, "What is wrong with my idea?" She was stunned when she only got back puzzled stares from everyone in the room. Once she finally got the team talking, they made it clear that there was a lot wrong with her idea...but who wants to tell their new manager what is wrong with an idea they are obviously excited about?

Over time, Suzanne built trust with her team; they got used to her asking about what was wrong with her bold ideas, and she received a lot of help from them. She was new to the organization, but the team knew where the hurdles would be along her path to successful change. If she was going to be successful in driving effective change, she needed feedback from her team. More importantly, she needed them to tell her what they saw wrong with the change that she might not have seen or considered from her position and lens as a new leader in a growing organization.

The barriers Suzanne's team mentioned were wide-reaching and sometimes very random but important! For example, when Suzanne was talking about a potential change to project management software, a surprising but significant blocker was the team's concern over losing access to a specific, legacy reporting feature. This feature, although outdated, was integral to how several departments prepared their monthly progress reports. The attachment to this specific function, which Suzanne had initially thought would be an easy sacrifice for the benefits of a more modern system, turned out to be a major challenge she and her team needed to navigate to ensure a smooth transition.

In each case, she was able to create a list of barriers to the change–which was great! Once she had a list, she could go through each item, looking to find ways to resolve, mitigate, or minimize the barrier. Not all barriers can be removed entirely, but she assured her team that she would still do her best to mitigate, minimize, or at least explain the barrier.

She's found that people often need time to think about the change and identify the barriers. This can be considered reaction time–people need time to process the news and begin to think about what might go wrong. This is part of the process of change, but don't spend too much time here; get to identifying the barriers!

Once you have identified the barriers and started resolving, mitigating, minimizing, or explaining them, it's great to begin showing signs of success at this stage. If you are leading people or a project through a change, get in front of the people who are involved and share information about how it's been going, what barriers have been identified, and what you are doing about them. Naturally, a cycle of iteration may occur as you and the team work through the various barriers, striving to reach a point where the unknown is known, resolved, mitigated, or minimized.

The barriers to successful change, much like the waves in a storm, can seem insurmountable. Yet, these obstacles can be navigated, if not entirely overcome, with the right approach. Here's how you can lead your team through this challenging stage with empathy, strategy, and determination:

1. **Facilitate Inclusive Discussions**: Gather the people who will be impacted by the change and get them talking, ensuring everyone's voice is heard and valued.

2. **Comprehensive Barrier Mapping**: Identify all perceived barriers together, acknowledging every concern without judgment, even if it is small or ridiculous.

3. **Collaborative Problem-Solving Sessions**: Brainstorm with key stakeholders and impacted people to find creative solutions to remove any barriers

4. **Prioritization and Acceptance**: Agree on what can be minimized and identify which barriers cannot be moved. Plan to work around any barriers that cannot be moved.

5. **Dynamic FAQ Creation**: Develop and regularly update a list of FAQs to address common concerns and share information transparently.

6. **Provide Clear, Actionable Information**: Offer resources that give straightforward steps for adapting to the change.

7. **Establish a Feedback Loop**: Create avenues for continuous feedback, allowing for real-time adjustments to your strategies.

8. **Celebrate Small Wins**: Recognize and celebrate progress to boost morale and maintain momentum.

9. **Leverage Peer Support**: Encourage team members to share their strategies for overcoming personal challenges with the change.

10. **Offer Personalized Support**: Provide tailored support to individuals struggling with the transition, recognizing the varied impacts of change.

As the storm begins to recede and the seas calm, it's essential to reflect on the journey you and your team have undertaken. While daunting, the challenges faced in the Fear stage have provided invaluable lessons in resilience, adaptability, and teamwork. By employing a strategic and empathetic approach to removing barriers, you've navigated through the turbulence and emerged stronger and more united. This experience underscores the importance of facing fears head-on, working collaboratively to find solutions, and maintaining an open line of communication throughout the change process.

In the aftermath, as calm waters surround you, the narrative shifts from overcoming fear to charting new territories with confidence and insight. The journey through the Fear stage, with all its trials and triumphs, serves as a testament to the power of collective effort and a flexible approach to change management. As you look ahead to the next stage of change, you do so with the knowledge that whatever challenges may arise, you and your team are well-equipped to meet them with courage, creativity, and a shared sense of purpose.

Having charted a course through the tumultuous waters of the Fear stage, where we've worked collaboratively to identify and dismantle barriers to change, we find ourselves at a pivotal moment. The strategies and techniques we've learned and employed—ranging from inclusive discussions to celebrating small wins—have helped us navigate the initial resistance and prepared the ground for a deeper transformation. As leaders, we've witnessed our team's collective strength, resilience, and capacity to adapt. Now, it's time to shift our focus from the immediate challenges of fear and resistance towards a broader horizon where change is not just something to be managed but embraced.

Potential Re-frames for Fear of Change

This next phase in our journey requires us to understand the origins of fear and actively re-frame these fears, turning them into catalysts for growth, innovation, and personal development. The process of re-framing involves looking at change through a new lens that highlights its inherent opportunities rather than its potential threats. By adopting this perspective, we can transform the narrative around change, making it a source of empowerment for both individuals and the organization. Here are a few ways you can consider re-framing change:

- **Personal Growth**: Viewing change as an opportunity for personal development and skill enhancement. Ask how this change could potentially add to their skills/abilities.

- **Ambition**: Embracing change as a pathway to achieve career goals and aspirations.

- **Loyalty, Trust, Commitment**: Building a sense of shared purpose and reinforcing the idea that change is a collective journey.

- **Personal Gain**: Identifying and communicating the direct benefits of the change to individuals.

- **Self-Preservation (If I don't, I will lose my job)**: Understanding that adaptation is essential for career sustainability.

- **Conviction (Knows why and agrees)**: Ensuring everyone understands and aligns with the reasons behind the change.

- **Involvement (Helped with the change)**: Actively involving individuals in the change process to foster a sense of ownership.

- **Adventure (Could be fun)**: Highlighting the exciting aspects of change and the opportunities it presents.

These approaches don't just help us manage the fear stage better; they change how we interact with the whole process of change. Effectively reframing change equips leaders to navigate the Fear stage more effectively and empowers individuals to learn how to view change not as a threat but as an opportunity for growth and innovation.

Developing FAQs

One of the best tools change leaders have in navigating the fear stage is providing additional information to impacted people. In our opinion, no change is too small to benefit from a list of Frequently Asked Questions (FAQs), and the more complex or subjective the change, the more FAQs are needed to help ensure everyone understands the details and nuances of the change.

As you consider developing a FAQ for your change initiative, think about these elements:

- What are the main features of the change?

- What is the impact (financial, customer, etc.)?

- Are these changes global?

- What won't change?

- What are the worries about the change?

- Who designed the new structure?

- What other options were considered?

- What has been done so far? (Tested?)

- When will it go into effect? Immediate, phased? (What should I do in the meantime?)

- How will we see progress?

- How will we give feedback?

- Is that all that will change?

- What negative impacts do we expect?

- Who is handling communication, and what will the communication cadence be?

- Who or what team will be open to receiving additional questions?

In addition to covering these concerns, consider how you can provide a forum for impacted people to ask more questions or provide further feedback. By providing a forum for feedback, you make it part of the expected process of change and do not treat questions and feedback as not "buying in" to the change. The FAQs also establish that you expect questions and have anticipated some. The FAQ provides some answers to the questions you expect will be asked.

FAQ Example

One of the most impactful changes in business is when a company is acquired by another, and a merger or acquisition integration process begins. For employees of the acquired organization, everything about their job and the rules of engagement change seemingly overnight. From hearing the announcement in an all-hands meeting, employees, managers, and teams are thrown quickly into the change curve, which immediately launches them into the Fear stage.

The FAQ document can be an essential tool to help impacted people understand what is going on, and in some cases, the FAQ forces important conversations about how things will work. In practice, you should develop one FAQ for each set of stakeholders: acquired company employees, acquiring company employees, and customers. While the FAQ document is most overused leading into the Fear stage, FAQs can be relevant as you move through any stage.

Here is an example of the questions you may find in a FAQ for acquired company employees alongside an M&A announcement:

- Why has the company been acquired?

- Will I still have a job?

- Will my job change?

- Will my compensation change?

- Will my benefits change?

- Will anyone be leaving?

- Will the acquiring company be assuming operational control of the acquired company?

- What leadership changes have been made? What do those changes mean for me?

- Who will I report to?

- Will the acquisition delay any existing projects or initiatives?

- Will any office locations close because of the acquisition?

- Will I have to relocate?

- What is the acquiring company like? (culture, rules, policies, values)

- How can I learn more about the acquiring company?

- When and how will we meet people from the acquiring company?

- Will our company culture change?

- What systems will we be expected to use?

- How long will the integration take?

- What are we telling customers?

- Who should I contact if I have questions?

- What should I do if someone from the media calls to ask about the change?

Creating a comprehensive FAQ for each stakeholder group in the context of a merger or acquisition is not just about providing answers; it's a strategic step towards fostering openness and trust during a time of significant transition. These FAQs serve as a foundation for ongoing dialogue, ensuring that everyone involved has access to the same information and understands the implications of the change. Just preparing the FAQ document is a step in the process as it forces some decisions and explanations to be explored and solidified.

As important as it is to cover the knowns, acknowledging the unknowns is equally vital. A well-crafted FAQ document invites further questions and highlights areas for continued conversation and clarification. It's a living document that evolves as the change process progresses and new information emerges.

Remember, the goal of the FAQ is not to close off discussion but to spark meaningful conversations that address concerns, alleviate fears, and build a shared understanding of the future. It's a tool for change leaders to demonstrate their commitment to transparency and dedication to supporting their teams through the change.

Stories From the Field

It is helpful to learn from others who have navigated the change curve. For that reason, we have included Stories from the Field to provide a real-world view of how others have experienced change.

From Fear to Failure

At a manufacturing company, a family-owned business known for its close-knit culture and loyal customer base, the leadership team decided it was time to modernize its operations by introducing an automated inventory system. The goal was clear: to improve efficiency, reduce errors, and ultimately serve their customers better. The investment was significant but deemed necessary for the company's future growth. Excitement was in the air as the leadership team envisioned a seamless transition to a more streamlined operation.

However, as news of the change spread throughout the company, excitement turned into apprehension. The warehouse staff, many of whom had been with the company for decades, began to worry. Rumors swirled about the machines "taking over" jobs, and the personal touch that had defined the company's operations for years seemed under threat. The fear wasn't just about job security; it was also about the loss of identity and the value of the human element in their work.

Despite these growing concerns, the leadership team pressed on, convinced that the new system's benefits would eventually win everyone over. They had already paid for the system, and the installation was underway. Training sessions were organized, but attendance was low. The staff's fears, left unaddressed, had taken root and grown into staunch resistance.

An inflection point came when a beloved warehouse manager, who had voiced his concerns early on, decided to resign, citing the loss of the company's soul in the march towards automation. This move struck a chord with many at the company, leading to a domino effect. The resistance grew stronger, productivity dipped, and the atmosphere was charged with uncertainty and distrust.

Faced with mounting opposition and a palpable shift in company morale, the leadership team made the difficult decision to halt the implementation of the automated system. The financial loss from the aborted project was significant, impacting the company's operations and strategic plans. More importantly, the episode left deep scars on the company's culture. The staff's trust in leadership had been shaken, and the sense of family that had been the company's hallmark felt compromised.

This story serves as a poignant example of how fear, if not acknowledged and managed with empathy and open communication, can derail even the most well-intentioned change. It highlights the importance of engaging with employees at all levels, understanding their fears, and taking proactive steps to address them. By doing so, companies can navigate the complexities of change without losing sight of their core values and the people who make the change possible.

Dropped Calls and Key Barriers

What follows is an example from a company with 19 employees, many of whom were consultants working in the field with customers. The owner and leader of this organization was driving between the office in West Michigan and Detroit, where they often went for work. During the drive, many of the owner's cell phone calls dropped due to loss of connection. In most cases, these were calls with clients as the commute between West Michigan and Detroit was a few hours and a great opportunity to get phone calls done without the typical distractions of being in the office.

From the owner: I'm on my way to Detroit. I had calls stacked up to fill the commute time, and each call kept dropping. I was annoyed. On my way back home after a full day in Detroit, I gave up on finishing my calls because I couldn't stand to suffer through another few hours of dropped calls and missed connections. Along the way, I passed a billboard for a specific wireless carrier that promised the broadest and most robust coverage. At the time, I was on a different carrier, and the billboard promised more coverage than any other carrier. I, in my state of frustration, thought this was a sign that I needed to make a change.

I didn't even go home. First, I drove right to the wireless store, and not only am I a great person because I'm going to make a change for myself, but I bought 19 new phones so each of my staff could have a brand new, no-calls-dropping phone. I am a small business owner; I can do this. I can get a cool new phone and unlimited plans. I am going to be a hero on Monday morning! I know it is not in the financial plan…but my people deserve the best experience.

When Monday morning came, I unloaded 19 new phones on the conference table for our meeting. I announced, "We're all changing to Verizon!" Can you imagine how that went over?

I thought this change was brilliant. I spent my own money to solve a problem that had been causing communication problems within my company. I thought I would be a hero getting everyone a new cell phone.

Unfortunately, that's not how it went. I was not a hero. On this day, my staff made me painfully aware of the problems with my great idea, and there were lots.

The barriers identified by my staff included:

1. Some employees didn't like the color of the phone that I got for them.

2. A few people said they did not have Verizon wireless phone coverage in their home area.

3. My accountant told me we still had a two-year contract with the other phone carrier.

I went from hero to zero, all within the span of the first 15 minutes of our Monday meeting. I felt like such an idiot. I had spent my money trying to do the right thing, but I missed the mark because I didn't consider the impact of the change and the potential barriers to success.

I'd already spent the money; it was time to figure out how to make this work. I pivoted the group from complaining about why the change was stupid to discussing the barriers to success. We made a list of how stupid my idea was and all the things wrong with it.

A few additional things on the list included:

4. Employees said they didn't know how to use the new phones. (We were a training company, so we should have been able to get over that.)

5. Someone mentioned that they didn't know how to transfer contacts from their old phone to their new phone. (Yes, this was before the cloud.)

6. A tech-savvy employee complained that the new phone didn't support the app they liked to use to check their email and claimed that would greatly impact their productivity.

7. One of the employees who drove a lot was worried that their speed-dial contacts would not work and that they would not be able to make calls on the road as easily or successfully.

8. Many people shared worries about the quality of the camera.

9. I heard a concern about moving a custom ringtone to the new phones.

10. People were concerned that their preferred hands-free headsets would not work on the new phones, and that would force them to get a different (assumed to be worse) headset.

11. An employee in a long-distance relationship shared a concern about their partner not having an unlimited plan and them being on the same network we had been on previously, making the minutes "free" for them to talk. They were worried that this would negatively impact their relationship.

After all these barriers had been identified, I reiterated to my staff how I had gotten us into a two-year contract and that the money had already been spent, meaning we needed to figure out how to handle the money problem. My accountant suggested that we could donate the old phones to an organization that would benefit the community, and then we could get a tax write-off that would benefit us. That was the start of our momentum. We went through the list and resolved each item. If we decided it could not be resolved, we worked on how to deal with it.

After a shock, criticism of my idea, and some creative problem-solving, we had resolved most of the issues associated with the new phones. The experience of the ups and downs was painful—I felt like a complete idiot at times. I learned a valuable lesson here and didn't do that again. The next time I thought I had a brilliant idea, I brought it to the team. I said, "I have an idea, and I'd like your feedback."

This story illustrates that even what is considered a good change can cause disruption if not planned. The owners' intentions were noble, but had they worked with their team, the outcome might have been different, and the disruption would have been limited.

Exiting the Fear Stage

Exiting the Fear stage marks a pivotal moment in the change management journey. It's the point where the initial resistance and apprehension begin to wane, giving way to curiosity and a readiness to engage more deeply with the change. Recognizing the signs that your team is ready to transition from the Fear stage to the Near stage is crucial for maintaining momentum and ensuring the successful implementation of change.

Identifying the Transition

When team members start asking, "How is this going to work?" it's a clear indicator that their mindset is shifting. This question can arise from a place of concern, but more importantly, it signifies a move from merely reacting to the change to wanting to understand and navigate through it. It's an acknowledgment that while the change may be daunting, there's a willingness to explore its possibilities.

Encouraging Questions and Engagement

This stage is characterized by increased inquiries and engagement from the team. Questions about specifics—logistics, timelines, impacts, and benefits—begin to surface. This curiosity is a healthy sign that the team is moving beyond fear and looking toward understanding and action. It's important for leaders to encourage these questions, providing clear, concise, and honest answers that build trust and confidence.

Facilitating the Shift with Support and Information

As a leader, facilitating this shift from the Fear stage to the curiosity of the Near stage involves providing ample support and information. This may include:

- **Detailed Plans and Roadmaps**: Sharing detailed plans about the change process helps demystify what's to come and outlines the steps needed to achieve the change successfully.

- **Resources for Learning and Adaptation**: Offering resources for team members to learn new skills or adapt to new processes empowers them to take active roles in the change.

- **Opportunities for Involvement**: Engaging team members in decision-making processes or roles that allow them to contribute to the change fosters a sense of ownership and commitment.

Recognizing and Addressing Lingering Concerns

While the shift toward the Near stage is a positive development, it's also a time to be vigilant about addressing any lingering concerns. Leaders and organizations should host open forums and one-on-one meetings, and feedback mechanisms should be in place to capture and address these concerns. This ensures that no one feels left behind as the team moves forward.

Celebrating Progress

Acknowledging and celebrating the progress made in overcoming fears and embracing the change reinforces positive behaviors and attitudes. It's a way of marking the journey's milestones and motivating the team as they step into the Near stage, where the focus shifts to practicalities and the path toward realization.

Exiting the Fear stage is not just about leaving apprehension behind; it's about stepping into a phase of proactive engagement and preparation for the changes ahead. By recognizing the signs of this transition and supporting your team through it, you pave the way for a smoother, more effective change process that harnesses your team's collective energy and capabilities.

📌 Key Takeaways

- Change leaders must embrace the fear stage and actively help others enter and navigate the Fear stage for themselves. You cannot skip this or any stage.

- Understanding and acknowledging the origins of individual fears helps leaders effectively navigate their teams through the Fear stage of change.

- Leverage open communication to transform fear into constructive engagement while reducing resistance.

- It is your job as a change leader to identify and address specific barriers through empathy and flexibility; this paves the way for smoother transitions and acceptance of change.

- Help others demystify the change process by developing comprehensive FAQs to help address concerns and promote understanding.

- Reframing the perspective on change from a source of fear to an opportunity for growth and innovation can empower individuals and strengthen teams.

💡 Tips for the Fear Stage

Leaders actively navigating the Fear stage can help their teams understand and manage their fears more effectively, fostering a supportive atmosphere that encourages moving forward with confidence and openness to the next stage of change. Try out these tips:

- **Acknowledge Individual Experiences**: Recognize that each team member's fear and reaction to change are personal and varied. Openly discuss that it's normal to feel unsettled or doubtful during this stage.

- **Normalize the Feeling of Fear**: Share stories or examples of your own moments of fear in past changes to show that it's a common part of the process. This can help normalize the experience and reduce the stigma of expressing fear.

- **Provide a Safe Space for Expression**: Create an environment where team members feel safe sharing their fears without judgment. This could be through one-on-one check-ins, team meetings focused on emotional well-being, or anonymous feedback mechanisms.

- **Focus on Things Within Your Control**: Empower your team by encouraging them to concentrate on aspects of the change they can influence. Guide them to set small, achievable goals related to adapting to the change. This approach helps shift focus from the overwhelming aspects of change to actionable steps, reducing feelings of helplessness and boosting personal agency and resilience.

- **Re-frame the Narrative**: Guide your team to re-frame their fear by asking, "What opportunities does this change present for us?" Encouraging a shift from focusing on what's lost to what can be gained can transform fear into motivation.

- **Engage in Collaborative Problem-Solving and Fear Mitigation**: Facilitate group sessions where team members can collectively identify fears and brainstorm practical solutions or coping strategies. This collaborative approach addresses specific concerns and strengthens team bonds, as members see they are not alone in their feelings and can rely on each other for support and ideas.

- **Encourage Human Connection**: Weaved throughout eminent theories in psychology and grounded in neuroscience, a sense of connection with other human beings is a coping strategy we need to survive tough times, including change. Talking about the change with a friend can help us feel better.

- **Offer Perspective and Hope**: Highlight stories of past changes that initially sparked fear but led to positive outcomes. Emphasize the growth, learning, and successes that came from navigating through the Fear stage to the Near stage and beyond.

Dos in the Fear Stage

- **Do Listen and Validate Feelings**: Acknowledge the fears and concerns of your team members as valid. Understanding their perspective fosters a supportive environment.

- **Do Provide Clear Information**: Utilize FAQs and regular updates to demystify the change process, addressing common concerns and the specifics of how changes will be implemented.

- **Do Focus on Empowerment**: Highlight control points by emphasizing skill development, career advancement opportunities, and ways to contribute to the change process.

- **Do Encourage Open Dialogue**: Facilitate forums for discussion, whether through meetings, feedback sessions, or informal conversations, to allow team members to express their thoughts and concerns.

- **Do Celebrate Small Wins**: Recognize and celebrate milestones and successes along the change journey to boost morale and demonstrate progress.

- **Do Use Peer Support**: Promote the creation of support networks within the organization, allowing employees to share experiences and coping strategies.

Don'ts in the Fear Stage

- **Don't Ignore or Dismiss Fears**: Avoid brushing aside the worries of your team. All fears are valid and important. Ignoring fears can lead to increased resistance and disengagement.

- **Don't Overwhelm with Information**: While it's important to provide details, ensure the information is accessible and not overwhelming. Overload can increase anxiety.

- **Don't Oversimplify**: Avoid describing the change in general terms so that elements that cause fear are overlooked or missed.

- **Don't Make Promises You Can't Keep**: Be realistic about what the change entails. Overpromising can lead to distrust if those promises are not fulfilled.

- **Don't Tell People How to Feel**: Telling people their emotions minimizes their own intelligence, makes them suspicious, and distracts them from the message. It creates mistrust. It's judgmental, and it won't move you faster.

- **Don't Forget to Follow Up**: After addressing concerns initially, don't neglect the importance of continuous support and check-ins to see how team members are adjusting.

- **Don't Rush the Process**: Allow adequate time for team members to adapt to the change. Rushing can exacerbate fears and lead to mistakes or oversights.

- **Don't Neglect Personalized Support**: Recognize that people react to change differently and may require different forms of support. Avoid a one-size-fits-all approach to addressing concerns.

Quiz

Question 1:

Liz has just announced a major operational shift in her company to integrate a new technology system. During the announcement, she notices a mix of confused and concerned faces among her team. Based on the strategies discussed for navigating the Fear stage, which of the following should Liz do next?

A) Immediately start training sessions for the new system without addressing any concerns.

B) Acknowledge the team's concerns, provide a detailed FAQ about the change, and invite questions in a follow-up meeting.

C) Tell the team they just need to get on board with the change because it's happening regardless of their concerns.

D) Avoid discussing the change further to prevent additional fear.

Correct Answer: B) Acknowledge the team's concerns, provide a detailed FAQ about the change, and invite questions in a follow-up meeting.

A three-pronged strategy that involves acknowledging the team's concerns, providing a detailed FAQ about the change, and inviting questions in a follow-up meeting is the most effective because it directly addresses the fear and uncertainty accompanying change. By providing clear, accessible information and an open forum for discussion, Liz demonstrates empathy and leadership, which are crucial for guiding her team through the Fear stage. This approach not only helps clarify details and dispel rumors but also encourages team engagement and ownership of the change process.

Question 2:

After a merger is announced, Alex, a department manager, notices a significant drop in his team's morale and an increase in rumors about job security. What is Alex's most effective initial step to address his team's fears according to the dos and don'ts of the Fear stage?

A) Tell the team everything will be fine and that they should focus on their work.

B) Promise the team that no one will lose their job, even though he has not received confirmation from upper management.

C) Ignore the rumors, assuming they will eventually dissipate on their own.

D) Organize a team meeting to directly address the rumors and provide as much information as he can, acknowledging the challenges while also working to re-frame the scenario and highlight any positive aspects of the merger.

Correct Answer: D) Organize a team meeting to directly address the rumors and provide as much information as he can, emphasizing any positive aspects of the merger.

Organizing a team meeting to directly address rumors and provide as much information as possible is the best initial step for Alex. This strategy aligns with the principles of open communication and transparency, which are foundational elements in successfully navigating the Fear stage. By openly discussing the merger, Alex can offer reassurance, clarify misunderstandings, and help the team re-frame while highlighting the positive aspects, which can help shift the team's perspective from fear to cautious optimism.

Question 3:

Maria is leading a change initiative to shift the company culture towards more collaborative and innovative practices. She's aware that her team is currently in the Fear stage, worried about how these changes will affect their daily routines and job security. Which of the following actions best aligns with promoting an agile mindset to help her team navigate their fears?

A) Implementing the changes all at once to quickly overcome the Fear stage.

B) Discouraging any negative talk about the change to maintain a positive outlook.

C) Encouraging team members to share their thoughts and fears in a workshop, focusing on how the change might open up new opportunities for personal and professional growth.

D) Telling the team that the change is non-negotiable and they should adjust as quickly as possible.

Correct Answer: C) Encouraging team members to share their thoughts and fears in a workshop, focusing on how the change might open up new opportunities for personal and professional growth.

Encouraging team members to share their thoughts and fears in a workshop, with a focus on the new opportunities that change brings, embodies the agile mindset of flexibility, learning, and growth. This approach helps team members move from a place of fear to one of curiosity and potential enthusiasm for the change. It demonstrates the importance of involving the team in the change process, validating their feelings, and reframing the change as an opportunity for personal and professional development.

Question 4:

A company is transitioning to a new customer management software. During a team meeting, several employees express concerns about losing data during the transition and being unable to use the new system effectively. Based on effective strategies for the Fear stage, what should the team leader do?

A) Dismiss the concerns as resistance to change and urge the team to focus on the benefits of the new software.

B) Acknowledge the concerns, promise to provide detailed training on the new software, and set up a support system for issues that may arise during the transition.

C) Tell the team they can stick with the old system if they're uncomfortable with the new software.

D) Offer incentives for those who learn the new system the fastest, ignoring the broader concerns.

Correct Answer: B) Acknowledge the concerns, promise to provide detailed training on the new software, and set up a support system for issues that may arise during the transition.

Acknowledging the team's concerns about the software transition, promising detailed training, and setting up a support system is the most effective response because it directly addresses the fear of the unknown and potential loss (data, efficiency, etc.). This solution not only provides the necessary resources for a smooth transition but also reassures the team that their concerns are being taken seriously. It fosters a supportive environment crucial for moving through the Fear stage and towards successful adaptation.

Question 5:

Thomas, a project manager, has been leading his team through a significant organizational change. Over the past few weeks, he has noticed a shift in the team's conversations and attitudes towards the change. Which of the following signs indicate that Thomas's team is transitioning from the Fear stage to the Near stage?

A)   Team members openly express their concerns and skepticism about the change, with many still unsure about its benefits.

B)   Team members frequently discuss the negatives of the change and reminisce about how things used to be before the change was announced.

C)   Most team members avoid discussions about the change, preferring to focus on their current tasks.

D)   Team members have started asking specific questions about their roles in the new structure and how their daily tasks will be impacted.

Correct Answer: D) Team members have started asking specific questions about their roles in the new structure and how their daily tasks will be impacted.

The team members starting to ask specific questions about their roles in the new structure and the impact on their daily tasks is a clear indicator that they are moving towards the Near stage. This shift from expressing general concerns and fears to seeking detailed information about the change signifies a readiness to engage more constructively with the change process. It reflects a transition from fear and resistance to a more practical and problem-solving approach, indicating that the team is beginning to consider how they will operate within the new changes, signaling readiness for the next steps.

As we wrap up the Hear stage, you should have a solid foundation for setting the stage for change within your organization. The techniques and insights shared here are designed to ensure your change message is clear, compelling, and comprehensively received. Armed with the right tools and an understanding of how to effectively communicate at the outset, you are now ready to address the emotional and psychological aspects of change. Moving into the Fear Playbook, we will explore how to manage and mitigate the fears and resistance that typically arise following your initial announcements. Remember, this playbook is here for you at any time as you lead and navigate change. Return here if you feel stuck or need an extra nudge towards change success.

CHAPTER 4

NEAR

In the quiet before dawn, Alison lies wide awake, thinking about the new job that's been both a dream and a source of anxiety. Last week, when the offer came, she was tangled in a web of excitement and fear. "What if I'm not cut out for this?" she wondered, the unknowns casting long shadows over her enthusiasm.

But tonight, something shifts. Her mind, once preoccupied with doubts, now busily sketches plans. "How will I tackle the first day? How will I fit into the new team?" Fear hasn't vanished, but it's no longer in control.

Alison doesn't consciously realize she's moving beyond her apprehensions into a state of readiness; all she knows is that she's suddenly keen to dive into the "how" rather than dwell on the "what ifs." Imagining the route to work, picking out an outfit, and planning her lunch become acts of quiet defiance against her fears.

The thought, "How can I make a positive impact right away?" crosses her mind. It's not laced with worry but tinged with excitement. She's on the brink of this new venture, ready to join and eager to contribute.

As the first light of dawn filters through Alison's window, her thoughts brighten, too. The fear of stepping into this new role lingers but is now mixed with anticipation and a readiness to engage. Today isn't just about starting a new job; it's about embarking on a journey. With questions of "how" guiding her, Alison is ready to embrace this change, step by step, ready to make the unknown her new familiar.

The Near stage is where apprehension shifts towards action, and thoughts of change become plans for how to enact it. This crucial stage moves us from asking "Can we?" to "How will we?" and marks a readiness to tackle change head-on. It's a time for laying out practical steps, turning the idea of change into a clear path forward. In short, the Near stage is when the journey through change really begins to take shape, guided by a newfound focus on making the change successful.

In this chapter, we'll dissect the Near stage, where individuals shift from fear to engagement with change, marked by probing "how" questions. We'll provide strategies for leaders to support this transition, emphasizing the importance of offering resources, facilitating training, fostering open dialogue, and celebrating early wins.

Entering the Near Stage

As you transition into the Near stage, you'll notice a distinct shift in the conversations surrounding the change. The focus moves from expressing doubts and concerns to actively seeking solutions and understanding the practicalities of the change. Suddenly, people go from having many problems with the change to needing to understand how it will all work. Questions begin to pivot from "Why is this happening?" to "How will we do this?"

In the Near stage, people will start to ask detailed "how" questions, demonstrating an eagerness to learn and adapt. The near stage is often the longest, but it is the least emotional as this stage sees people moving from worrying about the impact on themselves to considering the broader implications and logistics of the change. In this stage, the concept of change starts to feel real, and its implementation becomes a topic of constructive discussion rather than resistance.

In Chapter 1, we discussed the moveable kitchen example where people could stand in their own kitchen and imagine the space. Helping people with the "how" would mean asking them questions such as, "How would you clean out the dishwasher?" When they can show you how they would do this task, they are imagining living in the kitchen and not thinking about its cost. These questions help make the mental transition from Fear to Near.

The Near stage occurs when an individual starts to believe the change is real and going to happen and makes the switch from worrying about the change to participating. The easiest way to spot an individual moving from Fear to Near is they will start to ask "how" questions and imagine living in the new change.

- How will we do this?

- How should we organize the work?

- How does the system work?

Consider this example of Greenwood Marketing moving through the stages of change. As you review this example, imagine the transitions from stage to stage and the key indicators of transitioning to the next stage.

The team at Greenwood Marketing had always prided themselves on their close-knit office culture. Nestled in their well-loved, albeit slightly cramped, office space in the bustling downtown area, they had celebrated countless successes and faced challenges head-on together. So, when the announcement came that they were moving to a new building just a few blocks away, reactions were mixed. Initially, there was a palpable sense of loss among the team. "Why leave a place filled with so many memories?" they wondered collectively, apprehensive about the change.

For the first few weeks after the announcement, the team found themselves engulfed in a cloud of uncertainty and resistance that is all too common in the Fear stage of change. The office buzzed with hushed conversations and speculative whispers. "Will the new space stifle our creativity?" "What about the charm of this old place that felt so much like home?" The questions reflected a deep-seated apprehension about leaving behind the familiar comforts and memories embedded within the walls of their current office.

During team meetings, the air was thick with tension as discussions about the move inevitably circled back to concerns over potential disruptions to their workflow and fears of losing the close-knit culture that had become their hallmark. The team's once vibrant brainstorming sessions were now shadowed by a sense of mourning for what was perceived as the end of an era.

Karla, the team leader, noticed the shift in morale. She saw firsthand how fear had cast a pall over the team's usual dynamism and enthusiasm. In an effort to steer the team through this turbulent stage, Karla initiated open forums, inviting everyone to voice their concerns and hesitations. These meetings were crucial in acknowledging the team's fears, providing a space for vulnerability and honesty that had been missing in the initial announcement.

Through these candid discussions, the Greenwood Marketing team began to confront and unpack their fears. Karla addressed each concern with empathy, reinforcing the value of their collective spirit and assuring them that the essence of what made them a great team wouldn't be left behind but would instead be carried into the new space. Slowly, the narrative began to shift. The team's focus gradually moved from what they were losing to what they stood to gain—a larger, more versatile space that offered new possibilities for growth and creativity.

As the moving date drew closer and after much conversation about the fears surrounding the move, the team's conversation started to evolve. Seated around their usual lunch table, cluttered with blueprints of the new office and neighborhood maps, the dialogue shifted. "How will we set up the new workspace to maintain our collaborative spirit?" they pondered, recognizing the need to plan how to preserve their team dynamics in a new environment.

Karla, the team leader, noticed this change in tone. She organized a meeting to brainstorm the possibilities of the new space. "How can we make the most of the additional meeting rooms? What's the best way to utilize the larger break area?" The team began to engage with these "how" questions, signaling their transition into the Near stage. Together, they started to visualize their new office layout, discussing furniture arrangements and decor to make the space their own.

Excitement bubbled up as they contemplated the opportunities the new location presented. "How can we explore this part of town together? Maybe we can find a new favorite lunch spot," they mused, thinking beyond the office walls. This shift from concern over the move to curiosity about their new surroundings underscored their collective move towards embracing the change.

The process wasn't without its moments of doubt, as worries about the disruption to their routine surfaced. Yet, these were quickly countered with collaborative problem-solving. "How will we manage our projects during the move? Let's create a transition plan," they proposed, tackling potential challenges as a united front.

The Greenwood Marketing team navigated the Fear stage and moved into Near, finally getting planful and more excited about their move to a larger space. This transition from Fear to Near didn't happen overnight. It took weeks of open dialogue, reassurance, and careful planning. But as the moving date drew closer and the team began to engage more with the practicalities of the move, their questions and conversations started to reflect a change in perspective. No longer were they asking, "Why do this?" but instead, "How can we make this work?" This shift marked their collective step into the Near stage. They were ready to tackle the challenges and opportunities that lay ahead in their new environment.

Now, as we head toward talking about the goals of the Near stage, you might be wondering, "Wait, are there some people that do not make it out of the Fear stage?" Unfortunately, the answer is yes; some people will have been so opposed to the change that they cannot now publicly support it, or they still believe it is not a positive change, or they chose not to change. This is the unfortunate reality of change; some fall flat in the Fear stage because people just can't overcome the fear. It is important in the Fear stage to allow people to get out of their emotions and move on, but there is also a time to move on. Not everyone will move together.

Consider people who refused to learn to drive cars when they were invented and instead rode horses until the end of their lives. In today's terms, that would look like the person who exclusively uses cash at every establishment or only pays bills with checks. In these cases, the change moved forward, and the individual was left behind to do things their way, inconveniencing the world around them. Sometimes, this is an option, but at work, typically, every person is required to adapt to the change, meaning either the change will fail or the person will fail, neither of which is a desired outcome.

Transitioning to the Near stage requires an understanding that while not everyone may leave their initial fears behind, the majority who do are ready to engage with the change more constructively. It is here, in the

Near stage, where the focus shifts from overcoming fear to actualizing the change. This stage is characterized by a readiness to accept change and a proactive effort to understand and implement it.

Here's a quick reference for how to identify if your change is entering the Near stage:

Indicator	What You Will Observe	What People Will Be Doing
Shift in Conversations	Conversations shift from concerns and doubts to constructive discussions on implementation and solutions.	Asking detailed "how" questions, discussing practicalities of the change, planning for implementation.
Focus on Practicalities	A noticeable increase in discussions about the specifics of the change, such as logistics, timelines, and impacts.	Actively seeking solutions, engaging in problem-solving discussions, and planning the next steps.
Engagement in Planning	Team members participate in planning sessions, showing eagerness to contribute to how the change will be managed.	Collaborating on new systems or structures, organizing work around the new changes.

Indicator	What You Will Observe	What People Will Be Doing
Readiness for Implementation	A readiness to engage with the change, indicated by proactive involvement and acceptance of the upcoming transitions.	Engaging with training, attending workshops, and preparing themselves for the new processes.

This table reflects the key behaviors and activities that indicate those impacted by the change are moving from the Fear stage to the Near stage. This transition is marked by a shift from apprehension and resistance to active involvement and planning, focusing on how to implement the change effectively. Now, on to what you need to do in the Near stage to continue to help people along the change journey.

Goals of the Near Stage

The goal of the Near stage is to harness the energy and engagement of those impacted by the change as they transition from fearing the change to engaging with it and being ready to learn how it will happen. It is in these moments when you can lead people to collaboratively plan or understand "how" the change is going to happen. Here's how to approach it:

- **Highlight Feedback Integration**: Inform the team about incorporating their feedback into the change plan. Highlight specific alterations made to address their concerns, underscoring the direct impact of their input. This approach clarifies the transition towards actionable steps and emphasizes the importance of their contributions, boosting engagement and readiness for the upcoming changes.

- **Enhance Clarity and Participation**: Repeat the mantra, goal, and why of the change while working to shift the team's focus from questioning the necessity of the change to understanding its implementation or "how" of the change. Provide concise, transparent information on forthcoming steps and expectations, illustrating each team member's important role in achieving a successful transition.

- **Cultivate a Collective Vision**: Help the team imagine their world in the new state and visualize the positive outcomes and benefits of the change. This can involve sharing success stories, taking field trips to see how others have done it, and identifying potential growth opportunities and how the change aligns with the organization's broader goals. Creating a shared vision helps to rally the team around the change, strengthening their commitment to the process.

- **Provide Tools and Resources**: Equip your team with the necessary tools, training, and resources to empower them to confidently engage with the change. Whether it's training sessions, workshops, or access to experts, providing these resources helps to transform apprehension into action.

- **Celebrate Progress and Adaptation**: Acknowledge and celebrate the milestones, no matter how small, as the team progresses through the Near stage. Recognizing individual and collective efforts reinforces the value of their contributions and builds momentum towards the next stage of the change.

In short, the Near stage is about helping everyone grasp "how" the change will unfold. Leaders should look to demonstrate how feedback influences the plan and aim to dispel any uncertainties by outlining the journey ahead and emphasizing everyone's crucial role in achieving success. By highlighting success stories and potential benefits, leaders can equip impacted people with the knowledge, skills, and abilities they need to navigate the change.

Near Stage Responsibilities

In the Near stage of change, the focus shifts from addressing and managing fears to actively engaging with and facilitating the change. This stage involves individuals, leaders, and the company working together to harness the momentum built by overcoming initial apprehensions. Here's an overview of the responsibilities by role during the Near stage:

Individuals:

- **Clarify Needs**: Individuals should communicate their specific needs for resources or support to effectively engage with the change. This could involve identifying gaps in their knowledge, skills, or tools required to navigate the new landscape.

- **Engage Proactively**: Take an active role in learning sessions, training, and discussions. Engagement shows readiness to adapt and contributes to shaping the path forward.

- **Contribute to the Collective Vision**: Share insights and ideas that can help refine the approach to change, emphasizing collaborative efforts to achieve the envisioned future.

Leaders:

- **Supply Resources**: Leaders must ensure that all necessary resources, such as training, access to experts, and supportive tools, are readily available to the team. Leaders must be especially careful to ensure individuals have the time to participate in the change or training as this empowers individuals to engage with the change confidently and feel supported by their leader in doing so.

- **Celebrate Progress**: Acknowledging and celebrating even the smallest sign of forward movement is crucial. Recognition fosters motivation and reinforces the value of everyone's efforts in the change process. A quick acknowledgment of progress or a shoutout to someone who finished even the smallest task creates momentum.

- **Foster Open Communication**: Maintain transparent and continuous communication, updating the team on progress, addressing any emerging concerns, and highlighting successes along the way.

Company:

- **Provide Comprehensive Support**: The organization should offer a range of resources —from formal training sessions to informal learning opportunities and access to consultants or playbooks. These resources equip the team to handle the change effectively.

- **Promote and Celebrate Adaptation**: Highlighting and celebrating adaptation and progress company-wide encourages a culture of resilience and flexibility. This motivates the team involved in the current change and sets a positive precedent for future transformations.

- **Iterate Based on Continuous Feedback**: As the team progresses through the Near stage, continuous feedback may reveal areas for further refinement. The company should remain open to making iterative changes to the plan, ensuring it meets the team's evolving needs.

In the Near stage, the collaborative effort pivots towards deep engagement, practical preparation, and collective problem-solving. By providing the necessary resources, fostering an environment of open communication, and celebrating each step towards adaptation, the organization solidifies the foundation for successful change implementation. Moving through the Near stage to fully embracing and living the change becomes a smoother transition, marked by a shared commitment to the new direction and a strengthened resolve to achieve the desired outcomes.

Navigating the Near Stage

Expect that people slide from Fear to Near and back to Fear in this stage. It is quite common for the person's emotions to change from "This will never work" to "This will be hard" to "How do we get this done?" Because people start to work with the change, they will discover more things that they did not know prior, hence causing the slide back into Fear momentarily.

The Near stage is pivotal. It's the bridge between resisting change and embracing it. At this juncture, individuals are looking for guidance and clarity. They want to understand how the change will impact them and how they can adapt.

A team of people rarely all move from Fear to Near at a similar time. It is common for a few people to quietly start working on how to get the change done while most other people are still in Fear. Once 25 percent or more of the team is in Near, it is time to move away from eliciting what is causing Fear and toward supporting those in the Near stage. This is also the time to provide the team with as many resources as possible. Think of resources as the things that will empower a person or team to do the work and understand how to move forward. Below is a list of potential resources:

- Training
- Time to work on the change or attend training
- Field trips (going to see someone or an org that has made this change)
- Buddy Programs (partnering with someone who has adopted the change)
- Experts and consultants
- Access to technical support
- Documentation

Remember: Your early adopters may move fast into Near. It is important to acknowledge them and give them resources and room. Once you start getting momentum, it will accelerate at an increasing pace because people like safety in numbers. Start celebrating micro wins and team accomplishments to give this momentum a boost.

In the following sections, we will explore strategies to effectively navigate the Near stage. We'll discuss how to provide clear, actionable steps that demystify the transition, offering a detailed roadmap to guide individuals through the practical aspects of change. By focusing on specific methods to deepen understanding and participation, such as step-by-step guides, interactive workshops, and role-specific training, we can transform uncertainty into a well-structured pathway for implementation. Additionally, we will examine techniques for addressing residual fears and empowering individuals with the knowledge and resources needed to embrace and drive the change. Through these approaches, we aim to foster an environment where team members not only adapt to new realities but also thrive, turning the challenges of today into the achievements of tomorrow.

Providing the "How"

A leader should provide the "how" in the Near stage and go beyond merely outlining steps. The "how" involves immersing the team in the practical aspects of the change, ensuring they grasp not just what is changing but precisely how those changes will affect their daily operations and responsibilities. In the Near stage, leaders should ensure they are effectively demystifying the change, transforming uncertainty into a roadmap for action, and equipping people with the knowledge, skills, and abilities they need to operate effectively in the changed environment. Here are ten ways you can work to provide the "how" for people navigating a change:

1. **Step-by-Step Guides**: Create comprehensive, easy-to-follow guides that break down the change and the new behaviors people need to exhibit into manageable steps. These guides should cover all new processes and highlight the differences from old processes.

2. **Interactive Workshops**: Organize workshops where employees can actively engage with the new changes. Use real-life scenarios to demonstrate how daily tasks will change and allow hands-on practice.

3. **Detailed FAQs**: Compile a list of frequently asked questions that address common concerns and detailed explanations of how specific changes will work in practice.

4. **Role-Specific Training**: Offer training sessions tailored to different roles within the organization to address specific needs and concerns related to the change.

5. **Virtual Tours and Demonstrations**: If the change involves a physical space or new software, provide virtual tours or live demonstrations to show the end-state in a tangible way.

6. **One-on-One Support Sessions**: Give employees the opportunity to schedule one-on-one sessions with change leaders or experts to

discuss how the changes will affect their individual roles and to address any personal concerns.

7. **Checklists for Transition**: Distribute checklists outlining the key actions employees must take to transition to the new systems or processes. This helps ensure that nothing is overlooked.

8. **Simulation Exercises**: Use simulations to help employees understand and practice new workflows or to interact with new systems before they go live.

9. **Progress Tracking Tools**: Implement tools that allow employees to track their progress in adapting to the change. This could include dashboards highlighting completed training, milestones reached, or proficiency levels.

10. **Feedback Mechanisms**: Establish robust mechanisms for employees to provide feedback on the change process, which can help leaders quickly address any issues or additional needs that arise during the transition.

Example: Applying the Near Stage at Home

Providing the "how" in Near is not only important at work; it also applies at home. Moving to a new house is a profound change for a family, particularly for children who may be leaving behind familiar surroundings, friends, and routines. The Near stage in this context involves diving in on "how" the change will happen by preparing children for the move, taking field trips, and helping the kids feel informed and involved in the change. Imagine these tools to help the family get to the Near stage of their move.

- **Touring the New Home Together**: Before the move, if possible, take your children to visit the new house. Walk through each room, discussing how you'll use the space and where their things will go. This tangible experience helps children visualize living in the new house and can spark excitement about their new rooms or a bigger backyard.

- **Creating a Moving Adventure Book**: Work with your children to create a "moving adventure book." Include photos of the new house, a map of the neighborhood, and pages where they can write down what they're looking forward to in the new place. This activity not only focuses on the "how" of the move but also allows children to express their feelings and expectations.

- **Involvement in Packing**: Involve your children in packing their belongings. Give them boxes and let them decide (with guidance) what goes inside. You can explain the process: "First, we put in your books, then your toys, and don't forget your favorite pillow." This hands-on involvement demystifies the moving process and gives children a sense of control.

- **Exploring the New Area Online**: Sit down with your children and explore the new area online. Look up parks, schools, and interesting places to visit. "How close is the nearest ice cream shop?" "Let's find the best route to your new school." This research makes the new environment feel more familiar and exciting.

- **Scheduling Farewell Visits**: Acknowledge the sadness of leaving behind friends and favorite places. Schedule farewell visits or a goodbye party. Discuss how you'll keep in touch with old friends and the possibility of making new ones. "We can use video calls to show your friends your new room!"

- **First Night Box**: Together with your children, pack a special "first night" box with items they'll want immediate access to in the new house, like a favorite toy, book, or pajamas. This ensures they have comforts from the start, making the new house feel like home sooner.

- **Establishing New Routines**: Once moved in, establish new routines together. Decide where you'll eat breakfast in the new house or choose a spot for family movie nights. This helps children adapt to their new environment while maintaining a sense of continuity.

By focusing on these "how" aspects of moving to a new house, parents can help children navigate the transition with curiosity and enthusiasm. It shifts the experience from a daunting change to an adventure they are prepared for and even excited about. Engaging children in each step provides them with reassurance, a sense of involvement, and the tools to positively adapt to their new surroundings.

When you are leading in the Near stage, you can be a great help and source of reassurance or cause for significant concern. If you want to drive successful change, work to demystify the process in this stage by employing tactics to help people understand what is changing and how those changes will affect their daily operations and responsibilities. This approach clarifies the transition and empowers individuals to embrace and adapt to the new changes and move through the Near stage successfully.

Addressing Residual Fears

While the Fear stage primarily addresses concerns, residual fears might still linger in the Near stage. In addition, as individuals start understanding the "how," new questions or challenges might emerge that might cause them to lose hope or agreement with the change. In these instances, it is your job as a change leader to provide even more support to those who need it to help these individuals deal with any residual fears caused by the change and get everyone back on the rails and moving through the near stage.

Let's look at this through an example that might hit a little close to home for some who work in the technology space.

Amid a major collaboration and productivity system change at a mid-sized software development company, the leadership and project management teams noticed that while many employees were adapting well, a few were still struggling with the transition and refusing to use the new tools and processes. The project manager, Lisa, decided to take a proactive stance to address these residual fears and ensure no one felt they were dragged into the change kicking and screaming or, worse, left behind.

Lisa employed multiple intentional tactics to address residual fears and get people back on track. First, Lisa implemented weekly check-in sessions. These were not just standard team meetings but specifically designed to uncover and address ongoing concerns that employees might not feel comfortable bringing up in larger settings. During these sessions, team members could share their experiences with the new system, highlight specific issues, and discuss any personal challenges they faced. While this got most folks on track, Lisa also met one-on-one with a few key struggling employees to get their feedback and thoughts about the change while also encouraging adoption.

Through these check-in sessions, it became adamantly clear that some team members had more complex questions that required detailed answers from technical experts. To address this, Lisa set up bi-weekly Q&A forums. These forums were facilitated by IT specialists who were instrumental in the system upgrade and could explain how everything worked piece by piece. They provided a platform where employees could get real-time solutions and clarifications, helping to dissipate fears about the new technology.

There were also some problems with the training. While the training was thoughtfully crafted and facilitated, feedback from the check-in sessions revealed that several employees found the initial training materials too technical and difficult to apply. People were afraid they wouldn't know what to do when it was time because they didn't understand the training well enough. Lisa collaborated with the training department to create a set of simplified, step-by-step guides that were better tailored to the needs of the team. These new materials were distributed and made available on the company's internal resource portal so that folks using the new system had something quick and easy to refer to as they adapted to the change.

Next, Lisa addressed individuals who were change-resistant. Through the trainings and Q&A forums, Lisa noticed that Mark, a long-standing developer, was particularly hesitant about the new software and processes. He was being such a stick in the mud! Mark's attitude was negative, his productivity had declined, and he was actively disengaged in the training sessions. Lisa arranged for one-on-one mentoring sessions for Mark with a senior developer he respected and who had quickly adapted to the new system. The intent of these sessions was twofold: inspire confidence in the change from someone Mark trusted and help Mark understand specific functionalities crucial to his daily tasks. Lucky for Lisa, after a few weeks of working together, Mark and his mentor were able to make the system work for Mark such that he adopted it and became a power user in the first quarter of using the new system.

It was only after Mark got on board that Lisa could finally exhale a sigh of relief as Mark was an important talent on the team, and others looked to him for cues as to what to do at work. Finally, topping off the tactics to address residual fears and change avoidance, Lisa requested time in the company's upcoming all-staff meeting to highlight the successes of the change and share stories from employees like Mark, who had overcome their initial hesitations and were now thriving with the new system and achieving results beyond what was possible in the old system. These stories motivated others and demonstrated the tangible benefits of embracing the change.

Through these targeted strategies, Lisa and her team managed to significantly reduce the anxiety surrounding the new system. The team's morale improved as they saw their concerns being addressed in real-time, and their confidence in using the new system grew steadily. Lisa's leadership and taking the time to care for each impacted person meant the difference between success and failure in her change initiative. Thanks to her careful consideration of everyone's needs, Lisa led a smooth and successful transition to the new system.

Lisa is not a superhero; she's a regular person trying to help people through the Near stage. You can be like Lisa, but to be like Lisa, you need to pay attention to what is happening in your organization. You need to listen to people's residual concerns and fears and provide tailored support to those who need it most.

Using Visualization in Near

Visualization is a powerful tool in the Near stage as it helps individuals and teams to clearly picture the upcoming changes and their potential impacts. This technique not only assists in overcoming residual fears but also helps make abstract changes more tangible and understandable. Here's how leaders can effectively use visualization to facilitate change:

1. **Create the Condition You Describe**: Leaders should actively help team members visualize the organization's future state or their work environment after the change has been implemented. For example, if a company is moving to a new office, leaders might provide virtual tours of the new space or detailed blueprints that employees can explore to see where their new workspaces will be located.

2. **Practical Visual Tools**: Incorporating visual tools such as diagrams, flowcharts, and digital mock-ups can help individuals understand the practical aspects of a change. For instance, if a new software system is being introduced, showing screenshots and step-by-step guides can help demystify how daily tasks will be performed using the new system.

3. **Visualization Exercises**: Conducting workshops where employees can engage in visualization exercises, such as imagining a day in their role after the change has been implemented, can be beneficial. These exercises should encourage them to think through their daily routine, interactions with new tools or colleagues, and the outcomes they expect to see.

4. **Learning from Others**: If you're facing a challenge or change, it's likely someone else has already faced something similar—learn from them! When possible, arrange for field trips or virtual sessions with organizations that have successfully implemented similar changes to learn how they did it, what challenges they faced along the way, and how they overcame them. Seeing how others have navigated similar transformations can provide inspiration and practical insights that can be adapted to the current change initiative.

When visualization strategies are incorporated into the Near stage, leaders can help their teams move beyond merely understanding the "how" of the change to actively engaging with it and visualizing their success within the new setup. This helps smooth the transition and builds a more resilient and adaptive team culture where individuals feel more empowered to participate in change.

Empowering Individuals

In the Near stage, as team members start to engage more actively with the change, it becomes crucial for leaders to empower them effectively. Empowerment will switch the driver of change from the leader to the team or individual. As long as the leader is driving everything, the change has not been absorbed into reality. This empowerment is not just about providing tools and resources but also about nurturing an environment where individuals feel confident to embrace and drive the change. Here are strategies leaders can use to empower their team members effectively:

- **Delegate Meaningful Roles**: Assign roles that allow team members to participate actively in the change process. For example, a leader could appoint a dedicated "change ambassador" from among the staff who would be responsible for gathering feedback, disseminating information, and helping to troubleshoot issues as they arise. This role not only empowers the individual but also helps to bridge gaps between leadership and the rest of the team.

- **Foster Initiative and Innovation**: Encourage individuals to propose solutions that improve the change process. Create platforms such as innovation labs or suggestion boxes where team members can safely propose new ideas without fear of criticism. For instance, if transitioning to a digital-first approach, employees could suggest apps or tools that might enhance efficiency. Leaders should recognize and seriously consider these contributions to foster a sense of involvement and ownership.

- **Support Risk-Taking**: Promote a culture where calculated risks are encouraged, and failures are viewed as opportunities for learning. This could involve setting up pilot programs or trial runs that allow employees to test out new methods or tools in a controlled environment where the stakes are not prohibitive.

- **Enhance Peer Learning**: Establish mentorship programs and peer learning opportunities that allow individuals to learn from each other. This could be as simple as pairing newer employees with veterans or organizing regular peer-led workshops where team members can share insights and strategies.

- **Recognize Contributions**: Make a concerted effort to acknowledge and celebrate individuals' contributions toward the change process. This could be through public acknowledgments during meetings, recognition in internal newsletters, informal shout-outs in team chats, or one-on-one. If you see someone doing well in adopting the change, let them know you see them and appreciate their effort!

- **Provide Ongoing Feedback**: Ensure that feedback flows both ways. Regular check-ins and review sessions allow leaders to provide guidance and encouragement and enable team members to voice their concerns and suggestions. This ongoing dialogue is necessary for adjusting strategies and processes as needed.

Adopting these strategies equips leaders to significantly enhance team empowerment during the Near stage of change. When team members feel empowered, they are not only more inclined to accept and support the change but also become proactive contributors to its success. Their active participation can inspire and motivate their colleagues, fostering a collaborative and dynamic work environment that benefits the entire organization.

Celebrating Small Wins

As individuals navigate the Near stage, recognizing and celebrating small victories becomes essential. This practice is not just about acknowledging success; it's about creating momentum. Every time someone masters a new skill, overcomes a challenge, or simply becomes more comfortable with the change, it's an opportunity to boost morale and encourage progress. These moments of acknowledgment reinforce the positive aspects of the change and motivate everyone to advance toward the Cheer stage.

Imagine a university that is transitioning to a new digital student record system, which affects faculty, administration, and students alike. The transition is complex, involving changes to how courses are registered, grades are entered, and student progress is monitored.

To facilitate this transition and encourage buy-in, the university decides to celebrate small wins by recognizing individual departments and their successful adaptation to the new system. Each month, they highlight a "Department of the Month" in the university newsletter, which features stories about how the new system has improved efficiency or solved previous challenges within that department.

One of the first successes comes from the Registrar's Office, where staff successfully migrate over ten years of backlogged academic records into the new system without errors. This accomplishment significantly enhances the accessibility and reliability of student records, benefiting both staff and students. The Registrar's Office is recognized in the university's communications, and the team is rewarded with a special mention during the annual university conference.

Additionally, to make these achievements relatable and tangible, the university hosts a small celebration in the department's office, complete with a cake that reads "We Did It!" and an informal Q&A session where staff can share tips and tricks they've learned while using the new system. These celebrations boost morale and facilitate knowledge sharing across departments, helping other areas of the university see the practical benefits of the new system and learn from each other's experiences.

When the university celebrates these small wins, they help keep the morale high and demonstrate the practical benefits of enduring the change, encouraging widespread adoption and smoother transition across its entire community. This approach ensures that all stakeholders see the positive impacts of the change, fostering a supportive and collaborative environment as they move toward full implementation.

You might not be able to have a cake to celebrate your achievements, but you probably hold large forum meetings where you can recognize success. Consider adding the small wins and progress of your change initiatives to your next all-staff meeting, and don't forget to thank the team involved in the change in your messaging!

Stories From the Field

Below, you will read another story from the field to provide a real-life perspective on how people have navigated change successfully and unsuccessfully. These stories provide more context about the reality of navigating change.

Failure to Launch

In the city of Greenview, the city council was eager to introduce a new waste management system featuring high-tech recycling kiosks across the community. Envisioned as a modern solution to improve recycling rates and reduce waste, the council was captivated by the technology's potential and quickly moved to implement the project without extensive community consultation.

The enthusiasm within the council translated into a swift, decisive rollout. They were so convinced by the technology's benefits that they overlooked the crucial Near stage of change management, which focuses on engaging with the community to explore how the new system would be integrated into their daily routines. This oversight meant that the practicalities of operating the new kiosks were not communicated effectively, nor was there a trial run to gather initial public feedback.

When the recycling kiosks were unveiled, the reality of the situation quickly became apparent. The kiosks, which required users to scan each item to determine its recyclability, proved too complex for many residents. The technology that was supposed to simplify recycling instead created confusion and frustration due to its user-unfriendly interface and the lack of prior instruction or engagement from the council.

As complaints mounted and recycling rates did not improve—instead, the areas around the kiosks became cluttered with improperly disposed of waste—it became clear that the initiative was a failure. The council's failure to engage with the community during the Near stage, to understand and address their concerns and to provide adequate instruction on the new system's usage, led to the project's downfall. The council had moved too quickly, driven by their confidence in the technology, without securing the necessary buy-in and understanding from the people it was meant to serve. This resulted in a well-intentioned initiative falling short, leaving the city to grapple with the repercussions of a failed system and a disillusioned public.

As you can read from the previous story, the move to the new waste management system was unsuccessful. These failed changes can be costly in both monetary terms and in trust with your colleagues, constituents, and organizations.

Membership Modernization

In Dufur, Oregon, a small town of about 300 households, the local all-volunteer Fire and Ambulance Department faced a significant challenge when transitioning their annual ambulance transportation memberships from a mail-in paper sign-up process using checks or cash to an online enrollment process that allowed credit card processing and automatic renewals.

The Dufur Volunteer Fire and Ambulance department wanted to modernize the enrollment process to minimize mistakes and speed up the processing of membership enrollments, but there was concern that the less technical residents of Dufur would not enroll or become aware of the online enrollment process. The department's secretary, who also handled IT responsibilities, led the initiative. She was keenly aware of the town's apprehension towards online transactions and knew that a direct approach was necessary to ensure the success of this new system during the Near stage. Dufur residents would need hands-on assistance to navigate the change.

The change was initiated by sending pre-renewal notices to all existing members, letting them know about the upcoming change, why it was happening, when, and what would happen next. When it was time to start enrollments, the secretary worked to accommodate Dufur residents who were not confident in their use of technology by mailing out notices that included easy-to-locate website URLs, which then had instructional guides and videos to help people learn how to enroll using the new online system. Additionally, she utilized various communication platforms, including social media, local newspapers, announcements at recurring community events, and community bulletin boards to inform and reassure the community about the new enrollment process and the town's member sign-up progress throughout the enrollment period.

Once the change was underway, online enrollments flooded in, but they plateaued after a few weeks. Looking at the membership list for the previous year, it became clear that online enrollment was not reaching some of the older residents of Dufur. To address this, the secretary organized an in-person enrollment event at the fire department to help people who were hesitant to enroll online or preferred to enroll in person or via mail.

During the event, instead of requiring residents to enroll themselves using computers, fire department personnel were at the ready. They helped each person enroll without having to type or use a piece of technology, including helping these members turn on auto-renewal for their membership for ease of use in the future. Community members simply needed to provide their names and payment information, and the fire department team took care of the rest. This approach made the process less intimidating and fostered a sense of trust and personal attention for community members who were hesitant to enroll online.

The transition to online enrollment, including the in-person enrollment event, was a resounding success, reaching new households who had never signed up through the previous paper-based system and facilitating renewals for existing members. The secretary's thoughtful, hands-on approach during the Near stage overcame initial resistance and demonstrated the new system's tangible benefits, leading to improved data handling and member management for the fire and ambulance department.

The successful transition to online enrollment in Dufur's Fire and Ambulance Department didn't happen by chance. It resulted from careful planning, strategic communication, and a time-taught understanding of the community's needs. The secretary's approach to managing this change offers valuable lessons that can be applied to any change initiative, especially when we break down her actions through the lens of the change curve.

Let's take a closer look at what the secretary did right at each stage of the change process up through the Near stage and how these strategies ensured the success of the new system.

Hear

- **Pre-renewal Notices**: The secretary informed residents well in advance about the upcoming change. She communicated why the change was happening, when it would occur, and what to expect next. This helped set the stage for the transition and addressed initial concerns by making residents aware of the upcoming shift.

- **Communication Strategy**: She used multiple communication channels, such as social media, local newspapers, and community bulletin boards, ensuring the message reached a broad audience. This comprehensive communication strategy helped minimize confusion and resistance early on.

Fear

- **Addressing Hesitation**: When online enrollments plateaued, the secretary noticed that some older residents were not enrolling. She responded by organizing the in-person event, which directly tackled the fear and hesitation around using technology. By offering a comfortable alternative, she alleviated concerns and made the change more inclusive.

- **Building Trust**: By having fire department personnel assist residents directly, the secretary fostered trust and showed that the department was committed to making the process as smooth as possible. This personal attention helped reduce anxiety and resistance.

Near

- **User-Friendly Tools**: The secretary provided easy-to-use enrollment URLs, guides, and instructional videos to help residents navigate the new online system. These resources made the transition more accessible, especially for those less familiar with technology.

- **Personalized Support**: Recognizing the community's specific needs, the secretary anticipated and planned for challenges by organizing an in-person enrollment event. This event addressed the concerns of less tech-savvy residents and those who preferred in-person interactions, providing hands-on assistance to ease the transition.

The secretary in this story used her change management expertise to lead effective change and modernize an important process. This initiative went so well because she took the time to address concerns and support people in each stage of the change. As a result, the town of Dufur can continue to modernize processes for efficiency while still meeting the needs of all residents, both old and new.

Exiting the Near Stage

Exiting the Near stage marks a critical juncture in the change management process, where the initial planning and preparation stage gives way to active engagement and realization of the change. This stage is characterized by a shift from exploring and understanding the "how" of the change to actually implementing these strategies and seeing tangible results. Recognizing when your team is ready to move from the Near stage to the next stage, Cheer, is essential for maintaining momentum and ensuring effective change implementation.

Identifying the Transition

A key indicator of transitioning from the Near to Cheer is when the team's focus shifts from planning and preparation to execution and results— when discussions and questions about the "how" or logistics and specifics of the change begin to dwindle, and the conversation turns towards refining and optimizing the processes. In the transition out of Near, team members might start showcasing independent problem-solving related to the new changes or demonstrating proactive adjustments to their workflows enabled by the change.

Encouraging Implementation and Independence

During the Near stage, leaders should encourage team members to apply their new knowledge and skills independently, facilitating the shift with adequate support and resources. This could involve:

- **Empowering Team Members**: Allow individuals to lead portions of the project or manage specific elements of the change, reinforcing their role in the success of the transition.

- **Providing Advanced Tools and Training**: Offer more sophisticated tools and further training sessions that enhance the team's capability to operate effectively within the new system or process.

- **Setting Up Feedback Loops**: Establish mechanisms to gather feedback on the implementation phase, which helps fine-tune the process and proactively address any emerging challenges.

- **Pointing to successes**: Highlight advancements and specific micro wins to drive momentum.

Acknowledging Readiness and Resolving Final Concerns

As the team prepares to exit the Near stage, be sure to address any remaining uncertainties or last-minute concerns. This might involve:

- **Conducting Review Sessions**: Hold meetings to review the outcomes of the preparations and initial implementations, discussing what has worked well and what needs improvement.

- **Refining Processes**: Make necessary adjustments to the change plan based on feedback and early outcomes from the initial implementation phase.

- **Reinforcing Commitment**: Reiterate the organization's commitment to the change, highlighting the benefits and positive impacts observed thus far.

Your job in the Near stage is to hold the course, address any bumps along the road, and get everyone rolling on their own in the right direction, with a clear understanding of what they are expected to do, and the momentum to keep it going.

Celebrating Milestones

Celebrating the progress made during the Near stage is essential for boosting morale and reinforcing the value of the team's efforts. Recognize individual and group contributions that have led to successful outcomes and highlight how these efforts are paving the way for the final realization of the change.

Exiting the Near stage successfully sets the foundation for sustained change. It begins the transition into the Cheer stage, where the focus is on optimization, full adoption, and celebration of the change's success. By carefully managing this transition, leaders can ensure that the team remains motivated and aligned with the change objectives, ready to embrace and champion the new ways of working.

Key Takeaways

- Proactive engagement helps guide team members from initial theoretical acceptance to active participation in the change.

- Providing clear, detailed explanations and demonstrations helps people understand the change and reduces uncertainty.

- Supplying necessary tools, training, and resources equips team members to effectively engage with and navigate the changes.

- Regularly incorporating feedback into the change process improves implementation and increases team commitment.

- Helping team members visualize the positive outcomes and benefits of the change can inspire and motivate them.

- Recognizing and celebrating each milestone within the Near stage reinforces progress and encourages continued effort.

Tips for the Near Stage

When leading in the Near stage, focus on "how" the change will be executed, provide resources, and help people actively engage with the change to learn new ways of working and operating in alignment with the desired outcomes. Try out these tips:

- **Prioritize Clear Communication**: Ensure that all team members clearly understand the change processes by providing detailed explanations and answering "how" questions transparently. This helps demystify the change and aligns everyone's efforts.

- **Demonstrate the Practical Steps**: Use examples, simulations, or role-play exercises to show exactly how tasks will be carried out in the new system. This hands-on approach helps team members feel more prepared and less anxious about the changes.

- **Celebrate Early Adoption**: Your early adopters may move fast into Near. It is important to acknowledge them and give them resources and room. Momentum will accelerate at an increasing pace because people like safety in numbers. Start celebrating micro wins and team accomplishments to give this momentum a boost.

- **Facilitate Hands-On Training**: Provide training sessions that are not only informative but also interactive. Allowing team members to practice new skills or use new tools in a controlled environment builds confidence and competence.

- **Provide Access to Resources**: Make sure that all necessary resources, such as guides, toolkits, and access to expert advice, are readily available. Knowing these resources are at hand can significantly reduce anxiety and enhance engagement.

- **Cultivate a Solution-Oriented Mindset**: Encourage team members to focus on how they can contribute to solving any challenges that arise during the transition. This empowerment shifts their perspective from passive observers to active participants.

- **Foster a Collaborative Environment**: Promote teamwork by organizing collaborative sessions where team members can share insights, offer feedback, and support each other's learning. This speeds up the adaptation process and builds a strong team dynamic.

- **Encourage Ownership**: Empower individuals by assigning them specific roles or responsibilities related to the change. This helps them feel vested in the outcome and more engaged in the process.

- **Maintain Flexibility**: Be open to making adjustments based on feedback from the team. This adaptability shows that you value their input and are committed to making the change work for everyone.

- **Celebrate Milestones**: Recognize and celebrate small achievements and milestones as your team progresses through the Near stage. This recognition boosts morale and demonstrates the tangible benefits of embracing the change.

Dos in the Near Stage

- **Do Provide Detailed Instructions**: Offer comprehensive guides and step-by-step tutorials that clarify how to navigate the changes, ensuring that everyone understands the practical aspects of the transition.

- **Do Foster Hands-On Engagement**: Organize practical workshops or simulation sessions that allow team members to experience and practice with new systems or processes firsthand.

- **Do Empower Through Responsibility**: Assign meaningful roles related to the change, empowering team members to take ownership and feel more invested in the outcome.

- **Do Encourage Feedback**: Create a culture where team members feel comfortable providing feedback on the change process, which helps make necessary adjustments and improvements.

- **Do Offer Tailored Support**: Recognize the varying needs across your team and provide resources and support that address these specific requirements, facilitating smoother adaptation.

- **Do Celebrate Progress**: Make a point of recognizing and celebrating even minor milestones and successes to maintain morale and encourage ongoing engagement.

Don'ts in the Near Stage

- **Don't Assume Understanding**: Avoid assuming everyone fully grasps the new processes or changes. Continuously check for understanding and readiness to proceed.

- **Don't Neglect Training Needs**: Do not skimp on providing adequate training and resources needed for team members to feel confident in their new roles or with new tools.

- **Don't Forget to Provide Time for Training**: Training will speed up the change process. Consider all training modalities, including self-paced materials, videos, and live training. A pro-tip is to schedule downtime for training if it is self-paced to help people work it into their schedule and not just add to their workload at the end of the day.

- **Don't Overlook Individual Concerns**: While focusing on the team, don't ignore individual hesitations or struggles with the new changes.

- **Don't Minimize the Impact of Change**: Avoid downplaying the challenges associated with the transition. Acknowledge the effort required to adapt and the possible disruptions to routine.

- **Don't Delay in Addressing Issues**: Quickly address any issues or challenges that emerge during the Near stage to prevent them from escalating and affecting morale or performance.

- **Don't Rush the Process**: Resist the urge to push forward too quickly. Ensure the team is ready and has had enough time to fully engage with and understand the changes before moving on.

Quiz

Question 1:

After implementing flexible working hours, a project manager observes mixed reactions among the team. Some members are thriving, while others seem unable to manage their time effectively. In the Near stage, what strategy should the project manager employ to assist those struggling?

A)   Revert to the previous fixed working hours for all team members.

B)   Ignore the issue, assuming that team members will eventually adapt on their own.

C)   Criticize those who are struggling during team meetings to motivate them to improve.

D)   Offer personalized coaching sessions to help struggling members develop effective time management strategies.

Correct Answer: D) Offer personalized coaching sessions to help struggling members develop effective time management strategies.

Offering personalized coaching sessions aligns with empowering employees in the Near stage, providing them with the tools and skills needed to adapt to the change. This supportive approach addresses individual challenges and helps team members harness the benefits of flexible working hours, thus fostering a more productive and satisfied team. Also, be open to allowing people to "opt out" and tell you this is not the environment for them (yes, this means shifting roles or sometimes exiting the organization). While it would be great to bring everyone along in a change, the reality is that not all people make it through every change.

Question 2:

The local school district is transitioning to a new digital learning platform to enhance educational delivery. While teachers are generally supportive, there is some hesitation about integrating the technology effectively into their classrooms. To facilitate the Near stage of this change, what strategy could the district employ to increase teacher confidence and practical understanding of the new system?

A)   Ignore the teachers' concerns and insist on the immediate full-scale implementation of the platform.

B)   Provide extensive documentation on the platform's features without any hands-on training.

C)   Organize field trips to nearby schools that have successfully implemented similar technology, allowing teachers to observe and discuss practical uses in real classrooms.

D)   Limit training to online tutorials and email support for troubleshooting.

Correct Answer: C) Organize field trips to nearby schools that have successfully implemented similar technology, allowing teachers to observe and discuss practical uses in real classrooms.

Organizing field trips to schools that have successfully implemented similar digital learning platforms provides teachers with a tangible understanding of how the technology can be effectively integrated into their teaching practices. By witnessing firsthand the practical application and benefits of the new system, teachers can gain insights, ask real-time questions, and see positive outcomes, which can alleviate their concerns and increase their confidence in using the technology. This hands-on approach helps bridge the gap between theoretical knowledge and practical application, essential in navigating the Near stage of change.

Field trips do not always have to be in person; a virtual meeting with a team that has had a similar experience is also helpful.

Question 3:

Just like the scenario of Greenview's waste management system change, a small town is introducing a new recycling program to improve its environmental footprint. Initially, there are some resistance from residents who were unsure about the program and how to participate correctly. What should the town council do to help residents move through the Near stage?

A) Rapidly deploy the new system without any preliminary adjustments based on community response.

B) Conduct pilot programs in select neighborhoods to practically demonstrate how the new system would function and refine it based on real-time feedback.

C) Keep the existing system unchanged while the new system's benefits were discussed in council meetings.

D) Launch a large-scale promotional campaign about the system's benefits without practical demonstrations.

Correct Answer: B) Conduct pilot programs in select neighborhoods to practically demonstrate how the new system would function and refine it based on real-time feedback.

Conducting pilot programs in select neighborhoods effectively engages residents in the Near stage of accepting a new recycling program. This method allows for a hands-on demonstration of how the new system operates, which can help alleviate uncertainties and misconceptions. By providing a practical experience, residents can see firsthand the benefits and functionality of the system, and city leaders can get valuable feedback that can help refine the program.

Question 4:

The HR department of a large corporation is rolling out a new online self-service portal for employee benefits. While the rollout has been communicated, several employees have expressed confusion about how to use the portal effectively. What should the HR manager do to address this in the Near stage?

A) Organize a series of drop-in sessions where employees can come and learn about the portal features with the help of HR staff.

B) Send out a general email reminding employees that the portal is now available.

C) Assume that employees will figure it out eventually and take no further action.

D) Punish employees who fail to use the portal by the next benefits enrollment period.

Correct Answer: A) Organize a series of drop-in sessions where employees can come and learn about the portal features with the help of HR staff.

Organizing drop-in sessions where employees can actively engage with the new system with the support of HR staff is an excellent way to facilitate the Near stage. These sessions provide a hands-on learning experience, help clarify any confusion, and demonstrate the company's commitment to ensuring all employees feel comfortable and supported during the transition. This approach enhances understanding and promotes effective use of the new portal.

Question 5:

A local government office is transitioning to a digital permit application system to streamline processes and reduce paper use. Shortly after implementation, users report problems with uploading documents and payment processing, leading to a backlog of unprocessed applications. Faced with mounting complaints and the risk of losing public trust, what strategy should the department head adopt in the Near stage to effectively manage these setbacks and maintain progress towards full implementation?

A) Continue to enforce the use of the new digital system exclusively, assuming that users will adapt to the system with time.

B) Temporarily reintroduce the old paper-based application process for critical permits while the digital system issues are addressed, and communicate openly with the public about expected timelines for resolution.

C) Ignore user complaints and focus on training staff internally to work around the technical issues without altering current processes.

D) Blame the software provider publicly for deflecting criticism from the department and pressure the provider to speed up fixes.

Correct Answer:

B) Temporarily reintroduce the old paper-based application process for critical permits while the digital system issues are addressed, and communicate openly with the public about expected timelines for resolution.

Opting to reintroduce the old paper-based system temporarily for critical permits allows the department to manage urgent needs effectively while the technical issues in the new digital system are resolved. This approach shows responsiveness to public concerns and preserves the integrity of the service during the transition. Open communication about the issues and clear timelines for resolution help maintain public trust and demonstrate the department's commitment to transparency and customer service. This strategy ensures that the transition does not hinder access to essential services and supports a smoother eventual transition to a fully functional digital system.

CHAPTER 5

CHEER

As the final applause fades in the conference room, Eric stands amidst his team members, each awash in a mix of relief and triumph. Just months ago, the daunting prospect of their project seemed like a distant summit. There were days when the path forward was shrouded in the fog of uncertainty, and their steps were tentative and unsure. But today, as they review their journey, the air is electric with celebration—not just for reaching their goal but for the journey that brought them here.

On this otherwise ordinary Wednesday, as Eric looks around at the faces of his colleagues, there's a palpable shift in energy. The anxious glances and furrowed brows that once marked their meetings have been replaced by smiles and nods of satisfaction. Conversations buzz around the room, not about the hurdles they faced but how they overcame them and the lessons they learned. There's a sense of completion, yet a new kind of excitement bubbles beneath the surface.

"I never thought we'd get here when we started," Eric overhears someone say, their voice a mix of awe and pride. It's a sentiment echoed in his own heart. What seemed impossible has become a part of their daily lives, and their routines are now seamlessly integrated with the changes they've implemented. They're not just adapted; they're transformed.

As Eric prepares to close the meeting, his thoughts turn to the future. The Cheer stage is more than just a finale—it's a catapult into what's next. It's about harnessing the energy of success to fuel future ventures. "Today we celebrate," Eric begins, addressing the room, "not just our achievements but our potential. Tomorrow, we build on what we've learned, aim higher, and set new challenges."

The room quiets, every team member reflecting on the gravity of the moment. They've not only changed; they've grown stronger, more cohesive. They've turned challenges into stepping stones and skepticism into confidence. Now, as they stand in the glow of their accomplishments, they're ready to carry this momentum forward.

In this chapter, we'll explore the Cheer stage, where hard-fought efforts culminate in celebration and strategic advancement. We'll delve into effectively recognizing and consolidating gains, ensuring the changes become deeply rooted within the organization. From planning impactful recognition events to setting the stage for future innovations, this stage is crucial for sustaining change and building a culture that adapts to and thrives on continuous improvement.

Making it to Cheer

Reaching the Cheer stage of change is a significant milestone as it signifies that the initial resistance has been overcome, the change has been implemented, and people are starting to exhibit the behaviors the change sought to create. At this time, change leaders should celebrate loudly, as the journey to Cheer is never simple, easy, or straightforward.

You know you've reached the Cheer stage when there is visible enthusiasm and neutral or positive attitudes among the team. Team members are not just compliant but genuinely satisfied or even enthusiastic about the change. They talk about it without negativity and encourage others to embrace it. For instance, employees in a company that has successfully transitioned to a flexible work schedule might share their positive experiences, creating a ripple effect of acceptance and enthusiasm.

Another clear indicator of reaching the Cheer stage is when the changes have been fully integrated into daily routines. The new practices or behaviors are no longer seen as temporary adjustments but have become part of the daily routine. People have integrated the changes into their lives and are comfortable with the new normal. For example, after a community adopts a new waste sorting system, residents who initially resisted now use it seamlessly in their daily routines.

Recognition of success is another hallmark of the Cheer stage. Acknowledge and celebrate achievements related to the change. Encourage your team to share success stories, highlighting the benefits and improvements brought by the change. Hospitals might celebrate the successful implementation of a new patient care protocol by recognizing the dedication and adaptability of the staff who embrace the latest procedures to enhance patient outcomes.

In the Cheer stage, you will likely observe a forward-thinking mindset. The organization or community starts to look forward, setting new goals and challenges that build on the successful implementation of the change. There is a sense of readiness for future changes, driven by the confidence gained from navigating the current one. For example, a neighborhood that has successfully established community gardens might start planning for additional green spaces and sustainability projects.

It's important to note that not everyone in the Cheer stage will be visibly happy or enthusiastic, but they will be exhibiting the desired behaviors of the change. They will be participating, engaging, and contributing to the new normal. For example, in a town that has adopted new recycling practices, not every resident might be excited about the change. Still, they are all sorting their waste correctly, contributing to a cleaner environment.

Reaching the Cheer stage is a testament to the collective effort and resilience of the entire organization or community. It's a moment to pause, reflect, and celebrate the journey while setting the stage for continuous growth and improvement. As we move forward, understanding the goals of the Cheer stage will help us consolidate our gains and leverage our success for future initiatives.

Here's a quick reference for how to identify if you've made it to the Cheer stage:

Indicator	What You Will See	What People Will Be Doing
Visible Enthusiasm and Positive Attitudes	Team members showing genuine satisfaction or enthusiasm, openly positive about the change. Conversation shifts from "How?" to "Look at what we have done" or "Congratulations."	Discussing the change positively, encouraging others to embrace it, sharing personal success stories, praising each other, celebrating wins they feel with the change.
Integration into Daily Routines	The new practices or behaviors are seamlessly incorporated into everyday activities; they are the "new normal."	Engaging with the new systems or processes as routine, comfortably using new tools or methods.
Recognition of Success	Formal and informal celebrations of achievements related to the change, as well as acknowledgment in meetings and communications.	Celebrating successes, participating in recognition programs, and sharing beneficial outcomes of the change.

Indicator	What You Will See	What People Will Be Doing
Forward-Thinking Mindset	A proactive approach towards future challenges and changes, setting new goals based on past successes.	Planning for future initiatives, using gained confidence to explore further improvements and changes.

This table outlines the observable behaviors and activities that signify people impacted by a change are entering the Cheer stage, where the change is not only realized but embraced, forming a foundation for future growth and ongoing positive transformation.

Goals of the Cheer Stage

The Cheer stage is all about consolidating gains, celebrating successes, and reinforcing the change to ensure it becomes a lasting part of the organization. This stage focuses on acknowledging the hard work, embedding the change into the organizational culture, and using the momentum to foster future change. Here's how to approach it:

- **Acknowledge and Celebrate Successes**: Recognize and celebrate the achievements and hard work of everyone involved in the change. This can include organizing celebratory events, giving personalized commendations, and sharing success stories that highlight the benefits of the change.

- **Embed the Change**: Work to integrate the change into the organization's culture, policies, and standard operating procedures. This involves reinforcing the new behaviors and processes until they become the norm, ensuring the change is sustained over time.

- **Monitor**: Assure the change is working long-term as intended

- **Facilitate Retrospectives**: Conduct retrospective sessions to gather feedback and lessons learned from the change process. These insights are crucial for continuous improvement and preparing the organization for future changes.

- **Showcase Progress and Impact**: Regularly highlight the progress made and the positive impact of the change. This could involve sharing metrics, testimonials, and case studies demonstrating the tangible benefits and improvements resulting from the change.

- **Encourage Ongoing Engagement**: Keep the momentum going by setting new goals and challenges that build on the success of the change. Encourage continuous engagement and innovation by fostering a culture that values and supports ongoing improvement.

- **Provide Continued Support and Resources**: Ensure that support and resources remain available to help sustain the change. This could include ongoing training, access to experts, and providing tools that reinforce the new ways of working.

- **Leverage Success for Future Changes**: Use the success of the current change as a case study or motivator for future change initiatives. Demonstrating the organization's capacity for successful adaptation can inspire confidence and readiness for future transformations.

In short, the goal of the Cheer stage is to solidify the change, celebrate the journey and the achievements, and create a foundation for future success. By recognizing the efforts of everyone involved, embedding the change into the organizational fabric, and maintaining momentum, you ensure that the change is implemented, sustained, and built upon for continued growth and improvement. Woohoo, Cheer!

Cheer Stage Responsibilities

In the Cheer stage of change management, the roles and responsibilities of individuals, leaders, and the company are distinct yet interconnected, focusing on celebration, consolidation, and forward-looking strategies. Here's an overview:

Individuals:

- **Reflect and Celebrate:** Individuals should take the time to reflect on their own journey through the change process, recognizing their personal growth and contributions.

- **Share Experiences:** Actively participate in sharing experiences and insights gained throughout the change process. This helps in cultivating a learning culture and reinforces a sense of accomplishment.

- **Embrace and Consolidate Change**: Fully embrace the new changes, integrating them into daily routines and practices. This is the stage where the change becomes part of the "new normal."

Leaders:

- **Acknowledge and Celebrate Successes**: Leaders should publicly acknowledge and celebrate their teams' achievements and hard work. This could involve organizing celebratory events or giving personalized commendations.

- **Facilitate Retrospectives:** Lead retrospective sessions to gather feedback and lessons learned. This is essential for continuous improvement and preparing for future changes.

- **Sustain Momentum:** Keep the momentum of change going by setting new goals and challenges. This ensures the change doesn't stagnate once the initial objectives are met.

- **Monitor the outcomes**: Measure and report the outcomes to ensure that the goals continue to be met and share these with the team to reinforce the impact of the change.

Company:

- **Institutionalize Change:** The company as a whole should work to institutionalize the change, integrating it into the organization's culture, policies, and standard operating procedures.

- **Broad Recognition and Celebration**: Organize company-wide recognition events or communications to celebrate the success of the change initiative, highlighting how it contributes to the broader company goals.

- **Continued Support and Resources:** Provide ongoing support and resources to ensure the changes are sustained and continue to evolve as needed.

- **Leverage Success for Future Changes**: Use the success of the current change as a case study or motivator for future change initiatives, demonstrating the organization's capacity for successful adaptation and growth.

In the Cheer stage, the focus shifts from managing the change to embedding it into the fabric of the organization and using the experience as a springboard for future initiatives. Leaders at this stage must reinforce a positive outlook towards change.

Navigating the Cheer Stage

As organizations move through the Cheer stage, the celebration of success is naturally complemented by efforts to embed these changes into everyday practices and processes. In this stage, the joy and recognition experienced during celebratory events are complemented by strategic efforts to integrate these changes into the organizational culture. This ensures that achievements are not only celebrated but also solidified as enduring elements of the organization.

In this section, we will explore strategies to effectively leverage the Cheer stage as a change driver, leader, or representative of organizational change. We'll discuss how to organize meaningful celebration events that honor contributions and foster a sense of community and achievement across the organization. Additionally, we will delve into conducting retrospectives and post-mortems to reflect on the change journey and identify lessons learned and areas for improvement, which can drive further growth and development. By combining celebrations with reflective evaluations, leaders can ensure that the momentum of change is maintained and used as a springboard for continuous organizational enhancement and readiness for future challenges.

Celebrating Success with Events and Recognitions

In the Cheer stage, your job as a leader is to recognize the achievements of individuals and teams who have contributed to the successful implementation of the change. These celebrations not only acknowledge hard work but also reinforce positive behaviors and boost morale.

Consider hosting a company-wide celebration event to honor the team's efforts. For instance, a healthcare organization that successfully implemented a new patient management system might hold an event to recognize the contributions of its staff. During the event, the CEO could give a speech highlighting the journey and achievements, followed by a dinner and awards ceremony.

In addition to large events, personalized recognition is so important! Personalizing recognition shows you understand the value of the individual's contribution versus a generalized comment. For example, a sales manager who excelled in adapting to a new CRM system could receive an "Excellence in Innovation" award. Personalized thank-you notes from leadership or shout-outs during team meetings can also make a significant impact.

If you give gifts, they don't need to be big! Little tokens of appreciation can go a long way in helping people feel recognized. A talented project manager at a software company has a reputation for giving trophies after a project to all involved. Each trophy is themed in alignment with the project and works to recognize contributions while having a little bit of fun! A fan favorite trophy she has given are small disco ball trophies for a big project and the cans of Spam when a team worked to migrate spam filtering from one system to another.

Sharing Success Stories and Testimonials

Sharing stories and testimonials helps to reinforce the benefits of the change. A tech company might publish a series of blog posts or internal newsletters featuring employees who have thrived in the new work-from-home policy, sharing their tips and success stories. This not only celebrates their achievements but also provides a roadmap for others. When employees see their peers successfully adapting to and thriving in the new environment, it fosters a sense of possibility and motivation across the organization. Here are a few ideas for how to share success stories and testimonials in the Cheer stage:

- **Internal Newsletters and Blogs**: Publish blog posts or news-letters featuring employees who have thrived after adapting to the change. Include detailed accounts of how they adapted and what they love about their new routine. For example, when shifting to remote work, highlight how employees set up home offices, managed their time, and balanced work with personal responsibilities.

- **Video Testimonials and Interviews**: Create video interviews showcasing success stories. Highlight how new strategies have improved team performance. For example, a project manager might discuss how the new strategy allowed their team to meet tight deadlines more efficiently, providing insights and motivation for others.

- **Case Studies and Presentations**: Compile case studies detailing the successful implementation of changes to be shared internally and beyond your organization as data privacy rules allow. Present challenges, solutions, and outcomes. An example could be a retail store reducing stock discrepancies by 50 percent within six months by implementing a new inventory process, offering a clear demonstration of the benefits of the new system.

- **Social Media and Public Platforms**: Share success stories on social media and public platforms to enhance external visibility and brand reputation. First, consult with your marketing team and work with them to create feature testimonials from volunteers, customers, or employees highlighting the benefits of the change. For example, a donor might explain how a new fundraising platform encouraged them to increase their contributions, inspiring others to consider doing the same.

- **Interactive Workshops and Panels**: Host workshops and panels where employees can share their experiences and success stories either internally or in the public view. Include Q&A sessions to allow others to ask questions and gain insights directly from their peers. (This serves as field trips or case studies for others driving change, too!) For example, a nurse might share how a new patient care protocol improved outcomes in their unit while also sharing some practical tips and things to watch for when implementing a change of this type.

These tactics celebrate individual and team successes, creating a ripple effect of positivity and motivation throughout the organization. Whether through internal newsletters, video testimonials, or recognition programs, these stories provide practical tips and inspiration for others, fostering a culture of learning and celebration.

While celebrating successes is essential (and fun), taking a step back and critically evaluating the change process is equally important. This leads us to the next element of the Cheer stage: retrospectives and post-mortems. By reflecting on the entire journey, organizations can identify what worked well, what didn't, and how to improve in future change initiatives.

Retrospectives & Post-mortems

Retrospectives and feedback sessions are essential for learning from the change process and making continuous improvements. These sessions provide a structured way to reflect on what worked, what didn't, and how to move forward more effectively. In the Cheer stage, these reflections help consolidate success and lay the groundwork for future initiatives.

Change and project leaders have historically relied on post-mortems to conduct lessons-learned sessions. These traditional post-mortems involve analyzing the outcomes of a project after its completion, identifying what went wrong, and determining how similar issues can be avoided in the future. While these sessions can clarify past mistakes, they often focus on assigning blame and can create a negative atmosphere that hinders constructive dialogue.

In a more modern organizational culture, the approach has evolved toward blameless retrospectives. Unlike post-mortems, blameless retrospectives emphasize learning and improvement rather than fault-finding. The focus is on understanding the underlying causes of issues and developing strategies to enhance future performance as a cohesive team. This shift fosters a more positive and collaborative environment where team members feel safe to express their thoughts and ideas without fear of retribution.

When conducting retrospectives and post-mortems with your team, we hope that you lean towards the blameless approach and focus on learning from mistakes and missteps so that your future change initiatives will run more smoothly. In the Cheer stage, retrospectives are crucial for recognizing the hard work put in, celebrating successes, and planning for sustained progress and future changes.

Retrospectives

Retrospectives are a powerful tool for continuous improvement, bringing together the team to discuss what went well, what didn't, and what could be improved. Remember, the goal is not to assign blame but to foster a culture of learning and growth. For example, after rolling out a new project management tool, a construction firm could hold a retrospective meeting with project managers, site supervisors, and workers. They could discuss challenges, such as initial technical difficulties, and how they were overcome. This method should focus on understanding what happened and what could be done differently in the future.

Retrospectives are a good practice for any team across any context. Whether implementing a new technology, launching a marketing campaign, or reorganizing a department, retrospectives can help your team reflect and improve, especially in the Cheer stage when the immediate pressure of change has lifted and there is an opportunity to consolidate and celebrate.

Facilitating a Retrospective

Anyone can facilitate a retrospective, but it's often helpful to have a neutral party lead the session to ensure unbiased discussions. This could be a project manager, a team leader, or an external facilitator—someone not directly involved in the development, change, or problem. This neutrality helps to host the conversation without injecting personal opinions or biases into the framing of the problem or understanding of feedback.

When you (the facilitator) begin the session, start with a clear agenda and create a safe and open environment where team members feel comfortable sharing their thoughts. Emphasize that the goal is to learn and improve, not to criticize or blame.

Common formats include the "Start, Stop, Continue" method, where team members discuss actions to start, stop, and continue based on their experiences. Another popular format is the "4Ls" – what they Liked, Learned, Lacked, and Longed for during the project.

As you work through the prompts with the group, ensure that discussions lead to actionable items. Summarize the key takeaways and assign responsibilities for implementing changes. Follow up on these actions in subsequent meetings to track progress. Plan to hold retrospectives regularly at the end of each milestone or iteration so that the next portion of the change or project can be better than the last.

Imagine a software development team adopting retrospectives as part of their agile process. After completing a sprint or release, they gather to discuss what went well, such as successful collaboration and meeting deadlines, and what didn't, like encountering unexpected technical debt. They then brainstorm ways to improve, deciding to integrate more thorough code reviews and increase cross-team communication.

Retrospectives can be applied to multiple contexts, changes, projects, and initiatives. Anything that involves people working together or changing behavior can benefit from a retrospective. Whether you're a university implementing a new digital learning platform, a retail company transitioning to a new inventory management system, or a healthcare organization adopting new patient care protocols, retrospectives can help you refine processes and achieve better outcomes.

In the Cheer stage, retrospectives play a vital role in celebrating successes, learning from experiences, and setting the stage for future improvements. By continuously reflecting on what has been achieved and what can be improved, organizations can build on their successes and create a culture of continuous improvement and celebration.

Retrospectives are a great way to reflect, refine, and determine how to improve in the future. However, retrospectives are only one part of the process. To ensure the long-term success of any change initiative, it's essential to embed these changes into the organization's culture and processes. This means integrating new behaviors into standard operating procedures (SOPs), reinforcing these changes through ongoing training programs, and encouraging leaders to model the new behaviors desired so the change can be long-lasting.

Embedding Change into Culture and Processes

Embedding change into the fabric of an organization's culture and processes is crucial for ensuring the longevity and success of any change initiative. During the Cheer stage, solidify these changes by integrating them into the organization's daily routines, behaviors, and standard operating procedures (SOPs). This integration helps maintain the momentum gained and ensures that the new practices become second nature to employees. By reinforcing these changes through continuous training and strong leadership, organizations can foster a culture that embraces and sustains positive change. In this section, we will explore key strategies for embedding change into the culture and processes of an organization, ensuring that the improvements made are both lasting and impactful.

Integrating New Behaviors into SOPs

Updating standard operating procedures (SOPs) to reflect new practices is an important part of the Cheer stage. It marks the new way of working as standard procedure. This step ensures that new behaviors and processes become a part of the organization's daily routine for both existing and new employees, reinforcing the changes that have been celebrated.

For example, consider a retail company that has successfully implemented a new customer service initiative. To embed this change into the culture, the company needs to update its SOPs to include new customer service protocols so that existing employees can reference them. New employees will be trained in the "new way" as the company standard. Updating SOPs may include revising guidelines for handling customer inquiries, updating processes for returns and exchanges, and establishing new standards for in-store customer interactions. By doing so, the company ensures that every employee follows the same enhanced service guidelines, which helps maintain high levels of customer satisfaction and brand consistency.

Encouraging Leaders to Model New Behaviors

Leaders play a crucial role in embedding change. During the Cheer stage, leaders must model the new behaviors to set an example for the rest of the organization. Leaders' behavior will model what is expected of others. For instance, a financial services firm that has implemented a new client relationship management (CRM) system needs its senior advisors to use it consistently, effectively, and visibly. By doing so, they demonstrate their commitment to the change and set a standard for the rest of the team to follow. When employees see a leader's commitment to the new system, it encourages them to do the same, fostering a culture of adoption and consistent use. This leadership behavior emphasized during the Cheer stage reinforces the importance of the change and helps embed it into the organization's daily operations.

As a change leader, it is your job to communicate your expectations of leaders and how they can help move themselves and their teams through change. Explicitly communicate and train leaders on what they can do to help. Consider manager or leadership-specific workshops, training sessions, and support materials to equip leaders with the necessary knowledge and skills while highlighting the importance of modeling the new behaviors. Better yet, work with leaders to add accountability mechanisms related to the change. Consider how leaders can support the change by modeling it to their team and upholding it as the new normal. Encourage them to reject work that is not aligned with the changed process or behavior.

Reinforcing Change Through Training & Support Programs

Continuous training and support complement leaders' efforts, help reinforce new behaviors, and ensure no one is left behind. These sessions should continue as long as individuals adjust to the change in the Cheer stage—typically, this period is longer than you might anticipate. When people stop attending the sessions and error rates are low, it is time to stop having them.

We've seen this approach work effectively in healthcare organizations that adopted a new electronic health records (EHR) system. In the Cheer stage, change leaders introduced regular workshops to ensure all medical staff were proficient in using the system. These workshops benefitted both new and existing staff as they adjusted to the EHR software, providing a platform to bring specific questions to the support team while also receiving information on best practices for data entry and new features that improve patient care. Even after reaching the Cheer stage, people still sought support and guidance as they worked through various scenarios and unforeseen issues or patterns in using the new system. Once participation dwindled and error rates dropped, the sessions were concluded, signaling a successful transition.

By embedding these changes into everyday practices, leadership modeling, and ongoing support, organizations can ensure that the successes celebrated in the Cheer stage are not ephemeral but become a permanent and positive force within the company. This approach reinforces the changes made and sets the stage for future initiatives, demonstrating a commitment to continuous improvement and innovation. The Cheer stage, therefore, is not just a conclusion but a stepping stone to further growth and development, leveraging the positive outcomes of past changes to inspire and inform future successes.

Monitoring Change

Consistent monitoring is essential to ensure that the change has the intended impact. Ideally, the desired outcomes were clearly defined during the planning stage, and monitoring will now serve as a comparative analysis against that plan. This could involve demonstrating ROI, tracking throughput time, or assessing other key metrics. Monitoring and reporting will determine whether the change was successful or if further improvements are necessary. Be wary of adopting a "set it and forget it" mindset.

Monitoring isn't just about looking at the big picture—it's also about tracking the behaviors and processes that underpin the change. For example, after launching a new company website, it's important to check all links for functionality, analyze traffic with SEO tools, and measure other key performance indicators (KPIs) to ensure the site is performing as expected. This involves looking at metrics such as page load times, user engagement, and conversion rates.

Imagine you hire a new employee, and your only check-in is a 90-day feedback survey to determine whether the hire was the right decision. If you congratulate them on getting the job, put them through onboarding, check in at 90 days with a survey, and never check in again, you miss crucial opportunities to guide their development and address any issues early on. Just as with new hires, organizational changes need ongoing support and feedback to ensure they are integrated successfully.

Similarly, when rolling out a new software tool, simply training employees once and moving on isn't enough support to ensure long-lasting change. In addition to the launch, you must track adoption rates, gather feedback, and provide additional resources or training to ensure the tool is being used effectively. Monitoring in this context means continuously assessing whether the change delivers the expected benefits and adjusting your approach as necessary.

Further Growth and Development

While the Cheer stage may seem like the end of the change, this stage is not just about celebrating successes—it's about leveraging those successes to set new goals, encourage ongoing improvement, and spark innovation, ensuring the organization remains dynamic and forward-looking. Support your organization's ability to change and adapt to the future by engaging in forward-looking activities in the Cheer stage.

Encouraging a Culture of Feedback and Continuous Improvement

During the Cheer stage, transitioning from reinforcing new behaviors to continuously improving them involves actively seeking and utilizing feedback. This transition serves as a bridge between celebrating current successes and planning for future enhancements. By listening to employees and making adjustments based on their insights, organizations can fine-tune their processes and ensure the change is effective and sustainable.

Taking feedback seriously and implementing changes based on it shows that the organization values its employees' opinions. For example, a retail company that has transitioned to a new inventory management system might find through feedback that employees need more training on certain features. Acting on this feedback by organizing additional training sessions can enhance the system's overall effectiveness and demonstrate to employees that their feedback is valuable. This, in turn, encourages employees to provide additional feedback in the future, creating a positive feedback loop that drives continuous improvement.

Setting New Goals and Challenges

The end of one change cycle in the Cheer stage is an opportune moment to set new targets. This ongoing goal-setting is required to maintain the momentum of change and prevent stagnation. For example, after a successful rollout of an eco-friendly packaging initiative, a manufacturing company might set new sustainability targets, aiming to reduce its carbon footprint further by optimizing logistics to decrease transportation emissions. By doing so, the organization keeps the enthusiasm alive and pushes continuous improvement. A successful site opening might be the opportunity to brainstorm how to do site openings faster in the future.

Providing Opportunities for Innovation

Encouraging employees to innovate during the Cheer stage can lead to breakthroughs and sustained enthusiasm. Organizations should create opportunities for innovation by fostering a spirit of creativity and experimentation. A tech startup, for instance, might hold hackathons where teams compete to develop new features or solve existing problems. These events stimulate innovative thinking and build camaraderie and excitement among team members. Similarly, a healthcare provider might organize innovation days where staff can propose and work on new patient care solutions, driving engagement and practical improvements.

Building Readiness for Future Changes

Building on current successes during the Cheer stage prepares the organization for future changes, enhancing its capacity for adaptation.

When an organization successfully navigates a change, it gains valuable experience and confidence to be leveraged in future initiatives. For example, a publishing company that has successfully transitioned to digital media can use its newfound expertise to tackle innovations in content delivery and marketing strategies. This readiness for change ensures that the organization remains agile and responsive in an ever-evolving market landscape.

In the Cheer stage, organizations that double down on preparing for the future by learning from, celebrating, and planning their next change can ensure that the positive changes do not end with initial success but continue to evolve and contribute to the company's long-term vision and strategy. This ongoing cycle of improvement and celebration is essential for building a resilient and adaptable organization.

Stories From the Field

Example stories help us understand the impact of the change curve through a real-life lens. The example of Losing Loyalty Programs will illustrate the need to operationalize change to ensure success in the long term.

Losing Loyalty Programs

A regional retail chain introduced a new customer loyalty program designed to enhance shopping experiences and increase customer retention. The initiative was launched with great enthusiasm, and the initial uptake was promising. The Cheer stage was marked by a celebratory atmosphere as the company's leadership praised the new program during a series of store visits and in company-wide communications, highlighting the surge in sign-ups and initial positive feedback from customers.

However, as time progressed, several issues began to surface, undermining the sustainability of the change. One major problem was the lack of integration between the loyalty program and the existing sales strategies of the stores. Store managers, who were initially enthusiastic, began to see the program as an added burden rather than an asset. They felt the rewards undermined their pricing strategies and complicated inventory management.

Moreover, the training provided to the store staff on how to promote the program and handle related queries was minimal after the initial rollout and was not present in new hire training. This lack of ongoing training led to inconsistencies in how the program was presented to customers, causing confusion and diminishing the perceived value of the loyalty rewards. The staff, feeling unsupported and unclear about the program's benefits, gradually lost their initial enthusiasm and began reverting to their old routines of customer engagement without emphasizing the loyalty program.

Customer engagement with the program started to wane as the perceived value of the rewards did not match the effort required to participate. The initial celebrations and positive rhetoric from the leadership did not translate into sustained practice on the ground. The failure to embed the new loyalty program into the daily operations and culture of the stores, combined with inadequate ongoing support and training, resulted in the program fizzling out. Eventually, the retail chain saw a significant drop in participation rates, and, more critically, customer feedback began to reflect dissatisfaction not only with the loyalty program but with the store's overall service, which was now seen as inconsistent.

This example illustrates how a change initiative can reach the Cheer stage but still fail to be sustainable if it is not fully integrated into the operational and cultural fabric of the organization. Continuous support, clear alignment with existing practices, and consistent reinforcement are crucial to ensuring that new initiatives live beyond the initial excitement and become a lasting part of the organization's strategy.

Cheer for Holistic Health

The management team at a large healthcare facility introduced a significant initiative to integrate holistic health into their patient care model. This approach aimed to treat physical, mental, and emotional wellness comprehensively.

Initially, the change was met with apprehension. Staff members were concerned about the complexity of implementing new treatment protocols and the additional time it might require during patient assessments. Nurses worried about how to integrate mental health discussions into routine physical health checks, and doctors were skeptical about the efficacy of blending such diverse practices. To address these fears, the facility held multiple information sessions where staff could voice their concerns. Experts in holistic practices were invited to discuss the benefits and logistical details, helping to alleviate misconceptions.

As the initiative began, training sessions were introduced to equip the staff with the necessary skills. These sessions included practical workshops on conducting integrated health assessments and handling sensitive patient interactions. The staff began to see the potential benefits of this approach through guided real-life scenarios and role-playing exercises, which helped them understand the "how" behind the change. Gradually, the questions shifted from "Why are we doing this?" to "How can I effectively implement this in my daily routine?"

With the successful integration of holistic practices, the facility moved into the Cheer stage. Positive patient feedback accumulated, showing improvements in patient satisfaction and health outcomes. The facility celebrated these successes by organizing an appreciation event that recognized the efforts of all staff involved, from medical personnel to administrative support. During this event, the CEO highlighted specific success stories related to the organization's mission and reinforced the value of the holistic approach.

Additionally, the management team launched a monthly newsletter feature called "Holistic Highlights," which shared success stories from staff and patients. These narratives detailed how the new approach had positively impacted patient care, boosting morale and solidifying the initiative's value.

Ongoing training sessions continued to be a cornerstone of the Cheer stage, ensuring that the staff remained adept at the latest holistic practices and that any new staff were fully trained as part of the new hire onboarding process and were ready to join the team's endeavor to support and promote holistic health. These were paired with regular feedback sessions, creating a loop of continuous improvement and adaptation.

Leadership consistently modeled the new behaviors, with senior doctors and management regularly participating in holistic health treatments and discussing their benefits during staff meetings. This visible endorsement helped to embed the holistic approach deeply within the facility's culture, demonstrating a long-term commitment to these practices.

By actively celebrating the successes, continually reinforcing the new practices through training and leadership, and maintaining open channels of feedback, the healthcare facility successfully implemented the holistic health approach and ensured its sustainability and acceptance as a core component of its patient care philosophy.

What's Next?

As the Cheer stage reaches its culmination, it marks a significant milestone in the lifecycle of change management, but it is far from the end of the journey for a change leader. This stage represents not just the successful implementation and acceptance of a particular change but also serves as a crucial turning point where the focus shifts from celebrating current successes to preparing for future challenges. For change leaders, this is a time for reflection on both the achievements and the lessons learned throughout the process. It is an opportunity to consolidate the gains, ensuring that the new practices are not merely temporary but are deeply embedded within the organization's culture and operational norms.

Moving forward, change leaders must adopt a proactive stance, anticipating the next set of challenges and opportunities for growth. The end of one change cycle seamlessly transitions into the preliminary stage of the next, whether refining the current change or initiating a new project. Leaders should use the insights from the current change to inform their strategies for future initiatives, continuously striving to enhance their approach to change management. By doing so, they ensure the sustainability of implemented changes and foster a culture of continuous improvement within their organizations. This ongoing cycle of planning, action, and reflection distinguishes exceptional leaders who can maintain momentum and keep their teams engaged and evolving in an ever-changing business landscape.

📌 Key Takeaways

- Change leaders must actively celebrate successes to reinforce positive behaviors and foster a supportive environment.

- Continuous engagement through training, support, and welcoming feedback is essential to maintaining the momentum of change.

- Leaders should exemplify the new behaviors to encourage widespread adoption across the organization.

- Integrating new practices into daily routines and procedures helps to cement the change as a permanent aspect of organizational life.

Leverage retrospectives to provide insights into what worked and what didn't, promoting a culture of continuous learning. Leveraging current successes prepares the organization for future challenges, demonstrating its capacity for growth and adaptation.

Tips for the Cheer Stage

In the Cheer stage, concentrate on reinforcing and celebrating the successful execution of change by acknowledging individual and team contributions, providing ongoing support, and ensuring that the new behaviors or processes are fully integrated into everyday activities. Next, encourage the organization to embrace and build upon the changes, setting the stage for future initiatives and maintaining the momentum of success. Try out these tips:

- **Celebrate Achievements Publicly**: Highlight and celebrate every success, no matter how small, to reinforce the positive impacts of the change. This could involve public acknowledgments in meetings, newsletters, or through company-wide emails.

- **Lead by Example**: Ensure leaders at all levels are visibly committed to the new changes, using the new systems or behaviors themselves, and sharing their positive experiences with the team.

- **Facilitate Reflective Retrospectives**: Regularly schedule retrospectives to reflect on what has worked and what can be improved. This helps the team learn from the change process and apply these lessons to future initiatives.

- **Incorporate Change into Daily Routines**: Work to make new practices part of the standard procedures by updating training materials and SOPs to reflect the new status quo.

- **Support Sustained Engagement and Training**: Continue providing support and training opportunities to ensure everyone is comfortable and proficient with the new changes, adapting training as needed based on feedback and the evolving needs of the team.

- **Create Spaces for Continuous Feedback**: Establish ongoing channels for feedback to keep improving the change implementation. This can be through regular check-ins, feedback forms, or open-door policies.

- **Set New Goals to Build on Success**: Keep the team engaged by setting new objectives that build on the successes of the implemented changes, ensuring continued growth and development.

- **Use Success as a Springboard for Future Changes**: Demonstrate how the successful change can be a model for future initiatives, enhancing confidence in the organization's capacity to adapt and innovate.

Dos in the Cheer Stage

- **Do Celebrate Achievements**: Actively recognize and celebrate the successes of individuals and teams. Use events, awards, and public acknowledgments to highlight contributions and reinforce the positive aspects of the change.

- **Do Institutionalize the Change**: Ensure that the new practices are fully integrated into the organization's procedures and culture.

Update policies and standard operating procedures to reflect the new ways of working.

- **Do Provide Ongoing Support**: Continue to offer training and resources to support the new changes. Ensure all team members can access the help they need to fully adapt to the new systems or processes.

- **Do Encourage Continuous Improvement**: Foster an environment where feedback is sought and valued. Use insights gained from the team to refine and improve practices continuously.

- **Do Set New Goals**: Keep the momentum of change by setting new challenges and objectives that build on the current success and encourage ongoing engagement and growth.

- **Do Maintain Open Communication**: Continue facilitating open dialogue through regular meetings and feedback sessions, ensuring that communication remains transparent and inclusive.

Don'ts in the Cheer Stage

- **Don't Assume the Work is Done**: Avoid the mistake of thinking that once the Cheer stage is reached, no further action is needed. Continuous monitoring and engagement are crucial to sustain the change.

- **Don't Ignore Feedback**: Do not dismiss the insights and feedback from employees as the change becomes institutionalized. Ongoing adjustments may be necessary to fully embed the change.

- **Don't Stop Recognizing Efforts**: Avoid halting recognition programs after the initial success. Ongoing appreciation is key to maintaining morale and motivation.

- **Don't Isolate Skeptics**: Continue to engage with those who are still adjusting to the change. Provide support and resources to help them fully integrate into the new system.

- **Don't Neglect Long-Term Planning**: Ensure that the success of the change is not just a short-term win but is used as a foundation for future strategies and improvements.

- **Don't Overlook New Opportunities**: Be open to leveraging the success of the change to explore further innovations and improvements. Don't become complacent with the current success.

Quiz

Question 1:

The management team at a marketing agency has just completed a significant rebranding initiative and is in the Cheer stage. What is the most effective way to ensure that the success of this initiative is sustained and built upon?

A) Start planning the next change immediately without taking the time to review the outcomes of the rebranding.

B) Organize a celebratory meeting to acknowledge the team's hard work, provide detailed feedback on the rebranding results, and collaboratively discuss future steps.

C) Move on from discussing the rebranding to avoid dwelling on past achievements. People must be tired of hearing about rebranding.

D) Avoid bringing up the rebranding in future discussions to keep the team focused on upcoming projects.

Correct Answer: B) Organize a celebratory meeting to acknowledge the team's hard work, provide detailed feedback on the rebranding results, and collaboratively discuss future steps.

Organizing a celebratory meeting not only recognizes the hard work and achievements of the team but also solidifies the importance of the rebranding effort by reviewing its outcomes and discussing future applications. This approach encourages a culture of acknowledgment and continuous improvement, which are crucial for maintaining the momentum and integrating the change more deeply into the organization.

Question 2:

A software development company has reached the Cheer stage after successfully migrating to a new agile project management system that has improved team collaboration and project delivery times. To further enhance the benefits of this change, what step should the company consider next?

A) Discontinue all previous project management practices immediately to avoid confusion.

B) Organize celebratory events every month to maintain enthusiasm for the new system.

C) Implement a feedback loop where team members can suggest further improvements to the agile process.

D) Limit the use of the new system to only a few teams to assess long-term effectiveness.

Correct Answer: C) Implement a feedback loop where team members can suggest further improvements to the agile process.

Implementing a feedback loop allows team members to actively participate in the continuous improvement of the agile project management system. This approach capitalizes on the initial success by fostering an environment of ongoing engagement and innovation and ensures that the system evolves to meet changing project demands and team dynamics. Encouraging team members to contribute their insights and suggestions reinforces their commitment to the new system and enhances the overall effectiveness and adaptability of agile practices.

204 · THE CHANGE CHEAT CODE

Question 3:

An engineering firm has updated its project management SOPs to include sustainability assessments at every project stage. To reinforce this change, what should senior engineers do during project meetings?

A) Only focus on cost-saving aspects and ignore the sustainability criteria.

B) Actively use the new SOPs to guide project discussions and decisions, highlighting the importance of sustainability.

C) Avoid discussing the updates in meetings to reduce the burden on the team.

D) Delegate the responsibility of sustainability assessments to junior team members only.

Correct Answer: B) Actively use the new SOPs to guide project discussions and decisions, highlighting the importance of sustainability.

By actively using the updated SOPs in project meetings, senior engineers model the importance of the new sustainability assessments. This behavior demonstrates their commitment to the updated procedures and sets a standard for the team. Highlighting sustainability in discussions and decisions reinforces the change and ensures it is consistently applied, helping embed the new practices into the organizational culture. When questions arise for clarification of the process, the SOP should always be referenced to encourage use.

Question 4:

In the Cheer stage, a company has implemented a new workflow process that has been well-received. What actions should the company take next to maintain the effectiveness of this new workflow and ensure it becomes a permanent aspect of operations?

A) Update new hire training to reflect the new process, schedule regular training refreshers for existing employees, and encourage leaders to consistently use and refer to the new workflow in their daily activities.

B) Prevent any modifications to the new process to maintain its original integrity and stability.

C) Celebrate the initial success extensively but avoid ongoing discussions or training related to the workflow.

D) Immediately cease all training and reference to previous workflows to force a quicker adaptation to the new process.

Correct Answer: A) Update new hire training to reflect the new process, schedule regular training refreshers for existing employees, and encourage leaders to consistently use and refer to the new workflow in their daily activities.

Updating new hire training material, in addition to hosting regular training refreshers and encouraging leaders to actively use and promote the new workflow, ensures that the change is continually reinforced and properly integrated into daily operations. This strategy helps maintain the effectiveness of the workflow and supports its permanent adoption by making it a standard part of the organizational processes.

Question 5:

Following the successful implementation of an eco-friendly packaging initiative, what should be the focus in the Cheer stage to inspire and inform future organizational changes?

A) Discourage further discussion about the initiative to ensure it does not overshadow upcoming projects.

B) Create a detailed case study of the initiative, documenting the challenges faced, strategies used, and successes achieved to share with the organization.

C) Provide significant bonuses only to the team directly involved in the initiative, focusing rewards narrowly.

D) Quickly shift focus to new projects without evaluating or learning from the recent change's outcomes.

Correct Answer: B) Create a detailed case study of the initiative, documenting the challenges faced, strategies used, and successes achieved to share with the entire organization.

Creating a detailed case study of the eco-friendly packaging initiative allows the organization to capture valuable lessons and successes that can inform and inspire future changes. This documentation serves as a valuable resource for understanding what worked and what can be improved, providing a foundation for ongoing innovation and ensuring the organization's adaptive and sustainable growth.

PART 2: YOUR PLAYBOOK FOR SUCCESSFUL CHANGE

Welcome to Part 2 of our exploration into change management, where we transition from theory to practice. This section of the book is designed as a comprehensive playbook for successfully navigating each stage of change. Here, you will find a detailed guide through the four pivotal stages of change—Hear, Fear, Near, and Cheer—including practical strategies, tools, and real-life examples to support your journey.

Each stage is delineated with clear goals and responsibilities, tailored communication tips, and a checklist of tasks to ensure thorough preparation and execution. We delve into the intricacies of each stage, highlighting the unique challenges and opportunities they present. This section is structured to help you not only understand what to do but also how to think critically and adaptively about the changes you are implementing or experiencing.

- **Hear**: We begin by setting the foundational understanding of the change. This stage focuses on communication strategies that ensure all stakeholders are informed, engaged, and ready to embark on the journey of change.

- **Fear**: Next, we address the natural emotional responses to change. Here, you will learn to navigate resistance and uncertainty, employing empathy and support to transform apprehension into positive engagement.

- **Near**: As we move closer to the moment the change is realized, this stage concentrates on implementation. You'll be equipped with tools to facilitate adaptation and ensure all team members are not just compliant but competent and confident in their new roles or processes.

- **Cheer**: Finally, we celebrate success. This stage emphasizes recognizing achievements, consolidating gains, and setting the stage for sustained change and future growth.

This playbook includes case studies that illustrate both successful outcomes and cautionary tales, providing a nuanced perspective on how different approaches play out in real scenarios. Additionally, we offer a variety of resources, such as examples, templates, and communication samples, to provide you with tangible tools that can be adapted to your specific needs.

Whether you are a manager leading a team through organizational change, a business owner implementing new technology, or an individual navigating personal transitions, the strategies outlined in this playbook will empower you to manage change with skill and confidence.

Now, let's dive in and transform your theoretical knowledge into practical mastery as we navigate the complex yet rewarding landscape of leading effective change.

CHAPTER 6

PLAYBOOK FOR HEAR

We began this book by acknowledging that change is happening faster than ever before, and it is an inevitable and constant force in both personal and organizational landscapes, often evoking a spectrum of reactions. In order to lead yourself and others through change effectively, you must acknowledge the stages of change.

In Chapter 2, we discovered how the first stage, Hear, lays the foundation for what is to come and informs people that a change is coming. The Hear stage includes the moment of introduction, the point at which new information is presented. Whether it's a shift in company policy, the adoption of a new process, or a significant organizational restructuring, the Hear stage is where the seeds of change are sown.

Figure 6.1: The Change Cheat Code: Hear, Fear, Near, and Cheer

This chapter is dedicated to unpacking and mastering specific tactics and skills you can use in the Hear stage as a critical juncture in the journey of change management. We will explore how to craft and deliver messages about change that resonate and how to create an environment that fosters understanding and openness.

Hear Stage Goal

The goal of the Hear stage is to inform people about the upcoming change such that they understand what is happening and can begin their change journey with adequate support.

Hear Stage Responsibilities

In the Hear stage, roles and responsibilities are clearly defined across the organization to facilitate effective communication and set the groundwork for accepting change.

Individuals: Engage and Understand

Individuals are tasked with actively engaging with the presented information, listening attentively, and seeking to understand the implications of the change. This stage encourages individuals to internalize the change, preparing them to adapt their perspectives and behaviors accordingly.

Leaders: Communicate Clearly and Empathetically

Leaders play a pivotal role by clearly and empathetically communicating the details of the change. They are responsible for presenting the change comprehensively, addressing both the emotional and practical aspects, and engaging in open dialogue to address concerns and feedback. Their communication sets the tone for transparency, building trust and openness throughout the change process. Remember, resist the temptation to tell people their emotions. Work to avoid phrases such as "You are going to love this" or "This will be so great."

Company: Reinforce and Support Communication

The company supports these efforts by ensuring consistent messaging across all levels and providing resources for ongoing dialogue. This includes maintaining open channels for feedback and reinforcing the change narrative throughout the organization, helping integrate the change into the company's culture and operations.

Communicating in Hear

How information about change is communicated during the Hear stage can significantly influence the subsequent reaction and acceptance of that change. This stage is not merely about transmitting information;

it is about ensuring that the information is heard, understood, and internalized by anyone impacted by the change and anyone who supports those impacted. It sets the tone for how individuals begin to process and respond to the change.

Unfortunately, the importance of the Hear stage is often overlooked, and the consequences of mishandling it are underestimated. Communicating change is not just about the conveyance of facts and plans. It's about acknowledging the emotions and concerns that come with the unknown. It's about creating a space where dialogue can begin, questions can be raised, and the groundwork for acceptance and cooperation is laid.

In the Hear stage, your goal is to get people to really hear you! Keep these guidelines in mind:

- **Clear Communication**: Use clear, concise, and jargon-free language across appropriate channels to avoid misunderstandings and misinformation. Consider the timing of your announcements. You can follow this general rule:

Change Size	Amount of Notice Suggested	Change Example
Small change	No notice	New mailing address for accounts receivables
Small change	Some notice	Communication change (all-staff meetings going from bi-weekly to monthly)
Large change	No notice, followed by intense communication after the announcement	Confidential changes, restructuring, M&A

Change Size	Amount of Notice Suggested	Change Example
Large change	Extensive notice and preplanning	Office move, new company name, restructuring into divisions

- **Emotional Acknowledgment**: Recognize and empathize with the emotional impact of change, such as anxiety or excitement, to build trust and encourage positive engagement. Avoid telling people the emotions they are experiencing or will experience. Avoid saying statements like "You're going to love this idea" or "You're not going to like what I'm going to say next."

- **Dialogue and Collaboration**: Create an open space for dialogue, encouraging employees to ask questions, provide feedback, and discuss concerns. This fosters a sense of ownership and commitment.

- **Consistent Messaging**: Ensure that communication is consistent across all levels, setting a positive tone for the entire change process and facilitating smoother transitions in subsequent stages.

The Hear Stage Checklist

The Hear Stage Checklist is your practical guide for initiating change. It outlines key steps for planning, communicating, and reinforcing change effectively. Use this checklist to set clear goals and deadlines, ensuring a solid foundation for the change process.

☐ **Design, Understand, and Plan the Change**

   a. Clearly define the change's scope and details.

    b. Refine change details as best you can so the path forward is somewhat known. Write the Five Ws and include what is not changing.

☐ **Prepare Change Communications and Support Programs**

    a. Develop comprehensive communication strategies that clearly explain the change and include the Five Ws. Develop a FAQ and methods people should use to submit feedback or get help. Socialize the FAQ with key stakeholders or the CCN to be sure everyone is on the same page.

    b. Set up support systems and resources to help individuals understand the change and prepare to adapt.

☐ **Inform People of the Change**

    a. Officially announce the change to all stakeholders. Consider the cascade of information.

    b. Ensure the initial communication is clear, thorough, and accessible.

    c. Post internal and market-facing information, FAQs, and support information to your company's intranet or info hub and share the link.

    d. Plan to repeat the message with several modalities (emails, channels, FAQs, meetings).

☐ **Reiterate the Change, Collect Feedback**

    a. Regularly reinforce the key messages about the change. Make multiple impressions, talk to people one-on-one and in small groups about the change, and provide information that is relevant to them and offers the most support.

b. Open channels for receiving feedback to gauge reactions and address concerns.

☐ **Prepare to Enter the Fear Stage**

a. Anticipate and plan for emotional reactions and resistance.

b. Strategize how to ease the transition into the Fear stage.

Extra Support for Hear and Beyond with Change Champion Networks

Before we delve into the resources for the Hear stage, it's crucial to highlight a powerful strategy for leading change: Leveraging a Change Champion Network (CCN).

A network of change champions can be invaluable when spearheading large-scale, complex, or socially impactful changes. Change champions are advocates within your organization who are keenly aware of the impacts of proposed changes. They provide feedback, share insights, and help influence others to adapt to new ways of working. The concept of a Change Champion Network is utilized across various sectors, including healthcare, manufacturing, government, technology, and more, proving its versatility and effectiveness.

A CCN consists of individuals selected for their influential opinions, enthusiasm, and capacity to positively engage their peers. These champions are not just messengers of change; they are deeply involved in the process—solicited for feedback, informed of developments, trained in new processes, and empowered to facilitate and advocate for the change initiatives. Their insights are particularly crucial during transitions that deeply affect organizational dynamics, such as during mergers, acquisitions, or comprehensive policy shifts.

The absence of a CCN can lead organizations to mistakenly assume that employees are aligned with the change, potentially speeding towards failure. By integrating a CCN, leaders gain an otherwise unlikely communication channel that bridges the gap between executive vision and the every day realities employees face. This network serves as a sounding board, helping to refine strategies and ensure that change initiatives are grounded, realistic, and more likely to succeed. In essence, a CCN doesn't just support change; it ensures it is conducted thoughtfully and inclusively, significantly enhancing the likelihood of successful outcomes.

We use the label CCN, but you can use a name that works for your organization's culture. We have seen names such as Culture Club, Feedback Team, and Employee Ambassadors.

The Process of Utilizing a CCN

The process of leveraging a CCN typically involves several key steps:

1. **Decide to Implement a CCN**: Initiating a Change Champion Network begins with the strategic decision by leadership to use influential advocates within the organization to facilitate smoother transitions during organizational changes. These champions serve as a bridge between the change management team and the wider employee base.

2. **Selection and Training**: The individuals chosen as change champions are typically well-respected, exhibit a positive attitude towards change, and possess strong influence over their peers. They should represent diverse departments and levels within the organization. Typically, CCN tenure is six to 12 months, at which time CCN members should be replaced by another company employee who meets the criteria. Once CCN members are selected, they should be trained on the change process, how to support others in navigating change, how to manage resistance,

and how to impact as leaders in the organization on the mindset, engagement, and outlook of others experiencing change.

3. **Previewing and Feedback**: Before any major change is broadly communicated (in the Hear stage), it is first previewed to the CCN. This allows for testing the message and enables the collection of initial feedback, which can be used to refine the messaging and overall change strategy. For instance, changes in employee mobility policies can be vetted by the CCN to gauge potential reception and identify any concerns that might arise so they can be addressed proactively.

4. **Communication and Support**: Once the change is rolled out, CCN members act as primary communicators and supporters within their departments. They explain the rationale behind the change, discuss its benefits, and address any concerns, ensuring the message is not just disseminated but also understood and accepted.

5. **Monitoring and Feedback Loop**: CCN members continuously monitor the implementation and reception of the change across the organization. They provide regular feedback to the change management team, offering insights and suggestions for improvements. This ongoing feedback is essential for making real-time adjustments and ensuring the change remains aligned with employee needs and organizational goals.

Leveraging a Change Champion Network (CCN) significantly enhances the potential effectiveness of change initiatives by fostering a supportive and informed environment. By involving champions from within the workforce, organizations ensure that communications resonate deeply, minimizing resistance and accelerating adoption. These champions provide crucial feedback that tailors the change process to real-world conditions, enhancing employee engagement and commitment. Over time, this strategy smooths transitions and cultivates a culture of agility and openness, preparing the organization for future changes. Win-win!

Practical Application of a CCN

While we have described the steps of creating and leveraging a CCN in driving change, let's look at it through the lens of the stages of change. In this section, we'll use the example of a software system change to walk through the four stages of change and what you can do with the CCN in each stage to drive your change to success.

Stage 1: Hear

- **Initial Briefing to CCN**: Before the announcement of the new software system, the CCN is briefed about the change. This includes the reasons for the change, the benefits of the new software, and how it will impact different departments.

- **Feedback and Message Refinement**: CCN members provide feedback on the initial communication plan. They might suggest simplifying technical jargon or focusing on specific benefits relevant to different teams.

- **Initial Rollout**: When the change is communicated to the wider organization, CCN members help disseminate or support the delivery of the information within their respective departments, ensuring that their peers understand the "what" and "why" of the new software.

Stage 2: Fear

- **Relaying Feedback to Leadership**: CCN members gather insights on common fears and relay this information to leadership, suggesting possible ways to alleviate these concerns, such as offering additional training sessions. The CCN members may need to be specifically trained on gathering feedback and not furthering change resistance.

- **Addressing Concerns**: As employees start to express concerns or anxiety about adapting to the new system, CCN members are key in addressing these fears. They might organize informal Q&A sessions or facilitate discussions where employees can voice their worries.

Stage 3: Near

- **Facilitating Adaptation**: As employees begin to interact with the new software, CCN members play a supportive role. They might conduct hands-on workshops or share tips and tricks they've learned.

- **Tracking Progress**: CCN members monitor the adoption progress in their areas, identifying where additional support might be needed. They communicate successes and challenges to the leadership, helping adjust the ongoing support strategies.

- **Celebrating Small Wins**: By recognizing departments or individuals adapting well to the new system, CCN members help foster a positive attitude towards the change and bring forward examples of people who have had small wins with the change.

Stage 4: Cheer

- **Acknowledging Success**: Once the new software is fully integrated and employees are comfortable using it, CCN members help celebrate this success. They might organize team events or share success stories to highlight how the change has brought about improvements.

- **Maintaining Momentum**: Even after the successful implementation, CCN members stay alert to ensure that the new system continues to be used effectively. They might share updates about new features or ongoing training opportunities.

Example Scenario: Health and Wellness Program Launch in a Corporate Setting

Let's explore the role of a Change Champion Network (CCN) in launching a new health and wellness program within a corporate environment aimed at enhancing employee health and overall productivity.

Hear: Initially, the CCN is briefed on the new health and wellness program, which includes initiatives like onsite health screenings, subsidized gym memberships, and wellness workshops. The CCN members are encouraged to focus on how these initiatives benefit individual health and contribute to a positive workplace culture. They emphasize the program's ability to reduce healthcare costs and improve overall productivity, addressing key employee concerns about personal health and company support. The CCN members are also asked for their perception of barriers to successful implementation that might come up, and change facilitators get to work resolving or mitigating the concerns prior to the all-company announcement.

Fear: Following the program's all-company announcement, some employees express concerns about privacy and the time required to participate in the program. CCN members participate in informational sessions where change facilitators explain the confidentiality of health data and the flexible nature of the program. These sessions help alleviate fears by reassuring employees that their privacy is protected and participation is adaptable to their schedules.

Near: As the program rolls out, CCN members provide feedback on creating supportive materials, such as a guide on effectively utilizing the new health resources. They also help identify and spotlight early adopters who have benefited from the program, sharing their stories and tips in company newsletters and team meetings. This helps normalize the change and demonstrates real-world benefits, encouraging wider participation.

Cheer: Once the health and wellness program is fully launched, the CCN helps organize a celebration event to recognize its success and the positive outcomes achieved. Change Leaders, along with a CCN representative, present statistics on improved employee health metrics and testimonials from participants, highlighting both the personal and organizational benefits. This celebration marks the successful implementation and motivates continued engagement with the program.

In this scenario, the CCN plays an instrumental role throughout the stages of the change. Initially, they help tailor the communication strategy to ensure it resonates with employees. As the program is implemented, they help to address employee concerns and facilitate understanding and participation. Finally, they celebrate the program's success, reinforcing the benefits and securing its place as a valued part of the organizational culture. Great job, CCN!

The main point of the CCN is to serve as a conduit between leadership and the wider employee base, ensuring that change initiatives are effectively communicated and meaningfully executed. By tapping into the insights and influence of CCN members, organizations can significantly enhance their change management processes, making them more responsive, inclusive, and, ultimately, successful. If you're driving widespread change, consider launching a CCN to help you along your journey.

Case Study: Acquisition Announcement

In the scenario of a company acquisition, the Hear stage of communication plays a pivotal role in shaping the understanding and reception of this significant change. The process begins with a clear and detailed announcement of the acquisition. For instance, a company acquiring a technology firm might elucidate the benefits, such as new market opportunities and technological advancement, offering employees a comprehensive picture of the change. This initial communication sets the stage by detailing "what" the change is and providing the necessary context and background, helping employees grasp the full scope of the acquisition.

Simultaneously, the company delves into the "why" behind this strategic move. Perhaps the acquisition aims to expand market reach, diversify product lines, or harness technological innovations. By transparently sharing these motives, the company doesn't just dictate the change; it invites its employees to understand and align with the broader organizational vision. This transparency is crucial in building trust and minimizing resistance, as it helps employees see the acquisition as a strategic and beneficial decision rather than a sudden upheaval.

As part of the communication strategy, a thorough impact assessment is conducted and shared. This assessment clearly outlines who is affected by the acquisition and how. For example, the integration of departments or new collaborations with the technology firm's team can be significant changes. By understanding these impacts, employees are better prepared for the transitions ahead. Furthermore, the company provides a realistic timeline of the acquisition process, detailing key milestones and expected completion dates. This structured approach offers employees a sense of certainty and control amidst the change.

However, the company is also mindful of the uncertainties and challenges accompanying such a significant change. Recognizing these establishes open channels for feedback and dialogue, creating a supportive environment where employees can express their concerns and seek clarification. This empathetic approach is extended throughout the communication process, ensuring the messaging is inclusive and considerate of the diverse workforce. By inviting ideas and participation, the company fosters a collaborative atmosphere, making the acquisition not just a top-down decision but a shared journey.

The narrative of this acquisition is continuously reinforced through consistent messaging across all communication platforms. By repeatedly emphasizing the key aspects of the acquisition, the company ensures that the message is not only delivered but deeply ingrained. The consistent reiteration of these messages and an empathetic and inclusive tone pave the way for a smoother transition. Employees are not left to navigate this change alone; instead, they are equipped with the understanding, resources, and support needed to adapt to and embrace the new chapter that the acquisition brings.

At a very tactical level, the Hear stage might look like this:

Before Day 1

1. Inform high-level company leaders at the acquiring and acquired organization about the change, give them time to ask questions, and begin preparing them to help support their employees through the transition.

2. Partner with high-level leaders to plan Day 2 department-level meetings and initial integration messaging for all teams.

3. Gather critical feedback from leaders on key risks as you move into Day 1 announcements.

Day 1 (announcement)

1. Each employee at each company receives summary information about the acquisition and an invitation to an all-company meeting to receive more information.

2. Each company hosts an all-company meeting where they clearly announce the change and articulate the Five Ws (who, what, when, where, why, and what is not changing).

3. Following the all-company meeting, an FAQ is emailed to all employees, and a channel is opened for any questions.

Day 2

1. A joint all-company meeting is held with the new presiding CEO providing more detail about the acquisition, timing, and value that will be derived.

2. Each department leader hosts departmental meetings following the all-company meeting to describe what the acquisition means to each department (who will lead the department, will the work change, what is the new organization chart).

3. Information and feedback meetings are scheduled for the next two weeks to answer questions and listen to feedback.

When change leaders approach the Hear stage intentionally and with transparency and care, people impacted by the change have the best opportunity to understand what is changing and how it impacts them, which prepares them to enter the next stage of change.

Next, let's consider a change that experienced an issue in the Hear stage.

Change Cheat Code Error: Hear

Landon, a project manager at a medium-sized tech company, found himself at the center of a critical miscommunication during a major company transformation. The company had just announced its acquisition of a competitor, intended to significantly expand its market reach and product offerings. However, the announcement came as a surprise to many, including Landon, who was subsequently tasked with leading the integration efforts.

As Landon set to work, he quickly prepared a detailed presentation to outline the future of the merged companies. He focused on defining the acquisition's structure, leadership, and strategic benefits, using the term "acquisition" prominently throughout his slides. Working under tight deadlines, Landon sent his presentation late in the evening to both companies' leadership for review.

The next morning, Landon was inundated with urgent corrections and confused messages from his colleagues. The crux of the issue? The other company had been informed that the deal was a "merger," not an "acquisition." This fundamental discrepancy in terminology and its implications caused immediate distrust and confusion among the staff of the company being acquired.

The conflicting messages about the nature of the deal—merger vs. acquisition—created a significant barrier to successful integration. Employees from the acquired company felt misled and undervalued, leading to resistance and skepticism about the motives behind the change. The initial enthusiasm for the merger was overshadowed by frustration and a lack of trust, which slowed down integration processes and required additional resources to address misunderstandings and rebuild employee confidence.

Unfortunately for Landon and his colleagues, inconsistent communication and conflicting messaging in the Hear stage resulted in significant resistance across the newly combined organization. Key team members who could have been champions for the new company were instead leading the opposition due to the lack of confidence in their understanding of the expectations of operations across sides. The M&A integration, as a result, faced severe delays, and the company had to spend additional resources to manage the fallout and re-establish trust with its employees. Upon a check-in, even years later, people hadn't forgotten the inaccurate messages surrounding the acquisition of their company and the resulting chaos.

This case clearly illustrates the critical need for precise and unified communication during the Hear stage of change management. Had Landon and the leadership employed a consistent narrative and engaged in open dialogue from the start, they might have avoided much of the confusion and resistance that followed. In the next section, we provide a variety of tools and templates that could have supported Landon and his team. These resources are designed to help leaders effectively plan, communicate, and reinforce key messages during significant changes. By using these tools, leaders can ensure that all stakeholders are aligned, which is crucial for the successful implementation of change and for avoiding the pitfalls experienced in Landon's scenario.

Example Resources for Hear

As we conclude this chapter, we encourage you to check out the range of practical resources designed to help you effectively manage the Hear stage. These tools include communication schedules, agendas for change announcement meetings, FAQs, and more, all of which are intended to help you ensure clarity and engagement with your change from the start.

Communications Schedule for a Company Reorganization

This is a sample schedule for communications regarding an impactful company reorganization. In this case, the change is socialized with leadership and the Change Champion Network prior to being announced to the entire organization.

Day/ Time	Activity	Purpose	Channel
Day -7	Leadership Briefing	To inform executive and department leaders about the reorganization and gather initial feedback.	Private meeting (in-person/ virtual)
Day -7	Change Champion Network Member Selection	To identify and select members to form the Change Champion Network (CCN). Managers and HR to identify individuals.	Private meetings with leaders and HR
Day -5	Change Champion Network Formation	To create a network of influencers across departments to help facilitate the change process.	Email and virtual kickoff meeting
Day -3	Change Champion Feedback Session	To gather insights and initial reactions from the Change Champion Network, refining messaging and strategies.	Virtual meeting
Day -1	Final Leader Socialization	To finalize details with leadership and prepare them for company-wide communication.	Email summary and confirmation call

Day/ Time	Activity	Purpose	Channel
Day 1, 9 AM	All-Hands Meeting	To inform all employees about the upcoming reorganization and the reasons behind it.	Virtual meeting
Day 1, 10 AM	Initial Announcement Follow-up Email	To email all employees about the upcoming reorganization and the reasons behind it for anyone who missed the all-hands meeting.	Email blast to all employees
Day 1, 2 PM	Departmental Briefings	To discuss the reorganization details, specific department implications, timeline, and answer any immediate questions.	In-person/ Video calls per department
Day 1, 4 PM	FAQ Document Release	To address common questions and concerns that may have arisen after the initial announcements.	Email, Company intranet
Day 2-4	Team Meetings	To discuss the specific impacts of the re-org within each team, clarify team members' new roles and responsibilities, and address any immediate concerns.	In-person/ Video calls per team

Day/ Time	Activity	Purpose	Channel
Day 2-4	1:1 Discussions	To provide a private space for employees to feel heard, express personal concerns, and ask questions they may not feel comfortable raising in a group setting.	In-person/ Video calls per employee with their manager
Day 4	Change Champion Feedback Session	To gather insights and observations from change champions about the initial reception of the re-org across the company. This session will help identify common concerns, areas of confusion, and potential resistance, enabling the leadership to tailor ongoing support and communications more effectively.	Virtual meeting
Day 4	Leadership Feedback Update	To update leaders on the overall employee feedback, share insights from the change champions, and discuss necessary adjustments to the re-org strategy. This meeting ensures that leadership remains aligned and responsive to employee needs.	Private meeting (in-person/ virtual)

Day/ Time	Activity	Purpose	Channel
End of Week 1	Follow-up Email	To summarize the week's discussions and clarify next steps.	Email
Week 2	Open Office Hours with Leaders	To offer a forum for ongoing questions and personal discussions with leadership.	In-person or virtual as per location
Week 3	Feedback Survey	To collect employee feedback on the reorganization process and assess the impact of the communication efforts.	Online survey

This schedule ensures that the reorganization is thoroughly communicated at multiple levels before and after the official announcement, leveraging leadership and change champions to facilitate a smooth transition.

If you are planning a change of this type and find this exhaustive, that's an understandable reaction. However, planning and executing communications at this level of detail and frequency is required in order to fully socialize the change. You must also ensure everyone has enough impressions of the change content to hear and understand what is changing.

Communications Schedule for a Major Process Change

This is a sample schedule for communications regarding a major process change. In this case, the change is determined, documented, and socialized prior to announcements and training. The total time of the change implementation is about seven weeks. This schedule assumes all decisions are made and systems are fully up and running to support the process change prior to the change communications and process change implementation.

Day/ Time	Activity	Purpose	Channel
Day -7	Leadership Briefing	To inform executive and department leaders about the upcoming process change and gather initial feedback.	Private meeting (in-person/ virtual)
Day -5	Process Preview Webinar with Change Champions	To introduce the process change, select employees, explain the timeline and expected outcomes, and collect feedback.	Webinar/ Virtual meeting
Day -3	FAQ Document Preparation	To address common questions and concerns about the process change, creating a resource for employee reference.	Email/Company Intranet
Day -1	Final Leader Socialization	To finalize details with leadership, ensuring they are prepared for company-wide communication.	Email summary and confirmation call
Day 1, 9 AM	All-Hands Meeting	To officially announce the process change, discuss its importance, and outline the benefits and impacts.	Virtual meeting
Day 1, 10 AM	Detailed Announcement Email	To provide a written summary of the process change for reference and for those who could not attend the meeting.	Email blast to all employees

Day/ Time	Activity	Purpose	Channel
Day 1, 2 PM	Departmental Workshops	To delve into detailed implications of the process change specific to each department, including Q&A sessions.	In-person/ Video calls per department
Day 1, 4 PM	Release of FAQ Document	To address common questions and provide additional clarity following the initial announcements.	Email, Company Intranet
Day 2-4	Training Sessions	To provide hands-on training and demonstrations of the new processes, ensuring employees understand their new tasks.	In-person/Video training sessions
Day 4	Feedback Invitation	To start collecting initial feedback on the process change through surveys or suggestion boxes.	Online survey/ Suggestion boxes
End of Week 1	Feedback Review Meeting	To review initial feedback, discuss any immediate issues, and adapt the change plan as necessary.	Private meeting (in-person/ virtual)
Week 2	Follow-up Email	To summarize the first week's activities, provide updates on feedback actions, and outline the next steps.	Email

Day/Time	Activity	Purpose	Channel
Week 2	Cutover to New Process	To officially move to utilizing the new process.	Virtual meeting with Email follow-up
Week 2-3	Open Office Hours with Process Champions	To offer ongoing support and address specific questions from employees regarding the new process.	In-person or virtual as per location
Week 2-3	Open Feedback Invitations	To continue collecting feedback on the process change through surveys or suggestion boxes.	Online survey/ Suggestion boxes
Week 4	Progress Update Meeting	To update all employees on the status of the process change implementation and discuss any adjustments.	Virtual meeting
Week 6	Formal Review	To conduct a formal review of the process change with leadership and key stakeholders, assessing impact and long-term adjustments.	Private meeting (in-person/ virtual)

This schedule is designed to facilitate a smooth transition by keeping all parties informed and engaged throughout the implementation of the process change. It combines broad communication with targeted interactions to ensure everyone understands their role in the change and feels supported throughout the process.

Agenda for a M&A Change Announcement Meeting

This is a sample agenda for a meeting where a merger or acquisition is being announced. Typically, individual meetings will happen for each impacted group, such as the acquiring, acquired, or merging organization. The announcement meetings should be held in an appropriate order to ensure a proper flow of information, and after all meetings are complete, M&A leaders should follow up with a text-based announcement and a FAQ.

Note: This agenda works for acquiring, acquired, and merging organizations. Just be sure to tailor the content to the audience while honoring the contributions and success of both organizations. Also, be sure to paint a picture of a hopeful future and support employee needs. Plan ahead, rehearse, and have a backup facilitator and technology owner for the session.

1. **Welcome and Introduction (5 minutes)**

   - **Presenter**: CEO/President

   - **Purpose**: Open the meeting with a warm welcome and introduce the purpose of the gathering.

2. **Announcement of the Merger or Acquisition (10 minutes)**

   - **Presenter**: CEO/President

   - **Purpose**: Officially announce the merger or acquisition, highlighting the strategic reasons behind the decision and the benefits expected for the company and its employees.

3. **Combined Organizational Profile and Future Direction (8 minutes)**

   - **Presenter**: CEO/President or Strategic Planning Director

   - **Purpose**: Outline the details of both organizations involved in the M&A (company size, geographies, leadership, customers, main products), long-term vision for the merged entity, and how the integration aligns with the company's goals.

4. **Overview of Changes and Timeline (5 minutes)**

   - **Presenter**: Chief Integration Officer or Project Lead

   - **Purpose**: Provide a high-level overview of the key changes, including any immediate impacts on company operations and a timeline of upcoming milestones.

5. **Human Resources and Staffing Implications (10 minutes)**

   - **Presenter**: Director of Human Resources

   - **Purpose**: Discuss staffing implications, including any potential changes in roles, reporting structures, and job opportunities. Reassure employees about measures in place to support them through transitions.

6. **Support Systems and Resources (5 minutes)**

   - **Presenter**: HR or Change Management Team Lead

   - **Purpose**: Inform employees about available support systems such as counseling, training programs, and dedicated communication channels for ongoing updates and feedback.

7. **Closing Remarks (5 minutes)**

- **Presenter**: CEO/President

- **Purpose**: Summarize the key points discussed, reaffirm the company's commitment to a smooth transition, and express confidence in the company's future. Encourage continued open dialogue and teamwork.

After conducting these sessions, follow up with a text-based announcement and include access to an FAQ. Suggested FAQ questions for an M&A change are included in the Hear chapter.

FAQ for a Systems Change Announcement

The following is a list of Frequently Asked Questions that may accompany a change announcement. Consider building the FAQ prior to the initial announcement and including it in your follow-up immediately after the announcement. It is also recommended that the FAQ be posted to a place where it can be updated or expanded over time, such as a shared document or intranet page.

1. **What is the new system and why are we changing to it?**

- This system is a state-of-the-art platform designed to improve our workflow, enhance data security, and provide better customer service. We are making this change to stay competitive and efficient in our industry.

2. **How will this system change my daily tasks?**

- The new system will streamline many of the tasks you handle daily, reducing manual input and increasing automation. Specific changes to your workflow will depend on your department and role, which will be covered in detail in training sessions.

3. When will the new system go live?

- The rollout is scheduled for [specific date]. We will have several weeks of parallel running with the old system to ensure a smooth transition.

4. Will there be training provided?

- Yes, comprehensive training sessions will be scheduled for all employees. These sessions will cover all new features and functionalities, and support will be available to ensure everyone is confident using the new system.

5. What should I do if I encounter problems or errors with the new system?

- A dedicated support team will be available to address any issues. You can contact them via [support contact methods]. Additionally, we will have a troubleshooting guide and FAQ available on the intranet.

6. How secure is the new system?

- The new system includes enhanced security features such as [describe security features, e.g., encryption, multi-factor authentication]. It adheres to all our security policies and compliance requirements to protect our data and privacy.

7. Will I be able to access the new system remotely?

- Yes, the system is designed for both on-site and remote access to accommodate our flexible work policies. Specific instructions for remote access will be provided during training.

8. **Will this change affect current projects?**

- We have planned the implementation to minimize disruption. However, some project timelines may be adjusted to ensure alignment with the new system capabilities. Your project manager will provide updates if your projects are affected.

9. **Who can I talk to if I have more questions or concerns about the change?**

- Please feel free to reach out to your direct supervisor or email our change management team at [change team's contact email]. We encourage everyone to share their thoughts and questions to help make this transition as smooth as possible.

10. **What are the long-term benefits of this new system?**

- Beyond improving daily operations, the new system will provide better data analytics, support our growth strategies, and improve customer satisfaction. Over time, it will allow us to operate more efficiently and deliver greater value to our clients.

Email to Deliver FAQs

When you send a FAQ after an announcement, you will also need to include a body of the email. Use this template as a guide or example for writing the body text of the email you will send to deliver access to the FAQs related to your change.

Subject: More About Our Upcoming Changes – FAQ Available!

Hello Team,

Following our recent announcement about the upcoming changes at [Company Name], we have compiled an FAQ document to answer some of your questions.

This resource is designed to clarify points and address any concerns you may express about the [change initiative]. We aim to ensure that everyone feels confident and informed as we move forward.

Access the FAQ here: [link to the document or intranet page]

We encourage you to read through this document and reach out if your questions are not covered. Your feedback is crucial to us, and we are here to support you through this transition.

Thank you for your engagement and cooperation.

Your Name]

[Your Position]

Video Script for Leadership Change Announcement

In many cases, a video will help communicate change to impacted people. The following script is a sample that may be used by a CEO or HR Leader to announce a leadership change. Use this template as a guide or example when planning and writing an announcement that will be delivered via video, either recorded or live.

The Scene: CEO or HR Leader of the organization is in view. Audio is clear. Minimal slides may accompany the video of the leader.

The Script:

Hello, everyone. This is [Name], the [Role] at [Company Name]. Today, I'm here to talk about a significant moment in our journey—a leadership transition that marks both an end and a beginning.

As of [Effective Date], [New Leader's Name] will join us as the new [Position Title], succeeding [Current Leader's Name], who, after [X] years of remarkable leadership, will be retiring. We owe [Current Leader's Name] a debt of gratitude for [his/her/their] unwavering commitment and significant contributions, including [mention a specific achievement or personal story].

Who is [New Leader's Name]? Coming to us with extensive experience in [relevant industry or expertise], most recently as [Previous Role] at [Previous Company], [New Leader's Name] is celebrated for [notable achievements or qualities]. [He/She/They] brings a vision that aligns seamlessly with our core values and future aspirations.

What changes can we expect? This transition is designed to bolster our capabilities to better meet future challenges. [New Leader's Name] will infuse our strategies with new perspectives that promise to drive innovation and growth.

Where and when is this happening? [New Leader's Name] will officially start on [Transition Date] at our headquarters, with a period of overlap to ensure a smooth handover from [Current Leader's Name].

Why this change? It's about fortifying our leadership to steer through upcoming challenges and opportunities, which are crucial for our ongoing evolution and commitment to excellence.

Now, I know that change can bring uncertainty. Still, I assure you this decision aims to enhance our collective future. We're organizing sessions for you to meet [New Leader's Name] and discuss our path forward—your participation is crucial, as your insights and questions will shape our approach.

Thank you for your continued dedication and support. Let's welcome [New Leader's Name] and move forward together with renewed energy and commitment.

Email to Announce an Upcoming Change

In some cases, a change will be first communicated via email. This is not the best choice for large or highly impactful changes, but sometimes it is the only option. Consider this template as a starting point for an email announcing a change.

Subject: Exciting Changes Ahead for [Company Name]

Dear [Company Name] Team,

I'm reaching out today to share some exciting developments that will shape the future of our organization. As we strive for continuous improvement and innovation, it's crucial that we evolve to meet the dynamic demands of our industry and enhance our capabilities.

We are planning to [briefly describe the change, e.g., introduce a new software system, reorganize our project management structure, etc.]. This change is designed to [mention the main benefits, e.g., increase efficiency, improve customer service, enhance product quality].

What to Expect:

- Timeline: The initial phase will begin on [start date], with full implementation expected by [end date].

- Impact: You will receive detailed information about how this will affect your work and team in [describe upcoming communications and meetings to explain more].

- Support: Comprehensive training sessions and resources will be available to ensure a smooth transition.

We understand that change can bring about uncertainty, but we are committed to keeping you informed and supported every step of the way. Please keep an eye out for further communications, and feel free to reach out to your manager or the HR team if you have any immediate questions or concerns.

Thank you for your continued dedication and hard work. Together, we will make this a successful transition and emerge stronger as a team.

[Your Name]

[Your Position]

Email Invitation to Provide Feedback About Change

When you solicit feedback from people impacted by a change, you will likely need to notify them via email. Use this template as a starting point when looking to collect feedback about a change.

Subject: Your Feedback Matters – Let's Talk About [Change]

Dear Team,

As you are aware, we have recently begun implementing [describe the change], and your initial feedback is incredibly important to us.

We are committed to making this transition as smooth and beneficial as possible for everyone involved. To better understand your experience and any challenges you might be facing, we kindly ask for your feedback.

Please share your thoughts by [date] via:

- Filling out this quick survey: [link to survey]

- Emailing us directly at [email address]

- Joining one of our upcoming feedback sessions on [dates]

Your insights are valuable as they will help us adjust our approach and provide additional support where needed.

Thank you for your cooperation and commitment during this period of change. We look forward to making [Company Name] a better place for all of us.

[Your Name]

[Your Position]

As we wrap up the Hear stage, you should have a solid foundation for setting the stage for change within your organization. The techniques and insights shared here are designed to ensure your change message is clear, compelling, and comprehensively received. Armed with the right tools and an understanding of how to effectively communicate at the outset, you are now ready to address the emotional and psychological aspects of change. Moving into the Fear Playbook, we will explore how to manage and mitigate the fears and resistance that typically arise following your initial announcements. Remember, this playbook is here for you at any time as you lead and navigate change. Return here if you feel stuck or need an extra nudge towards change success.

CHAPTER 7

PLAYBOOK FOR FEAR

When entering the Fear stage, you will encounter one of the most challenging aspects of change: the emotional response it elicits. When faced with these challenges, use this playbook as a guide. Here, you can quickly reference the objectives of navigating the Fear stage, your responsibilities as a leader, and how you can support your team effectively. This chapter provides strategies for empathetic communication, a checklist for addressing concerns, and examples of common pitfalls to avoid. We'll also present a case study demonstrating successful emotional management during change, accompanied by practical resources to help you facilitate discussions and make it to the next stage, Near.

Fear Stage Goal

The goal of the Fear stage is to navigate through it with intention, acknowledging and then transforming fear into a constructive force that drives the change forward. By understanding, addressing, and communicating about fears, you can build a foundation of curiosity and trust that paves the way for achieving a successful change.

Fear Stage Responsibilities

In the Fear stage of change management, the roles of individuals, leaders, and the company are crucial in addressing the emotional responses to change and transforming fear into constructive engagement.

Individuals: Identify and Articulate Fears

Individuals are encouraged to identify and express their fears or concerns related to the change. By actively acknowledging these feelings, individuals can contribute to a deeper understanding of the change's impact, helping leaders tailor support and responses to mitigate these fears.

Leaders: Acknowledge and Address Fears and Facilitate Open Dialogue

Leaders must address fears empathetically and facilitate an environment where open dialogue is encouraged. This includes listening attentively to concerns, validating feelings, and discussing ways to mitigate fears. Leaders should also provide clear, continuous information and reassurances to help ease anxieties and foster a sense of security and trust among team members.

Company: Support with Resources and Foster a Supportive Environment

The company must ensure that adequate resources and support systems are in place to help individuals navigate through their fears. This includes providing access to information, training, and counseling services. Additionally, the company should reinforce a culture where expressing and addressing fears is supported and valued, ensuring that the change process accommodates time for adjustments and feedback.

Communicating in Fear

The Fear stage is marked by heightened emotions and potential resistance. People are going to come at you and react emotionally. Your job is to continue to provide change messaging and support while acknowledging and addressing fears.

Keep these guidelines in mind:

- **Empathetic and Reassuring Communication**: Acknowledge fears as natural and valid. Use a supportive tone to help alleviate concerns.

- **Soliciting and Addressing Feedback**: Create channels for employees to express concerns. Actively listen and respond by adjusting the change plan or increasing support as needed.

- **Transparent and Continuous Dialogue**: Keep communication transparent and regular. Update on the handling of concerns and progress, which builds trust and reassurance.

- **Engagement and Collaboration**: Involve employees in developing solutions to address their fears, empowering them to participate actively in the change process.

The Fear Stage Checklist

The Fear Stage Checklist serves as your actionable to-do list for navigating the complexities of the Fear stage in change management. Utilize this guide by setting specific goals with associated due dates for each task, ensuring you address and manage fears effectively to prepare for a seamless transition to the Near stage.

☐ **Acknowledge and Validate Fears**

a. Recognize signs of fear and validate these feelings among team members. Let people react without reacting yourself. Take in the information as feedback.

b. Ensure everyone feels heard and supported by acknowledging their concerns.

☐ **Enhance Communication Strategies**

a. Communicate consistently, clearly, and empathetically, providing honest and consistent information about the change.

b. Use various communication channels to reach all team members, ensuring no one is left out.

☐ **Engage and Solicit Feedback**

a. Create safe spaces for open discussions where team members can express their fears and concerns.

b. Actively listen to feedback and use it to understand the root causes of fear and resistance.

☐ **Develop and Implement Supportive Actions**

a. Based on feedback, develop solutions to address barriers, mitigate risk, and alleviate fears. Share early signs of success.

b. Modify aspects of the change plan as necessary to make it more acceptable and less daunting for everyone involved while still achieving the change goals.

☐ **Prepare for Transition to Near Stage**

    a.   Facilitate and monitor a shift in perspective from fear to curiosity, highlighting the change as an opportunity for growth and improvement.

    b.   Ensure team members are ready to progress by confirming that their fears have been adequately addressed and they understand the reality of the change.

Case Study: Cultural Transformation in the Sales Team

When Jessica Ramirez assumed the role of Head of Sales at a large medical corporation, she encountered a team fraught with apprehension and discord. Recognizing the challenges of the Fear stage in the team's response to her new leadership and the strategic changes she intended to implement, Jessica saw an urgent need to reshape the team's culture and restore confidence.

In her first move, Jessica orchestrated an in-person all-hands meeting. This was not merely a formal introduction but a strategic initiative to directly address the team's underlying fears, both of her new leadership and the future of the team and organization. To assist in her efforts, she introduced Marcus Lee, a new employee, as the Culture Realizer, tasked with the important role of listening to and addressing team concerns, fostering an environment of open dialogue and continuous feedback.

Jessica introduced a new idea, an "Elephant in the Room" segment of meetings where team members were encouraged to openly express their concerns about the changes and the new direction the team was heading. This strategy was not only about transparency but also about demonstrating empathy—acknowledging that their fears were valid and creating a platform for these issues to be addressed constructively.

To provide structure to the cultural shift, Jessica and Marcus developed a framework based on four pillars: integrity, accountability, innovation, and support. Each meeting dedicated time to discuss progress on these pillars, with Jessica sharing updates and tangible results directly linked to team feedback. This ongoing communication was crucial in showing the team that their input had a direct impact on decision-making processes, thereby fostering a sense of ownership and participation among team members. Each week, Jessica would share a full list of priority items to change based on the team's feedback, along with the group's progress. The team would review the results and celebrate their growth together.

Jessica's leadership was characterized by her commitment to being accessible. She held regular office hours and informal coffee chats, which helped break down barriers between her and the team, allowing for more personalized interactions and reassurances.

The turnaround of the team's morale and culture was gradual but evident. As the team began to see real changes implemented based on their feedback and witnessed Jessica's consistent and transparent communication style, their trust in her leadership solidified. The fear that once overshadowed the team's potential slowly transformed into a collective drive toward achieving their new goals under Jessica's guidance.

Bravo, Jessica and Team! This case study offers a compelling example of effective leadership in navigating the Fear stage, demonstrating how a leader can transform a toxic environment into a productive and positive one by prioritizing open communication, transparency, and empathy. This story highlights the importance of leaders being visible in their commitment to change, showing that they value team feedback, and ensuring that changes are made based on this feedback. By actively addressing the team's fears, fostering an environment where dialogue was encouraged, and being responsive and accessible, the leader was able to rebuild trust and morale while helping the team become prepared to move from a state of fear to one of curiosity and engagement.

Change Cheat Code Error: Fear

Dr. Emily Thornton, the lead oncologist at a regional hospital, was at the forefront of introducing a new patient management system integrated with genetic profiling technologies. This cutting-edge initiative promised to revolutionize treatment plans but also brought significant changes to the staff's daily operations.

As the system rolled out, it quickly became evident that many staff members were overwhelmed by the complexity of the technology. Initial training sessions were conducted but were too technical and sparse, leaving many feeling inadequately prepared. Concerns about mastering the new system led to widespread anxiety, with fears centering on job competence and increased workload.

Though Dr. Thornton and the hospital management were focused on the technological aspects, they initially underestimated the fear associated with the change. While Dr. Thornton and her team were excited about the opportunities enabled by the new systems, the team that would use the systems was overwhelmed with concern about how the new system would work, if they would be able to use it effectively, if they would like to use it, and if it would actually improve patient care. These fears piled up, resulting in poor communication and understanding and insufficient support structures. This oversight by change leaders allowed misinformation to spread through informal channels, exacerbating the staff's anxieties. Feeling unsupported and uncertain about their future roles, key team members began to express their frustrations openly.

The situation escalated when two senior nurses, valued for their expertise and experience, decided to leave the hospital. Their departure was a significant blow to the team's morale and highlighted the consequences of not effectively managing the Fear stage. Productivity and morale plummeted, and the hospital had to contend not only with implementing a new system but also with rebuilding trust and confidence among the remaining staff.

Dr. Thornton failed to acknowledge the needs of employees navigating the Fear stage, which resulted in a significant negative impact on the hospital. In the Fear stage, management failed to address employee's fears or adequately prepare and support staff, leading to considerable anxiety and frustration. The training provided was too early, technical, and infrequent, leaving staff feeling overwhelmed and insecure about their ability to use the new technology effectively.

Poor communication from leadership failed to address or alleviate these fears, allowing misinformation to spread and intensify staff concerns. As a result, two senior nurses resigned, severely affecting team morale and productivity. Four other nurses left in the following three months. The hospital scrambled for talent, leaving patients without the robust care the hospital and Dr. Thornton were previously so proud to deliver.

As we reflect on this scenario, it is clear that certain tools and strategies could have greatly assisted Dr. Thornton and her team. In the following section, we introduce a series of tools and templates specifically designed to navigate the Fear stage more effectively. These resources aim to equip leaders like Dr. Thornton with the necessary skills to foster open dialogue, provide adequate support, and maintain morale during transformative changes, ensuring a smoother transition and stronger team cohesion.

Example Resources for Fear

As we conclude the Fear Playbook chapter, we provide a selection of example resources tailored to effectively manage the Fear stage. These tools are designed to help you navigate the emotional and psychological challenges of change. Included are templates for conducting feedback sessions, strategies for enhancing communication to address concerns, and methods to facilitate open dialogue, ensuring that fears are acknowledged and addressed constructively.

In Fear, you will often facilitate feedback and keep people updated about the progress and adaptation of the change based on participant engagement. Here are a few examples:

Quick Brainstorm on Change Barriers and Potential Solutions

If you need to quickly identify barriers to a change, use this guide to facilitate a session (virtual or in-person) to solicit barriers or blockers and move forward productively.

Gather people who are going to be affected by the change in a virtual or a physical room. This could be the Change Champion Network (CCN) or folks directly affected by the change. Ask them questions to elicit feedback, emotion, and lists of worries (barriers). Questions to prompt people may include:

- What could go wrong with our plan?

- What did we not think about?

- What issues will this create?

Collect all feedback during the session and ensure it's visible to everyone. If you're leading the session in person, use a whiteboard, flip chart, or similar display to show that you're recording each comment accurately. For virtual sessions, choose a reliable digital collaboration tool that allows participants to see and contribute to the list in real-time. As you document feedback, do so openly to address any concerns participants might have about being misunderstood. Make it a point to write down everything shared, no matter how minor or trivial it may seem, demonstrating that all input is valued.

The next step after brainstorming is to consider possible solutions. Review your list of barriers one by one to do one of three things:

- Find a way to **mitigate or remove** the issues. (If an issue listed is that people don't know how to use a new software, it can be mitigated or removed with training.)

- Create a sub-team to **investigate and find a solution**. (Use this for bigger issues.)

- Agree that this issue cannot be removed and to move on. (An example could be that we just got through a change and have change fatigue. We cannot remove change fatigue, but we can acknowledge it.)

Once all brainstormed items are reviewed, you can start working on the action plan. You have now transformed a list of complaints into momentum to work on the items. Issues not listed or dealt with will create extra noise and work in the environment. It may take more than one of these sessions to get through the change because as you start a change, more issues will arise. However, this technique is very effective in bringing people along with you in change.

Agenda for a More Formal Feedback Session

When soliciting feedback from change participants in a more formal live session, consider using this format to gain valuable insight that can help refine the current change and improve the future change.

1. **Welcome and Introduction (5 minutes)**

   - Facilitator: Welcome participants, introduce the purpose of the session.

   - Outline the agenda and objectives.

   - Reinforce the constructive nature of the session.

2. **Overview of Change and Current Status (5 minutes)**

   - Facilitator: Provide a brief update on the current status of the change initiative.

   - Highlight the importance of feedback in shaping the transition.

3. **Ground Rules for the Session (5 minutes)**

   - Facilitator: Set the ground rules for the discussion to ensure a respectful and productive environment.
     - Encourage open and honest feedback.
     - Listen to understand, not to respond.
     - No interruptions when someone is speaking.

4. **Group Discussion: Experiences and Perceptions (20 minutes)**

- **Facilitator**: Lead a structured discussion on specific aspects of the change process.

   ◦ What has been working well?

   ◦ What challenges are participants facing?

   ◦ How has the change impacted their daily work?

5. **Breakout Sessions: Deep Dive into Key Issues (15 minutes)**

- **Participants**: Divide into smaller groups to discuss predefined topics in depth.

- **Facilitator**: Provide each group with guiding questions to explore solutions and suggestions.

- **Possible topics**: Training effectiveness, communication clarity, tool usability, etc.

6. **Share Back and Group Synthesis (10 minutes)**

- **Groups**: Share key points from their discussions with the larger group.

- **Facilitator**: Summarize common themes and unique insights, acknowledging contributions.

7. **Closing and Next Steps (5 minutes)**

- **Facilitator**: Outline how the feedback will be used to inform and adjust the change strategy.

- Announce the next feedback session or follow-up actions.

- Thank participants for their honesty and engagement.

Online Feedback Collection Form

If you are leading a larger-scale change, you might consider collecting feedback using an online form. Here is a sample of what might be good to include in the online form.

1. Personal Information (optional)

2. Description of Concern

3. Impact on Role or Department

4. Suggestions for Improvement

5. Preferred Method of Follow-Up (if requested)

It is best not to have a form where folks can just leave their complaints. By using this format, people are asked to think about the problem (or fear) they are concerned about and suggest what could be done to mitigate it. A great practice in small to moderate-size change environments is also to include a checkbox to allow the submitter to indicate if they would like to follow up on their feedback directly.

Training on Navigating Fear Associated with Change

You may have an opportunity to address fears and train your team to navigate change. This can both support the current change and prime people for further change down the road. Use these examples as outlines or templates to help you plan and facilitate sessions to help people navigate the Fear stage and set the stage for the Near stage.

The purpose of this session is to provide a structured forum for addressing fears and uncertainties related to the change, facilitating open discussions, and offering practical coping strategies.

Agenda:

- Introduction and Objectives (10 minutes)

- Group Discussion: Sharing Fears and Concerns (30 minutes)

- Facilitated Workshop: Understanding the Change and Its Benefits (20 minutes)

- Breakout Session: Problem-Solving Common Fears (30 minutes)

- Facilitated Workshop: Stress Management Techniques (20 minutes)

- Q&A and Wrap-Up (10 minutes)

If you plan to run this session, consider engaging a strong trainer or facilitator who has experience in helping others navigate change, as some of these discussions can become tricky to navigate or keep on track, especially when they become emotional.

Change Update Email

Change leaders should keep people impacted by the change up to date on progress and adaptations made as a result of feedback. In many cases, this will be done by email. The purpose of these emails is to provide ongoing updates that communicate not just progress but specifically how employee feedback is shaping the change process, thereby reinforcing the value of their input.

Subject: [Change Initiative] Progress Update: Adapting to Your Feedback

The body of the email should cover the following:

- Greeting and appreciation for continued engagement.

- Specific examples of how employee feedback has influenced recent adaptations.

- Details on the next steps and expected outcomes.

- Invitation to scheduled feedback sessions or workshops.

- Assurance of ongoing support and resources.

- Contact information for immediate concerns.

Personal Meeting Talking Points for Navigating Fear

In some cases, an individual may require personal attention in order to successfully navigate the Fear stage. A leader, close colleague, or support team member can engage those struggling in a conversation to help the individual identify their specific fears and look to build a plan to mitigate the fears and remove barriers. Here are some questions you can use to try to open up the conversation and get to the root of the fears with the individual.

- Can you share what aspects of this change feel most daunting to you?

- What specific concerns do you have about how this change will impact your day-to-day responsibilities?

- How do you feel about the changes that are happening? Is there anything in particular that's causing you anxiety or concern?

- Are there any obstacles that you feel are preventing you from fully engaging with the new system or process?

- What kind of support or resources would make this transition easier for you

- What is helping that we should do more of?

- Do you have any suggestions on how we might improve the implementation process to better accommodate your needs?

- Looking back, how have you handled changes in the past? What strategies have helped you adapt?

- How can I best support you through this transition? Are there specific areas where you'd like more guidance or clarity?

- What steps could you take in the next week to move forward with this change?

- Is there a particular part of the new process you'd like to learn more about or get additional training on?

Workshop on Documenting and Addressing Barriers

Visually documenting barriers to change can help bring people together to overcome them. Consider this format when planning to solicit barriers and work to solve or mitigate them. Use these examples as outlines or templates to help you plan and facilitate sessions to help people surface, document, and begin to address the fears that hold them back from entering the Near stage.

Duration: 60-90 minutes

Workshop Agenda:

1. **Introduction (10 minutes)**

   - **Welcome and Objectives**: Begin by welcoming participants and explaining the purpose of the workshop. Emphasize that the goal is to collectively identify barriers to adopting the change and determine how best to address them.

- **Overview of the Fear Stage**: Briefly explain the Fear stage in the change process, highlighting that this stage is where resistance, anxiety, and concerns often surface. Mention that addressing these fears proactively is crucial to ensuring the success of the change initiative.

2. **Identifying Barriers (15-20 minutes)**

- **Individual Reflection**: Ask participants to spend a few minutes reflecting on the change initiative and writing down any barriers they perceive on sticky notes—one barrier per note. Encourage them to think broadly about potential barriers, including emotional, logistical, and organizational challenges.

- **Sticky Note Placement**: Once participants have written down their barriers, have them place the sticky notes on a central board or wall. Allow everyone to view the notes as they are placed.

3. **Grouping and Reviewing Barriers (10-15 minutes)**

- **Group Similar Barriers**: As a group, review the sticky notes and start grouping similar barriers together. This can be done by having participants suggest categories or themes that emerge from the barriers listed. Move the sticky notes into groups as you discuss them.

- **Clarification and Discussion**: As you group the sticky notes, ask participants to clarify any barriers that might be unclear and encourage brief discussions to ensure everyone understands the issues at hand.

4. **Categorizing Barriers: Solve or Mitigate (20-25 minutes)**

- **Introduction to Categories**: Explain the difference between the "Solve" and "Mitigate" columns.

- **Solve**: Barriers that can be directly addressed and removed.

- **Mitigate**: Barriers that cannot be fully removed but can be minimized or managed.

- **Participant Involvement**: Ask participants to come up to the board, select a sticky note, and suggest whether it belongs in the "Solve" or "Mitigate" column. Encourage them to explain their reasoning. This can be done in rounds, allowing several participants to contribute.

- **Group Discussion**: For each barrier placed in a column, facilitate a group discussion on why it was categorized that way. Encourage input from other participants and reach a consensus on the appropriate categorization.

5. **Developing Strategies (15-20 minutes)**

- **Action Planning**: Once all barriers are categorized, focus on the "Solve" column first. For each barrier, ask participants to brainstorm potential solutions. Write down these solutions next to the corresponding sticky notes.

- **Mitigation Strategies**: Move on to the "Mitigate" column. Discuss ways to reduce the impact of each barrier. This might involve communication strategies, additional resources, or support systems.

- **Assigning Responsibility**: If applicable, discuss who in the organization might take ownership of implementing the solutions or mitigation strategies. This step helps translate workshop outcomes into actionable steps.

6. **Conclusion and Next Steps (10 minutes)**

- **Review**: Summarize the key barriers identified and the strategies developed. Reinforce the importance of addressing these barriers to ensure the success of the change initiative.

- **Follow-up**: Discuss how the outcomes of this workshop will be communicated to leadership or other relevant teams. Set expectations for follow-up actions and timelines.

- **Closing**: Thank participants for their engagement and contributions. Encourage them to continue thinking about and addressing barriers as the change process moves forward.

Facilitation Tips:

- Encourage open dialogue and make sure all voices are heard, especially when discussing sensitive barriers.

- Keep the energy positive and solution-focused, even when discussing challenging barriers.

- Be mindful of time, ensuring that each section of the workshop is adequately covered.

- Use the sticky notes creatively. Consider using different colors to represent different types of barriers (e.g., technical, emotional, logistical).

This workshop will help participants feel more confident navigating the Fear stage by collaboratively addressing the barriers to change and developing practical solutions or mitigations. When you're done, take a picture or screenshot of the board and save it with the information about the change.

Barriers   Solve   Mitigate

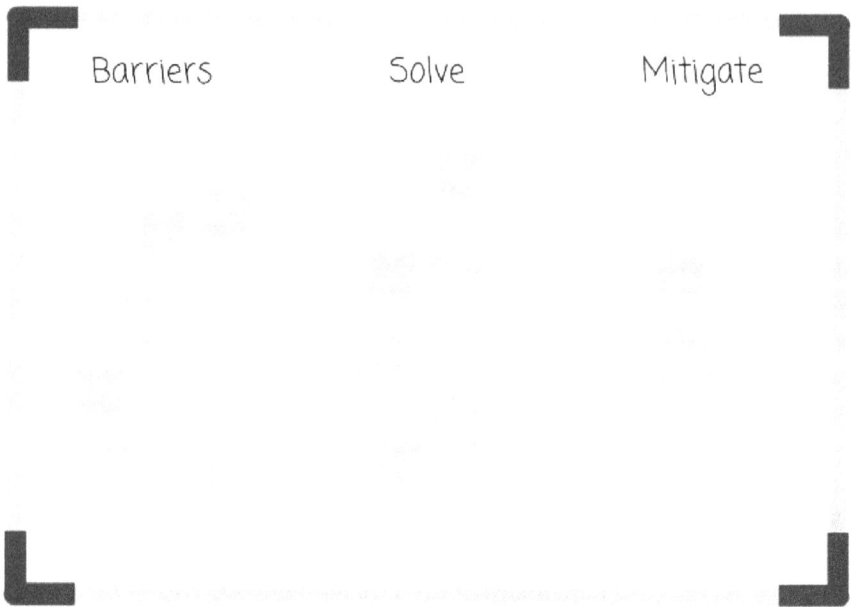

Figure 7.1: Fears Identified in Sticky Notes on a
Whiteboard to Solve or Mitigate

Measuring Progress Through the Change Curve

When leading change with a group, expect that not everyone will progress through the change curve at the same rate. You can ask people involved with the change to self-report their progress through the change curve, which will help you know where to apply support.

Get a view of how individuals are progressing through the change curve. In a facilitated session, either in-person or using a virtual collaboration tool, show the change curve and, if needed, explain the different steps in the curve. Next, invite individuals or department representatives to write their names on a sticky note and indicate where in the curve they feel they are in relation to the change.

As time progresses and the change proceeds, continue soliciting feedback about how individuals are progressing through the curve. You might even consider taking pictures or screenshots of the team's progress through the curve over time. Be sure to celebrate progress as the team moves through the curve and the change is realized.

Figure 7.2: An Example of Identifying Multiple
Individuals Progressing Along the Curve

Navigating the Fear stage in each change equips you with the necessary skills to handle emotional upheavals and resistance. With a better understanding of how to engage empathetically and maintain open lines of communication, you are set to transform potential obstacles into opportunities for growth. As we transition to the Near chapter of the playbook, the focus will shift from managing emotions to the practical implementation of change, where you will apply specific learning strategies and adoption techniques to ensure that the change is effectively realized.

CHAPTER 8

PLAYBOOK FOR NEAR

This chapter of the playbook guides you through the hands-on phase of change management in the Near stage. This section aims to detail the specific tasks and responsibilities necessary for the successful implementation and adoption of change. You'll find tips for maintaining engagement, a checklist to help people get on board, and strategies for addressing and solving unexpected challenges. A real-world case study will highlight effective implementation techniques, and we'll provide you with additional resources like training outlines and tool guide templates to ensure the change sticks.

Near Stage Goal

The goal of the Near stage is to transition individuals from apprehension to active engagement with the change, fostering an environment where they can learn, adapt, and contribute positively. This stage aims to clarify exactly who needs to do what to achieve the change while providing necessary resources, collaboration, and feedback to ensure everyone is prepared and motivated to implement the new change effectively.

Near Stage Responsibilities

In the Near stage of change management, the focus shifts to engaging people more deeply as they move from apprehension to active participation in the change process. This stage is pivotal for fostering a supportive environment that encourages interaction and involvement in shaping the future.

Individuals: Clarify Needs and Engage Actively

Individuals are encouraged to identify and clearly communicate what they need to adapt to the change. By engaging proactively in discussions, training sessions, and feedback mechanisms, they help to refine the change process and ensure it meets their needs and those of the organization.

Leaders: Provide Resources and Encourage Engagement

In the Near stage, leaders should focus on providing the necessary resources and support to facilitate engagement with the change. They should foster an environment where learning is paramount and open communication is encouraged, recognizing contributions and facilitating discussions that help individuals feel valued and understood. Leaders must also celebrate incremental progress, reinforcing the positive aspects of the change and maintaining momentum.

Company: Ensure Comprehensive Support and Foster Adaptation

The company must provide comprehensive support to ensure that all employees have the tools and resources needed to engage with the change effectively. This includes access to training, expert advice, and continuous learning opportunities. Additionally, the company should promote a culture that celebrates adaptation and resilience, reinforcing the importance of flexibility and continuous improvement in the face of change.

Communicating in Near

The Near stage is characterized by a shift towards practical engagement and planning. As individuals start to focus more on the logistics and implementation of the change, your communication should ease adoption challenges to support and guide this transition.

Keep these guidelines in mind:

- **Clear and Detailed Information**: Provide precise details about the change to ensure understanding. Clarify the steps involved and the expected outcomes to reduce ambiguity.

- **Facilitate Problem-solving**: Encourage open discussions about how the change will be implemented. Engage team members in brainstorming sessions to address potential challenges and create a sense of ownership.

- **Consistent Updates and Progress Sharing**: Maintain a steady flow of communication about progress and developments. Regular updates keep everyone informed and help align efforts towards common goals.

- **Interactive and Inclusive Communication**: Foster an environment where questions are welcomed and actively involve employees in planning and decision-making processes. This not only increases engagement but also enhances the adaptability of the team.

The Near Stage Checklist

The Near Stage Checklist serves as your roadmap for embedding change effectively within your team. It provides a clear structure for detailing the change, supporting your team with the right tools and resources, and ensuring that everyone is prepared for successful implementation. Set specific goals and deadlines for these tasks to maintain momentum and ensure everyone is ready to transition to the Cheer stage.

☐ **Clarify Details and Next Steps**

    a. Provide comprehensive explanations about the specifics of the change, breaking down processes and expectations to ensure clarity.

    b. Distribute detailed documentation and step-by-step guides to help team members understand their roles and responsibilities in the new setup.

☐ **Ensure Effective Communication**

    a. Maintain consistent, clear, and inclusive communication, ensuring all team members receive the same information and feel equally involved.

    b. Use diverse communication platforms to accommodate different learning styles and preferences, ensuring thorough understanding across the team.

☐ **Provide Training, Tools, and Resources**

    a. Equip team members with the necessary tools, resources, and access to expertise needed to engage confidently with the change.

   b. Organize training sessions and provide access to tutorials and support materials that help bridge any skill gaps. Consider field trips, role-specific training, one-on-one support sessions, simulation exercises, interactive workshops, and more.

☐ **Facilitate Problem-Solving Sessions**

   a. Organize workshops and brainstorming sessions to address potential challenges and develop practical solutions collaboratively.

   b. Engage team members in scenario planning to anticipate possible issues and plan appropriate responses.

☐ **Prepare for Transition to Cheer Stage**

   a. Monitor engagement and readiness for the next stage, ensuring team members are not only comfortable with the change but are also actively implementing new practices.

   b. Celebrate milestones and progress to build momentum and reinforce the positive aspects of the change, setting the stage for full adoption and optimization.

Case Study: Crafty Navigation of Near

At Craft Corner, a popular local craft store chain, the annual inventory weekend was a cherished tradition, transforming routine stock-taking into a lively, team-bonding event. However, a shift in corporate strategy to introduce a real-time digital inventory system to support online shopping spelled the end of these beloved weekends. Essential for business expansion, this new technology presented a significant cultural shift for a team deeply rooted in their established traditions.

Jenna, the store leader, understood the deep-seated cultural importance of these inventory weekends and the potential resistance to the new system. As she navigated the Near stage with her team, she crafted a strategy that focused on engaging the team and leveraging their strong cultural bonds to facilitate a smooth transition.

First, Jenna knew she needed to start a new tradition. Recognizing the need to preserve the spirit of their traditional gatherings, Jenna introduced a new annual staff appreciation event. This event was designed to sustain the team's culture of celebration and camaraderie, aligning with the store's updated operational goals.

To ease the team into the new system, Jenna organized an interactive demonstration, allowing everyone to engage directly with the technology and try it in a safe environment. This hands-on session aimed to alleviate any apprehensions by showing how the system could make their tasks easier rather than more complicated.

Understanding the power of firsthand experience in overcoming skepticism, Jenna implemented several practical learning opportunities. To build an understanding of the customer's experience, Jenna provided each team member with a gift card to purchase items online and pick them up at a nearby store that was already running the new inventory system. This allowed her staff to experience the convenience and efficiency of the new system from a customer's perspective, highlighting the improved service they were now capable of offering.

To further cement their understanding and acceptance of the system, Jenna arranged a field trip to a neighboring Craft Corner store that had already implemented the new technology. Watching their peers effectively manage the system helped demystify its daily operation and showcased its benefits in real-time. At the end of the field trip, each employee of Jenna's store was invited to work in the store they visited for a week for hands-on training, where the team could learn the intricacies of the system. The majority of Jenna's employees took this offer and worked a week in the store in the neighboring town, which significantly helped in building their confidence and proficiency with the new technology, turning initial skepticism into informed endorsement. The team was now ready to implement the new inventory system at their store.

These strategic interventions by Jenna facilitated a smoother transition to the new inventory system and preserved and adapted the store's cherished culture of communal celebration to fit their evolving business model.

Jenna's proactive and thoughtful handling of the Near stage at Craft Corner demonstrates the importance of leadership in navigating change, especially in contexts where team culture and traditions are strong. Her strategy was rooted in understanding and respecting the team's emotional and cultural ties, using them as a bridge to embrace new operational methods.

The introduction of a new annual event to replace the inventory weekend was a crucial move in maintaining the team's morale as it preserved the spirit of collective celebration and teamwork that the team had grown to love. This adaptability in preserving core cultural elements while steering the team towards new operational norms was key to the change's success.

Jenna led her team through the Near stage effectively, focusing on cultural sensitivity, hands-on learning, and continuous engagement. By transforming potential skepticism into informed acceptance through strategic interventions like experiential learning and cultural adaptation,

Jenna not only navigated her team through the complexities of operational change but also strengthened their commitment and readiness for future challenges. Her approach highlights how adept management of the Near stage can lead to a stronger, more adaptable team that is prepared to thrive in a changing business landscape.

Change Cheat Code Error: Near

In the ever-changing world of software, an acquisition of a highly innovative AI company by a large cloud infrastructure provider was poised to set a new industry standard. The newly combined company aimed to revolutionize the market by combining the newly acquired, smaller company's cutting-edge AI platforms with the bigger company's robust cloud infrastructure. The potential was enormous, but so were the challenges that lay in integrating these complex technologies.

As the combined company entered the Near stage of their integration, the initial excitement began to give way to the realities of harmonizing two distinct product lines. The teams were enthusiastic but soon found themselves at a crossroads due to a lack of a unified product vision. Each team understood its own product but had not yet learned the complexity, capability, and operational requirements of the other. The acquired company's innovative developers were eager to push the boundaries of AI, while the larger, acquiring company's teams were focused on ensuring scalability and stability. This divergence led to a fragmented approach to product development, with each team pulling in its direction and unclear of the final product's desired outcome.

The integration of the technologies was a daunting task that was underestimated from the start. Teams were instructed to blend sophisticated AI algorithms with an extensive cloud network without a clear roadmap or sufficient cross-functional training. Without proper information, they trudged ahead. Unfortunately, the training and full functional integration failure became apparent when data synchronization issues and performance bottlenecks emerged during the late testing phases, delaying product launches and frustrating the teams.

Communication barriers added complexity and made realizing the change much more difficult on a person-to-person level. The cultural differences between the teams and the physical distance between locations hindered effective collaboration. Online meetings intended to streamline the integration process often ended without clear resolutions, and in the absence of a unified management tool, teams reverted to working in isolation, each following what they believed was the merger's objectives while becoming increasingly frustrated with "the other guys."

As a result, the much-anticipated flagship product that was supposed to showcase the seamless integration of AI and cloud capabilities turned out to be less than stellar. The product was a disjointed mix of features that did not fully leverage the potential of either technology, leading to a not-so-favorable reception from the market and reviews that did not shy away from pointing out its flaws. What had started as a good idea turned into a very expensive mess.

The story of this product integration failure teaches a very important lesson about corporate merger integration, specifically, about how important leadership is in steering the integration process effectively and taking the time to ensure everyone understands the goals of the integration as well as providing the resources (tools, training, time, support) to transform into a combined team. In this case, leadership failed to establish a clear, unified vision for the merged product line, which was essential for guiding the diverse teams toward a common goal.

Without a coherent strategy articulated by the leaders, the teams from both companies struggled to prioritize their efforts and align their distinct technologies and cultures. The lack of detailed planning and a defined end goal led to confusion and inefficiency, ultimately manifesting in a product that did not meet market expectations. This scenario demonstrates how important it is for leadership to be actively involved in providing continuous support and clear directives throughout the Near stage of change. Leaders of the combined company needed to not only set the vision but also actively engage with teams to ensure that all members understood their roles and the broader objectives of their collective effort.

This combined company's story is a powerful reminder that the success of a merger hinges not just on the strategic fit between the companies but also on the effectiveness with which it is executed during the Near stage. Leadership must play a proactive and supportive role, ensuring that teams are not only well-informed but also well-equipped to navigate the complexities of integrating disparate systems and cultures. As we transition into the next section, we'll introduce a variety of tools and templates specifically designed to support change leaders through the Near stage. These resources aim to facilitate better planning, communication, and training to ensure a more successful integration of teams and technologies, preventing the kind of costly missteps experienced by the combined company.

Example Resources for Near

In wrapping up the Near Playbook chapter, explore this collection of practical resources that support the hands-on management of change. Here, you'll find detailed guides for implementing change, including training materials, troubleshooting aids, and step-by-step documentation. These resources aim to simplify the transition by providing clear instructions and support, helping your team to engage confidently with new processes and responsibilities.

Early Adopter Recognition

Use this template in the Near stage to recognize individuals or teams that are adapting to the change and progressing successfully through the change process. The intent of this communication is to celebrate progress and encourage others to follow suit.

> Subject: Celebrating Our Change Champions!
>
> Hello Team,
>
> As we navigate through our recent changes with [briefly describe the change, e.g., "the new digital reporting system"], it's inspiring to see how many of you are stepping up and embracing these new challenges. Today, we want to take a moment to recognize and thank our early adopters who have shown exceptional enthusiasm and adaptability.
>
> A special shout-out to:
>
> - **[Employee Name 1]** for being the first to complete all training modules and actively helping others in their learning journey.
>
> - **[Employee Name 2]** for providing valuable feedback, which has led to improvements in how the system functions.
>
> - **[Employee Name 3]** for innovating ways to integrate the new tools into our daily operations, making processes smoother for everyone.
>
> Your proactive engagement is not only enhancing our transition but also setting a fantastic example for the entire team. We appreciate your efforts and are excited to see how your leadership and initiative drive us all forward.

Let's all continue to support one another and make the most of the new opportunities this change brings. If you have stories of your own adaptations or suggestions, please share them with us—every insight helps us grow stronger together.

Thank you once again to our early adopters, and here's to everyone's continued success!

With appreciation,

[Your Name]

[Your Position]

Experiential Learning Examples

In the Near stage, you have a great opportunity to lead change participants in their experiences and help them adapt to the change. Here are a few examples of experiential learning opportunities you could leverage to help people through the Near stage. Consider implementing one or more of these hands-on experiences, which will engage change participants and help them see, feel, touch, and experience the change—the more creative and immersive, the better!

Role-Specific Training: Training sessions designed to address the specific needs and responsibilities of different roles within the organization. This type of training ensures that each employee receives relevant and targeted information that directly applies to their daily tasks and roles post-change. Partner with training or learning & development professionals for best results.

One-on-One Support Sessions: Personalized meetings between an employee and a trainer or a mentor can provide individual guidance on the new changes. Use these sessions to address specific concerns or challenges faced by the employee and offer tailored support to facilitate their adaptation to the change. Consider revisiting the one-on-one session questions provided in the Fear stage to help with these discussions.

Simulation Exercises: Activities that mimic real-life scenarios that employees might face after the implementation of new processes. Simulations use artificial settings or virtual environments to allow employees to practice behaviors and use new tools in a controlled and safe setting. If you are implementing a process or software change, look for ways to simulate the exact experiences, screens, or interactions that change participants will encounter.

Interactive Workshops: Engaging sessions that involve group activities, discussions, and hands-on practices related to the change. Workshops are designed to be participatory, encouraging active involvement from all attendees to explore new ideas, practice skills, and solve problems collaboratively. Again, it is best to partner with someone who is a professional in facilitating learning experiences to run these workshops.

Field Trips: Organized visits to sites where the new processes or behaviors have already been implemented successfully. Field trips allow participants to observe real-life applications of changes and gather insights from experiences outside their usual work environment.

Instructions for Facilitating Learning with a Case Study

Case studies can be very helpful in helping individuals impacted by a change learn how change has impacted others and how they can navigate and adapt to change successfully. Consider this model to facilitate learning of this type in the Near stage.

To facilitate learning through a case study in the Near stage, follow these steps:

1. **Select a Relevant Case Study**: Choose a case that closely mirrors the challenges and opportunities presented by the current change. The case should offer practical insights into similar transitions or implementations that the organization or its industry has faced. The case can be fully or mostly factual. Think "based on real-life events." You can use the case studies from this book, from your life, or from popular news and media. The best case studies are told as stories and are widely relatable. Think about how people connect to movies and television shows; these can be considered case studies in themselves! Look for examples within your industry or that relate specifically to the change you are facing, either directly or at a more strategic level. Well-aligned case studies prompt those studying them to draw direct connections from the example to the real-life scenario they are currently facing.

2. **Prepare Guided Questions**: Develop a set of questions that encourage critical thinking and relate directly to the key aspects of the change. These questions should help participants draw parallels between the case study and their own situations.

3. **Group Discussion**: Organize participants into small groups to discuss the case study. Encourage them to analyze the strategies used, the outcomes achieved, and any mistakes to avoid. Each group should identify actionable insights they can apply in their roles.

4. **Debrief and Share Insights**: Convene a larger session where each group shares their findings and discusses how these could influence their approach to the change. This helps consolidate learning and promotes a unified understanding of how to navigate similar challenges.

5. **Action Planning**: Ask participants to draft action plans based on lessons learned from the case study. These plans should

include specific steps they can take to contribute to the successful implementation of the change within their roles.

Using case studies in this way helps contextualize the change, offering a concrete example of successful navigation through similar challenges, thus reinforcing the learning and adaptation needed in the Near stage.

Field Trip Guide

When you take those impacted by the change on a field trip to experience the change in action, consider the preparation and facilitation of the field trip and how you will debrief afterward to reflect on the experience and glean insights that can be directly applied to the change you are working to facilitate.

The goal of the field trip is to provide team members with a firsthand experience of the post-change environment or process in action, followed by a debrief session to reflect on observations and discuss actionable insights.

Preparation for Field Trip:

1. **Selecting the Location:**

   - Choose a site where the change or new system or process has already been successfully implemented. It can be virtual or physical location or event.

   - Ensure the site visit will demonstrate clear benefits and operational improvements.

2. **Scheduling and Logistics:**

   - Coordinate transportation and timing.

- Schedule the visit during a time that minimizes disruption to your team's workflow.

- Collaborate with the host location to prepare them for your visit, specifying what aspects of the change you'd like to focus on.

3. **Pre-Visit Briefing:**

- Hold a briefing session to discuss the purpose of the visit and what team members should pay attention to. Let the team know that after the visit you will join together to debrief their experience and incorporate learnings from this field trip into the change you are experiencing.

- Distribute observation sheets or guidelines on what aspects to note, such as efficiency improvements, team interactions, or the use of technology. You can even make this fun by including a scavenger hunt in the field trip guides.

Be sure to encourage folks to note their questions, encouraging them that if they have a question, it's likely someone else will have a similar or the same question. When the field trip is concluded, gather the questions in a Q&A and consider creating a FAQ document to answer them for the impacted group.

Conducting the Field Trip:

- Encourage team members to ask questions and interact with their counterparts or representatives at the host site.

- Take notes and, if possible, capture video or photos (with permission) to use in the debrief session.

Post-Visit Debrief Session:

1. Organizing the Debrief:

- Schedule the session immediately after the field trip or within a day to ensure observations are fresh.

- Arrange a comfortable setting conducive to open discussion and reflection.

2. Discussion Points:

- What were the key observations?

- How do the observed practices align with or differ from current practices?

- What benefits or improvements were most noticeable?

- What challenges or obstacles were observed, and how were they managed?

- How might these observations be applied to our implementation?

- What questions did folks have along the way?

3. Actionable Insights:

- Identify specific practices or ideas observed during the visit that can be adopted or adapted.

- Assign team members or small groups to explore how these insights can be integrated into the ongoing change process.

- Consolidate questions folks had during the experience and generate answers.

4. **Feedback and Follow-Up:**

- Create and publish a FAQ document to address the questions and share the answers widely.å

- Gather feedback on the field trip and debrief experience to improve future excursions.

- Plan follow-up sessions to monitor the implementation of insights and continue the conversation as the change progresses.

Communications Template for Inviting People to the Field Trip

Use this template as a guide for writing the body text of the email you will send to invite people to the field trip. Be sure to include information about the field trip and reference the Hear stage checklist for this communication, as a field trip is a change in pace and routine in itself!

Subject: Join Us for a Field Trip!

Dear Team,

As part of our ongoing efforts to [describe the change, e.g., enhance our customer service platform], we have arranged a field trip to [Location], where this new system is already in action. This visit will allow us to see firsthand the improvements and efficiencies we are aiming for.

Date & Time: [Insert date and time]

Meeting Point: [Insert location]

Following our visit, we will hold a debrief session to discuss our observations and how we can integrate these learnings into our own processes. This is a great opportunity to get a clear picture of what to expect and contribute to how we manage our change.

Please RSVP by [Insert date] to secure your spot, as we have limited availability.

We look forward to an engaging and insightful day!

Best regards,

[Your Name]

[Your Position]

Change Implementation Announcement Template

Use this template to announce the implementation of the launch of a change. Whether it be a systems cutover or process change, the milestone must be marked so people officially know the change has happened, understand that they are to operate according to the change, and celebrate making it this far all together!

Subject: Introducing Our New [System/Technology] – A Milestone Achieved!

Email Body:

Hello Everyone,

I am pleased to share that we have successfully launched our new [System/Technology], a major step forward in enhancing our [describe the primary benefit, e.g., customer interaction, data management, etc.].

This advancement is a result of countless hours of hard work from teams across our organization, and it demonstrates our commitment to innovation and excellence. I want to thank each of you for your contributions, with special recognition to the [specific departments or teams] for leading this effort.

As we move forward, I encourage everyone to engage with the new system and explore its features. Training sessions and resources are available to help you get acquainted, and your feedback will be invaluable as we continue to refine and improve our processes.

Together, we are making [Company Name] a better place to work and setting new standards in our industry.

Onward and upward,

[Your Name]

[Your Title]

New Process or Tool Guide Template

Use this template to develop detailed guides that can help team members understand and adapt to new systems, software, or procedures introduced during the change. Present and distribute these guides before, during, and after training so people who are adapting to the change can use them as a reference and provide feedback about the guide. Once the change is solidified, store these guides in an easy-to-find location and use them to train future employees who need to understand the newly implemented process or tool.

Guide Structure:

- **Introduction**: Purpose of the new process/tool and its relevance to the change.

- **Step-by-Step Instructions**: Detailed steps on how to use the new process/tool.

- **FAQs**: Common questions and answers about the process/tool.

- **Troubleshooting**: Common issues and their solutions.

- **Contact Information**: Who to contact for further help or feedback.

Impact Dashboard Template

Use this template to build a dashboard that visually displays the key outcomes and metrics related to a change initiative to help stakeholders quickly assess performance and areas for improvement in the future.

Dashboard Structure:

- **Project Overview**: A brief description of the change initiative and its objectives.

- **Key Performance Indicators (KPIs)**:

    ◦ Employee Engagement Score

    ◦ Customer Satisfaction Level

    ◦ Operational Efficiency Improvements

    ◦ Financial Metrics (ROI, cost savings)

- **Data Visualization**:

    ◦ Graphs showing trends over time (pre- and post-change).

    ◦ Pie charts displaying satisfaction levels or adoption rates.

    ◦ Heat maps if geographical data is relevant.

- **Real-Time Updates**: Ensure the dashboard can fetch and display real-time data if applicable.

- **User Interaction**: Allow users to filter and drill down into specific data points for detailed analysis.

Example Tools for Creation:

- Microsoft Power BI

- Tableau

- Google Data Studio

In the Near Playbook, you've gathered essential tools for effectively implementing and monitoring the adoption change. This section has equipped you with resources from early adopter recognition to impact dashboards, enhancing your ability to observe and adjust the adoption of new practices. When you implement these tools, remember that the Near stage can feel daunting and incredibly slow. Keep moving forward and continue to help people in their learning, behavior change and adaptation to change. When done right, you'll soon get to the Cheer stage, where you can shift from implementing to celebrating these changes, ensuring that the momentum gained is carried forward.

CHAPTER 9

PLAYBOOK FOR CHEER

Congratulations! You have made it to the Cheer chapter of our playbook, where we celebrate the successful adoption of change and reinforce the positive outcomes of our efforts. In Cheer, we aim to cement the changes that have been implemented and acknowledge the hard work and dedication of everyone involved. In this chapter, you will learn how to effectively recognize and reward the contributions of others, create lasting impacts through celebration, and use success stories to inspire continued progress and adaptation. This chapter, like all that have come before it in the playbook, includes checklists, case studies, and practical resources to help you explore how to maintain the momentum of change and set the stage for future initiatives.

Cheer Stage Goal

The goal of the Cheer stage is to solidify and celebrate the successful implementation of change, ensuring it is fully integrated and sustained within the organization. This stage focuses on acknowledging achievements, embedding the change into the organizational culture, and leveraging the momentum for future improvements and innovations.

Cheer Stage Responsibilities

In the Cheer stage of change, the roles of individuals, leaders, and the company are integral in consolidating gains, celebrating successes, and preparing for future challenges.

Individuals: Reflect, Share, and Embrace

- Individuals are encouraged to reflect on their personal journey through the change process, share their experiences to foster a learning culture, and fully embrace and integrate the new changes into their daily routines, making the change part of the "new normal."

Leaders: Celebrate, Facilitate, and Sustain

- Leaders play a critical role by publicly acknowledging and celebrating team achievements, facilitating retrospectives to gather feedback and lessons learned, and maintaining the momentum of change by setting new goals. Leaders also need to monitor the ongoing success and impacts of the change to ensure its sustained effectiveness.

Company: Institutionalize, Recognize, and Support

- The company must work to fully institutionalize the change within the organization's culture and operational procedures, promote broad recognition and celebration of the change's success, and continue providing support and resources to ensure the changes are sustained. Additionally, the company should leverage the success of the current change as a springboard for future initiatives, demonstrating the organization's capacity for continuous adaptation and growth.

Communicating in Cheer

The Cheer stage is all about positive reinforcement for the change and keeping up the momentum as the change becomes integrated into daily routines. It is then that folks may look for the next thing to change. As you communicate with the people who have navigated the change in Cheer, be sure to do so in a way that celebrates success while paving the way for future initiatives.

Keep these guidelines in mind:

- **Celebrate Achievements and Recognize Efforts**: Use a variety of platforms, such as company newsletters, meetings, and social media, to celebrate milestones and individual contributions. Publicly acknowledging successes boosts morale and encourages continued engagement, but do not underestimate the value of a personal message thanking individuals for their contributions—a special note goes a long way!

- **Reinforce Positive Outcomes**: Provide detailed information on the benefits and improvements brought about by the change. Share specific data and anecdotes that demonstrate the positive impact on efficiency, satisfaction, or other targeted outcomes to reinforce the value of the new practices.

- **Encourage Ongoing Dialogue**: Maintain open channels for communication, inviting employees to share their experiences, any ongoing challenges they face, or even their ideas for the future. This continuous openness ensures that employees feel supported and valued, even after the initial goals have been achieved.

- **Project Forward-Looking Messages**: Communicate about upcoming opportunities that build on the success of the change. Discuss how the achievements can lead to further improvements and innovations, ensuring the organization remains dynamic and proactive, ready to adapt to further change.

The Cheer Stage Checklist

The Cheer Stage Checklist helps you celebrate achievements, reinforce changes, and sustain momentum. Use it to recognize contributions, communicate benefits, and prepare for future initiatives, ensuring that changes are deeply embedded and pave the way for continuous improvement. Set clear goals and timelines to maintain engagement and success.

☐ **Celebrate Achievements and Recognize Contributions**

    a. Organize events and communications to publicly celebrate the milestones and individual achievements that contributed to the change.

    b. Provide personalized acknowledgments and rewards that highlight specific contributions, enhancing a sense of accomplishment among team members.

☐ **Reinforce the Change**

    a. Regularly communicate the ongoing benefits and positive impacts of the change through various channels, ensuring all team members understand the value of their efforts.

    b. Create and distribute success stories and case studies that demonstrate the effectiveness of the new practices, solidifying the change as a permanent element of the organization.

☐ **Encourage Continuous Feedback and Dialogue**

    a. Maintain open channels for feedback to capture insights on the integration of the change and any ongoing challenges faced by team members.

b. Organize regular check-ins and feedback sessions to discuss how the change is affecting daily work and to identify areas that may require additional support.

☐ **Facilitate Reflection & Retrospectives**

a. Conduct retrospective meetings to review what went well during the change process and what could be improved, promoting a culture of continuous improvement.

b. Use insights from these sessions to plan and implement refinements to the change process, ensuring the organization is better prepared for future changes.

☐ **Sustain Momentum for Future Initiatives**

a. Use the success of the current change as a springboard to discuss and plan future initiatives, keeping the team engaged and looking forward.

b. Continue to provide training, resources, and support to ensure the organization is ready to embrace and drive upcoming changes effectively.

Case Study: Manufacturing Company Cheers for Sustainability

After working through the Hear, Fear, and Near stages, a manufacturing company had successfully implemented its "Green Horizon" initiative, aiming to significantly reduce its environmental footprint. As the company transitioned into the Cheer stage of this transformative change, the focus shifted to solidifying the gains, celebrating achievements, and leveraging the success for future initiatives.

To acknowledge their big accomplishment, the company organized a series of celebratory events to thank employees for their involvement and participation in the Green Horizon initiative. These events served as public acknowledgments of the team's hard work and dedication. The celebration was not just one point in time. Company leaders went beyond the present and began hosting annual sustainability conferences, inviting all employees and key stakeholders to participate. During this event, specific departments that excelled in implementing new processes, such as waste reduction and energy efficiency, were highlighted and celebrated.

The company also instituted a new annual award, the "Innovator of the Year," given to employees who made significant contributions to sustainability efforts. This recognition was not only about celebrating success but also about reinforcing the behaviors and practices that led to these achievements.

To ensure that sustainability efforts became a permanent aspect of the organizational culture, the company updated its training programs and internal policies to reflect the new sustainable practices. Workshops and training sessions were held regularly, keeping all employees up to date on the latest sustainable practices and how they could contribute on a daily basis. For new employees, a half-day of training activities was added to the existing onboarding program to ensure everyone was up to date on sustainability expectations and practices.

The company also incorporated sustainability into its core values and mission statement, embedding it deeply within the company culture. Success stories and testimonials from employees about the positive impact of Green Horizon were regularly featured in the company newsletter and on the intranet, serving as constant reminders of the initiative's benefits.

Company leaders did a great job implementing their change, including ensuring communication during the Cheer stage was strategically designed to maintain enthusiasm and commitment to the initiative. Company leadership continued the focus on sustainability and making the change stick by consistently providing updates on the initiative's progress and its positive impacts in all major communications. For example, during quarterly all-hands meetings, the CEO would discuss the ongoing benefits of Green Horizon, such as cost savings from energy efficiency and positive feedback from environmentally conscious customers.

With the solid foundation laid by the Green Horizon initiative, the company began planning future sustainability-related projects, looking to expand the work that was done during the Green Horizon change. The success of the initiative was used as a springboard to launch additional green projects, such as expanding into renewable energy products, which grew the company's product line and revenue. The company also organized innovation brainstorming sessions, encouraging employees to come up with new ideas that could further enhance sustainability.

The Cheer stage for this company was characterized by a robust celebration of past successes, a strong emphasis on integrating these successes into the company's ongoing operations, and a clear focus on leveraging this momentum for future innovations. By effectively employing strategies from the Cheer stage checklist, the company not only consolidated its gains from the Green Horizon initiative but also set the stage for continued growth and improvement, reinforcing its position as a leader in sustainable manufacturing.

Change Cheat Code Error: Cheer

Melissa Jennings, the Director of Project Management at ByteScale Inc., was the driving force behind the adoption of a new agile project management system involving specific timelines and iterative development methodologies. Melissa was certain that this shift from the traditional waterfall method would bring about faster project turnovers and better teamwork across the company. As the initial implementation phase concluded, she saw positive metrics that seemed to validate her expectations. Eager to mark this success, Melissa planned an elaborate celebration event.

At the grand event, the air was filled with a festive buzz as Melissa presented the successes—highlighting improved efficiency and faster project deliveries. The room was adorned with banners displaying impressive metrics and future tech upgrades enabled by the new agile approach to development. At the event, Melissa's speech was filled with figures and projections, praising the agile system's capabilities and outlining ambitious future projects.

However, the celebration overlooked the individual contributions of the team members who had worked tirelessly to adapt to the agile method. Developers who had put in extra hours, project managers who had innovatively restructured their teams, and QA specialists who had swiftly adjusted to new demands—none received the acknowledgment they had hoped for. The focus remained on the abstract success of the system rather than on the human efforts that made it all possible.

After the celebration, Melissa quickly moved on to other initiatives, assuming the agile transition was complete. No further training sessions were planned, nor were there any follow-up meetings to address ongoing challenges. Feedback from employees suggested a disconnect between management's declaration of success and the everyday reality of still adjusting to agile practices. Unfortunately, this feedback went unnoticed as Melissa was already engrossed in new strategic plans.

Gradually, without ongoing support or recognition, teams started slipping back into their old habits. The once vibrant stand-up meetings turned into routine status updates, and the agile tools for defining, planning, documenting, and tracking development were slowly abandoned. The lack of acknowledgment and perceived indifference from leadership led to a significant dip in morale, particularly among those who had been most engaged.

The team had fallen back into their old way of working. Eventually, project timelines began to suffer, the quality of deliverables declined, and the company undertook an external review. It revealed that the failure of the agile system at ByteScale wasn't due to its incompatibility with the company's needs but rather due to the poor handling of the Cheer stage. Melissa was left to reflect on the oversight, realizing too late that the celebration of change isn't just about acknowledging the initiation but involves sustaining and nurturing the change continuously, valuing and recognizing the people behind the transformation.

Melissa's experience highlights a poignant lesson in change management—celebrating a change effectively involves much more than a one-time event; it requires an ongoing commitment to the people and processes involved. The celebration of Melissa's team's shift to agile methodologies lacked a meaningful acknowledgment of individual contributions, focusing instead on broad systemic changes. This oversight diminished morale, as team members felt their personal efforts were overlooked. Furthermore, the initial enthusiasm waned due to a lack of ongoing support and training, which was crucial for embedding the new practices into daily routines. Feedback channels were absent, preventing Melissa from capturing essential insights into employee experiences and challenges with the new system. This lack of continuous engagement led to inconsistencies in applying the agile methods, undermining the long-term sustainability of the change.

To remedy these missteps, Melissa could have instituted a program for continuous recognition, celebrating individual and team milestones regularly to maintain high morale. Regular training and review sessions would have helped reinforce the new methodologies, smoothing over any practical difficulties. Establishing open lines for feedback would allow for real-time adjustments and show a genuine commitment to employee input, ensuring that the transition to an agile way of working was not only adopted but also effectively integrated into the company's culture. These strategies would likely have prevented the premature declaration of success and provided a more accurate measure of the initiative's impact, fostering a truly transformative change at ByteScale. In the next section, we'll show you a few of our favorite tools and templates for the Cheer stage.

Example Resources for Cheer

To complete the Cheer Playbook chapter, we offer a suite of example resources that focus on celebrating and sustaining the achievements of your change efforts. From planning celebratory events to conducting retrospective meetings, these tools help to ensure that the positive impacts of change are recognized and reinforced. They also provide strategies to keep your team motivated and prepared for continuous improvement and future initiatives.

Ideas for Celebration

Consider using ideas from this list for different types of events or activities you could do with a group in the Cheer stage to acknowledge success and celebrate with the team.

1. **Throw a Themed Party**: Organize a celebration with a fun theme that resonates with your team. Themes like "Retro Night," "Hawaiian Luau," or "Hollywood Glamour" can make the event memorable and enjoyable. In the summer of 2017, a team of ours threw a party-themed "The Summer of Sunsets" to celebrate the removal (often called a sunset) of a particular piece of technology from our product offerings. This party included signature cocktails, a shaved ice station, and Hawaiian-themed décor—so fun!

2. **Personalized Awards Ceremony**: Host an awards ceremony where employees receive personalized awards. Categories can include "Most Innovative," "Team Player," and "Customer Service Star."

3. **Team Outing or Retreat**: Plan a day out or a retreat. Activities like escape rooms, adventure parks, or a relaxing day at a spa can be great for team bonding. If your organizational culture supports it, plan to follow these events with a happy hour or other relaxing activity so the team can bond over their shared experience.

4. **Office Makeover**: Give the office a temporary makeover to reflect the celebration. Decorations, banners, and balloons can create a festive atmosphere.

5. **Catered Lunch or Dinner**: Bring in a catering service to provide a special lunch or dinner. Including favorite foods and a variety of options can make everyone feel appreciated.

6. **Personalized Gifts**: Give employees personalized gifts that show you know and appreciate their individual contributions. Custom notebooks, trophies, engraved pens, or personalized mugs can be thoughtful and practical.

7. **Extra Day Off**: Reward employees with an extra day off to rest and recharge. This gesture shows that you value their hard work and well-being. Do not dictate when this is to be taken by the recipient. Instead, work with the employee and their manager to allow the extra time to be taken at a time that serves the employee best.

8. **Professional Development Opportunities**: Offer opportunities for further professional development. This could be in the form of workshops, online courses, or conferences relevant to their field. Make it clear the company is investing in its employees.

9. **Public Recognition**: Acknowledge the milestone in a public forum. This could be during a company meeting, in a newsletter, or on the company's social media platforms. Continue reading this playbook chapter for templates and ideas for public recognition.

10. **Charity Donation**: Make a donation to a charity chosen by the team or the individual employee being celebrated. This can add a meaningful aspect to the celebration.

11. **Experience Gifts**: Give experience-based gifts such as tickets to a concert, a sporting event, or a theatre show. Experiences can be more memorable than physical gifts.

12. **Customized Company Swag**: Create special edition company swag to commemorate the milestone. T-shirts, hoodies, or tote bags with the milestone and company logo can serve as a lasting reminder of the achievement.

13. **Video Montage**: Create a video montage highlighting the team's journey to the milestone. Include messages from leadership and colleagues, photos, and memorable moments. You could even consider making a publicly shareable version to promote your team's accomplishments on LinkedIn or other social media platforms.

A note on bonuses: You may have noticed bonuses are missing from this list, and that's because, while valuable, they do not mark the occasion publicly or as a group. We suggest using bonuses sparingly but do keep them in mind if an individual or small team accomplishes a heroic feat that required time and energy beyond their typical contribution.

Announcement Templates

Use these templates to announce team and organizational achievements. When using these templates and announcing achievements, consider the organizational context, audience, and scale of the achievement relative to other achievements the team has celebrated publicly. Be sure the achievement is of great importance to the group to which you plan to send the message. Also, consider individual preferences for public recognition as not everyone appreciates having attention drawn to them, even if it is positive. When in doubt about this, just ask the person or group that accomplished the achievement how they wish to be celebrated; they will typically tell you exactly what will help them feel celebrated while also marking the milestone.

Subject: A Remarkable Achievement – [Goal/Milestone] Reached!

Email Body:

Dear [Company Name] Team,

Today, I am thrilled to announce that we have reached [describe the goal or milestone], a goal we set out to achieve earlier this year. This achievement reflects our collective effort and the dynamic spirit of our company.

This success impacts not only our current projects but also opens new doors for future opportunities. It is a testament to what we can accomplish together and a reason to look forward with excitement to what we can achieve next.

Let's take a moment to appreciate our hard work and the positive outcomes we've created. Celebrate this success with your teams, and let's use this energy to propel us into the next challenge.

Thank you for your outstanding contributions and for pushing the boundaries of what we can achieve.

With gratitude,

[Your Name]

[Your Title]

[Company Name]

Subject: Celebrating Success: [Project Name] Completion

Email Body:

Dear Team,

I'm excited to announce the successful completion of our [Project Name]! This marks a significant milestone in our journey towards [briefly describe the objective of the project].

Thanks to your hard work and dedication, we've achieved [highlight key outcomes]. This project not only improves our [mention the specific area, e.g., operational efficiency, customer service, etc.] but also positions us strongly for future challenges.

I would like to extend my personal thanks to everyone involved, especially [mention any specific teams or individuals who played a key role]. Your commitment has made this possible.

Let's keep this momentum going as we tackle new challenges and continue to drive our company forward.

Thank you for your continued dedication and hard work!

Best regards,

[Your Name]

[Your Title]

[Company Name]

Newsletter Highlight Template

Use this template to write a success story about a specific department or change.

Title: Spotlight Success: How [Department/Team] Overcame Challenges

Introduction: Join us as we explore the success journey of [Department/Team], who have effectively implemented significant changes and achieved remarkable outcomes.

Content Structure:

The Challenge: What were the initial obstacles?

The Strategy: What changes were made?

The Success: What has been achieved?

Voices from the Team: Insights and quotes from the members.

Takeaways: Tips and advice for others.

Conclusion: This story is a testament to our adaptability and teamwork. Got a story of your own? Share it with us and inspire others!

Individual Recognition Template

Use this template to recognize an individual's great work in implementing or adapting to change. When writing an individual recognition, consider your relationship to the individual and how they may perceive you in your role. For example, would it be most effective for the CEO to send an email to an individual contributor employee that they have never met before? Would it feel forced? Is there another leader closer to the employee who might have a greater, more genuine, and long-lasting positive impact when sharing praise? Avoid asking leaders above you to send thank you notes or individual recognition to your employees. Do what feels right, and don't force it.

To: Outstanding Employee, with a CC to their Manager and/ or Department Head

Subject: A Special Thanks to [Employee Name] – Outstanding Contribution!

Email Body:

Hi [Employee Name],

I want to take a moment to personally thank you for your exceptional work during our recent [mention specific project or change initiative]. Your expertise and unwavering commitment have made a significant difference.

It's team members like you who embody our values and drive us forward. Your contributions have not only helped us achieve our goals but have also inspired your colleagues to strive for excellence.

Please accept my deepest appreciation for your hard work and dedication. Let's continue to reach new heights together!

Best regards,

[Your Name]

[Your Position]

Team Recognition Template

Use this template to recognize a team's great work in implementing or adapting to change. Similarly to individual recognition, consider your relationship to the team you are planning to recognize and how they perceive you in your role. When recognizing a team, it is more common for a higher-level leader to acknowledge a group. However, there should often be a direct line of reporting or a direct line of impact between the leader and the team they are recognizing. Again, in this case, do what feels right and don't force it.

To: The Team adapting to the change, with a CC to their Manager and/or Department Heads

Subject: Celebrating Our Success and Looking Forward

Email Body:

Dear Team,

As we mark the successful completion of [describe the change or project], I want to express my heartfelt gratitude to each of you. This success is a direct result of the collective effort and spirit of collaboration that defines our team.

Looking ahead, we have many exciting opportunities to build on this momentum. Our success with [mention the project or change] has opened new avenues for growth and innovation that we will explore together.

Thank you for your dedication and hard work. Here's to continued success and new adventures!

Cheers,

[Your Name]

[Your Position]

Celebratory Event Guide

Use this guide to help plan and execute your next change milestone celebration. Consider the scale of the change relative to the celebration. Big change accomplishments may call for big celebrations, but smaller milestones may call for smaller events. Consider what others celebrate in your organizational environment and take cues from historical events, big and small.

Pre-Event Planning:

- Determine the purpose of the event (e.g., celebrating a successful project completion).

- Set a date, time, and location (consider virtual options if necessary).

- Create a budget for the event (including costs for venue, catering, technology, etc.).

- Develop an agenda that includes speeches, recognitions, and entertainment.

- Select speakers and prepare them with topics and guidelines.

- Send out invitations and manage RSVPs.

- Arrange catering and accommodations for special diets.

- Organize technical support for sound, lighting, and virtual participation.

- Plan decor and branding materials (posters, banners, etc.).

During the Event:

- Set up the venue and check all technical equipment.

- Provide name tags and welcome packets if necessary.

- Coordinate with speakers and entertainers on the schedule.

- Capture the event through photography or videography.

Post-Event:

- Send thank-you notes to attendees, speakers, and vendors.

- Gather feedback from participants to improve future events.

- Share highlights and photos from the event on company internal channels.

Celebratory Video Guide

Use this guide to create a video to share the success of a change initiative. A video can be a very personal way to thank an individual or a group, and it can also be very easy! If you can take a picture with your phone or record a meeting on your computer, you can make a video. Consider the message of the video before beginning your recording. Alternatively, you could also make a video to represent the change itself and document how far the team has gone. Do you

308 · THE CHANGE CHEAT CODE

have pictures from the field trips you took in the Near stage? This is a perfect place to showcase them and celebrate how far the team has come.

Planning Your Video:

- Define the purpose of the video (e.g., highlighting achievements, thanking the team).

- Identify key messages and themes to include.

- Choose participants for testimonials (diverse representation of the team).

- Write a script or outline major talking points.

Shooting the Video:

- Decide on locations (inside the office, where the change took place, etc.).

- Schedule shooting times with all participants.

- Use quality recording equipment to ensure clear audio and visuals.

- Capture additional footage (b-roll) of the workplace, events, and daily activities to enhance the video (optional).

Editing the Video:

- Use editing software that you or someone in your organization is familiar with.

- Include engaging visuals, company branding, and background music.

- Edit testimonials to focus on impactful statements.

- Add titles, transitions, and captions where necessary.

Distributing the Video:

- Share the video during company meetings or special events.

- Distribute via email, company intranet, or social media.

- Consider making a public version for external stakeholders if appropriate.

Feedback Survey Template

Use this template to invite people to participate in a survey to provide feedback about the change. Keep it simple, but always include a deadline to drive urgency in giving feedback.

Introduction: Help us keep improving! Please share your thoughts on the recent changes through this quick survey. Your input is valuable as we continue refining our approach.

Survey Link: [Insert Link]

Deadline: [Insert Deadline]

Sample Questions:

- How well are the new changes working out for you?

- What do you like best about the new processes?

- What challenges have you encountered?

- Any suggestions for improvement?

- Do you need more support or training in any areas?

Invitation to Retrospective or Feedback Meeting

Use this template to invite people to participate in a live session to provide or review previously provided feedback about the change. Help people understand what the session will contain and how they can best engage.

Subject: Join Us for a Post-Implementation Review Meeting

Body: Hi Team,

To ensure we continue to improve and build on our recent changes, we invite you to a Post-Change Implementation Review Meeting. Your insights and feedback are invaluable as we assess our progress and plan our next steps.

Meeting Details:

Date: [Insert Date]

Time: [Insert Time]

Location: [Insert Location or Virtual Meeting Link]

Agenda:

- Review of the change implementation
- Discussion of successes and challenges
- Brainstorming session for future improvements
- Open floor for feedback

Please prepare any thoughts or feedback you might have on the recent changes; we will have an opportunity for everyone to share their feedback and experience adapting to this change.

See you there!

Best,

[Your Name]

Retrospectives Meeting Agenda Template

Use this template to facilitate a discussion on the process and outcome of the change with the intent to improve future changes. To enhance objectivity during feedback sessions, consider having an external facilitator lead the discussion. This helps minimize any potential bias or defensiveness that might arise if the change leader conducts the session. Ensure all meeting notes, particularly action plans and lessons learned, are thoroughly documented. Securely store these documents for future reference to demonstrate a commitment to learning and improvement, reinforcing the value and seriousness of the feedback received.

Objective: To evaluate the outcomes of the recent change, gather feedback, and identify actionable steps for future improvements.

1. **Opening Remarks (5 minutes)**

   - Welcome and introductions by the meeting facilitator.

   - Brief overview of the meeting's purpose and objectives.

2. **Review of Change Objectives (10 minutes)**

   - Recap the goals and expectations set before implementing the change.

   - Presenter: Project Leader or Change Manager.

3. **Presentation of Outcomes (15 minutes)**

   - Presentation of key outcomes, successes, and challenges faced during the change process.

   - Data and examples should be shared to illustrate points.

- Presenter: Data Analyst or Project Team Member.

4. Group Discussion: Experiences and Observations (20 minutes)

- Open floor for team members to share their personal experiences and observations.

- Discussion guided by the following questions:

  o What worked well during this change?

  o What challenges did you encounter?

  o How did the change impact your daily work?

5. Identification of Areas for Improvement (20 minutes)

- Group brainstorming session to identify areas needing improvement.

- Discussion guided by questions:

  o What could have been done differently?

  o What lessons have we learned for future changes?

- Participants encouraged to provide constructive feedback and suggestions.

6. Planning for Action (15 minutes)

- Discuss and decide on the next steps to address the identified areas for improvement.

- Assign responsibilities for action items to specific team members.

- Set deadlines and milestones for follow-up and review.

7. **Closing Remarks (5 minutes)**

- Summary of the key points and actions agreed upon during the meeting.

- Thank everyone for their contributions.

- Outline the schedule for follow-up or the next meeting.

8. **Feedback on the Meeting (5 minutes)**

- Quick round of feedback on the meeting's format and discussion.

- Suggestions for improving future retrospective meetings.

Additional Notes:

- Ensure that the meeting is conducted in an open and respectful manner, where all participants feel valued and heard.

- Consider using tools such as whiteboards, sticky notes, or digital collaboration platforms for brainstorming and voting on ideas.

- If the meeting is conducted remotely, ensure all participants have access to necessary technology and encourage the use of cameras to maintain engagement.

As we conclude the Cheer Playbook chapter and wrap up our playbook, we celebrate the culmination of your journey through mastering the art of managing change. This chapter has equipped you with the tools to not only celebrate and solidify the successes of change initiatives but also to ensure these changes are deeply integrated into your organization's culture. By using the strategies, templates, and resources provided, you are now fully equipped to maintain the momentum and set the stage for continuous improvement and future initiatives.

Looking forward to Chapter 10, we shift our focus from celebration to continuous improvement. This next chapter will guide you through maintaining the momentum of current successes and leveraging them as a foundation for ongoing and future changes. You'll learn strategies to ensure that change is not a one-time event but a continuous opportunity for growth and innovation.

CHAPTER 10

CONTINUING YOUR CHANGE JOURNEY

Congratulations on reaching the final chapter of your journey through change management. This section is not just a summary but a forward-looking guide designed to prepare you for the ongoing journey of leading and adapting to change. As you step forward, equipped with the knowledge and strategies we've discussed, this chapter aims to reinforce your ability to apply these lessons to continuous personal and professional evolution. Here, we will examine the dynamic nature of change, emphasizing that the journey doesn't end here but rather shifts towards a sustained practice of growth and adaptation.

Over the course of this book, you have explored the four stages of change— Hear, Fear, Near, and Cheer—each providing you with a roadmap for navigating the exciting and sometimes tumultuous process of change. You've delved into real-life examples, analyzed both successful and unsuccessful change initiatives, and gained practical tools and strategies to apply in your own life and organization. By now, you should feel well-equipped to recognize where you or your team are within the change curve, anticipate the challenges that each stage brings, and implement the necessary actions to move forward effectively. You've learned that while managing change is challenging, it is also a skill that can be honed with thoughtful preparation, continuous reflection, and a willingness to adapt.

Our final exploration begins with the story of John, an individual who stands at a significant crossroads, faced with the opportunity to fundamentally alter his career path by moving internationally. John's decision-making process and subsequent actions provide a rich, real-world example of the complexities involved in embracing substantial change. Through his narrative, we'll highlight essential skills and mindsets that facilitate successful navigation through change—not just surviving but thriving in new environments and roles. As we delve into John's experiences, consider how the principles of effective change management can be applied universally, ensuring that you're not only ready for what's next but also proactive in shaping your future.

As John reviewed his work and life leading into his 28th year, he decided that if he was going to make a large change, now was the time to do it. John was successful at his company, working for three years under the same leader in the HR department as an HR Business Partner. Just two weeks after having the initial thought of embracing a big change, John's company announced a position opening for a Senior Business Partner in London, England. John had an initial spark of excitement reading the internal job posting and imagining the idea of living in a bustling city in another country "over the pond."

Just as fast as John lit up with excitement, his worries set in. John had always been close to his family and friends, living within blocks of his childhood friends his whole life in the Pacific Northwest of America. He had never left America and did not have many acquaintances from other countries. Nonetheless, John's thoughts kept rotating back to the excitement of travel, new friends, and a promotion. He was justifying how easy it would be to live in London since they speak English and he would still be in the same company and even in the same department. Worry turned to action when

John approached his leader about the possibility of applying for the position.

With the cat out of the bag and the discussion beginning, John's leader brought new information to the situation, sharing that in order to move forward with this change, John would have to obtain permission for a country transfer (which had never been granted), as the company would incur the cost of an attorney for a work visa, and his pay would need to be calibrated to the London employment market. John, faced with these new challenges, asked his leader for advice on whether it would be a good idea to apply. John trusted his leader and was confident her advice would be coming from a place of care and wisdom since she herself had been an expat in multiple countries. John's leader stated that she needed a bit more time to answer the question, but that she would review the cost of a work visa, the pay calibration, and senior leadership's appetite for such a request. John and his leader agreed to meet the following week to discuss the situation.

In the week between dreaming of moving to London and when he was scheduled to meet with his leader again, John had an enormous range of emotions. He was excited about the possibility of moving to London, traveling around Europe on weekends and holidays, and gaining international experience. He also lamented the possibility of only seeing his family one or two times a year and missing key milestones such as family celebrations. He wondered how he would return to the US should the job or transfer not be what he expected. Would he have to quit his job and start over again?

When John and his leader sat down for their discussion, John found a calm and balanced release of information from his leader. She stated that the cost of a work visa would not be prohibitory and would likely be offset by having someone familiar with the company and the US policies in London. In fact, the leader saw a

US staff moving to London as an advantage for the company as many London staff saw the US executives as a bit tone-deaf to the needs of the London staff. Additionally, the pay change for the new position would be an increase that would be enough to provide a good income for the area. She also explained in detail how difficult it is to live away from family and friends, plus the complete change in environment. Even though the population would speak English, there would be little common ground to start. Besides driving on the other side of the street, the city itself would be challenging to someone who had never lived in a metropolis. The leader ended the meeting by encouraging John to think about the decision and said that if he chose to apply, the leader would support the request.

To say John agonized over the decision would be an understatement. He went back and forth with benefits and drawbacks, searched for apartments in London, and talked to friends and family. At the end of the day, he decided to move forward with the application.

Fast forward to John receiving a job offer for the promotion to the position in London. With excitement and terror, John accepted the position and began to plan his move. He agreed on a date to move, negotiated a planning trip to London to apartment shop, and signed his paperwork for the work visa. All was in motion, and there was no changing his mind. The day for the planning trip grew closer, and John was by now a digital maps expert, having poured over every street, apartment building, gym, and grocery store within a reasonable distance of the company office. By the time he was on his way to London for the planning trip, he felt confident in his knowledge and decision.

Just as things seemed to feel right, the planning trip sent John backward in emotion. He lost three apartments he wanted to someone else, found navigating the public transportation system harder than he imagined, and realized there were many cultural differences between the US and the UK. He left London without an apartment, feeling desperate about his decision and questioning his own decision. Of course, when he arrived home, everyone wanted to hear all about his trip and see pictures of his new apartment. He felt like crawling under a rock and not speaking to anyone.

Two days after he arrived home, the consultant who was helping him find an apartment called with good news. One of the apartments he originally wanted was available due to the renter being transferred to another location. His luck had changed! He took the apartment and began moving on to deciding what to take with him to London. He agonized over every item he packed. He had two months to get ready, train his replacement at work, and say his goodbyes to friends and family. He was focused on his checklist of things to do and was making good progress. He also got connected with expats in London who would be living close to his apartment and started to make plans to meet. He would start off with at least acquaintances in London, hopefully soon-to-be friends.

If you had dropped in on John six months after his move, you would never know he initially doubted his decision. He has a robust friend group, has won accolades at work for his ability to bridge the two teams, and has traveled extensively around Europe. As with all change, there were ups and downs. Simple things were tough in the beginning, but he acclimated. The first week, it was soul-crushing to almost be hit by a car because he looked the wrong way before crossing the street. He would go to the grocery store and ask for simple things, like eggplant or arugula salad, only to find out they were called aubergine and rocket salad locally. Still, John adjusted. In fact, he started celebrating everything he had learned and the opportunities in front of him.

John's leader met with him at month seven of his time in London. She asked, "What did you learn, and how is it going?" John was quick to point out that it was the best decision he had ever made. He had learned and is learning so much. In fact, he felt he had grown as a person and would embrace the next change with greater ease. He recounted all the mistakes he made in the first few months, laughed about what he did not know, and gushed over the world he could now see in front of him. John's leader beamed with joy; she acknowledged that it was not easy to make that big of a change and that many people gave up at various times. She told John she was impressed by his ability to adjust and, in fact, let him know they were considering making him a director of HR for European operations. What an accomplishment!

As you read this last example, could you put yourself in John's shoes? Did you mentally note which stage of change he was in? Did you feel him slide from Fear to Near and back to Fear again? If so, then you have internalized the four stages of change, understand the path of change is not linear, and are ready to apply what you have learned.

One of the most powerful lessons from this book is the importance of not only understanding these stages yourself but also teaching others how to navigate them. Change is a collective experience, and the more you share these concepts with those around you, the more you will empower them—and yourself—to face change with confidence. Whether you're guiding your team through a corporate restructuring, helping a friend through a personal transition, or embarking on a new chapter in your own life, these stages offer a reliable framework to make sense of the process and emerge stronger on the other side.

For your quick reference, here are the four stages of change, along with tips to identify and navigate them:

POSITIVE

SENTIMENT

Cheer

Hear

Near

Fear

NEGATIVE

TIME

Figure 10.1: The Change Cheat Code Model

Hear Stage	
Identification:	This stage is about communication and preparation. It's when change is announced and explained.
Key Characteristics:	Initial announcements, broad communication, setting the stage.

Tips for Navigation:

- Ensure correct order of operations and clarity in messaging to avoid misconceptions.
- Use multiple channels to disseminate information, ensuring everyone is informed.
- Provide ample opportunity for questions and feedback to gauge understanding and concerns.

Fear Stage

Identification:	Recognized by emotional responses and potential resistance to change.
Key Characteristics:	Heightened emotions, uncertainty, and possible pushback.

Tips for Navigation:

- Acknowledge fears and concerns openly and empathetically.
- Facilitate forums for discussion to allow individuals to voice their anxieties.
- Provide clear, consistent information to combat misinformation and build trust

Near Stage

Identification:	This stage involves the practical application and gradual acceptance of change
Key Characteristics:	Initial implementation, troubleshooting, and adjustment.

Tips for Navigation:

- Encourage hands-on interaction with new processes or systems to build familiarity.
- Organize training sessions and provide resources to support adaptation.
- Monitor progress closely and make adjustments as necessary to ensure alignment with goals

Cheer Stage	
Identification:	Marked by the successful integration of change and celebration of milestones.
Key Characteristics:	Achievement of goals, recognition of efforts, and positive reinforcement.

Tips for Navigation:

- Celebrate successes and milestones to boost morale and reinforce the benefits of change.
- Use success stories as examples to motivate ongoing adaptation.
- Prepare for future changes by leveraging the momentum gained.

As you apply the change cheat code model to your current and future changes, remember it is completely normal for mistakes to happen along the way, and that's okay. Every change initiative, whether successful or not, is an opportunity to learn and improve. Reflect on what worked, what didn't, and how you can apply those lessons to future changes. In doing so, you not only build your own resilience but also contribute to a culture of continuous learning and growth within your organization.

As the Greek philosopher Heraclitus famously said, "Change is the only constant in life." This timeless wisdom should inspire you to embrace change not just as an inevitable occurrence but as an opportunity for growth and innovation. Your journey through change has been ongoing, but today, you have new tools to navigate it better than ever before. As you journey on, embrace the uncertainty, celebrate the milestones, and, most importantly, keep this model close at hand as you navigate future changes. By doing so, you'll find that you are not just surviving change—you are mastering it.

Thank you for taking this journey with us. Now, go forth and lead change with confidence and clarity. The more you practice and share these insights, the more adept you will become at guiding yourself and others through the inevitable changes that life and work will continue to bring.

BRING THE CHANGE CHEAT CODE TRAINING TO YOUR TEAM

If the strategies and insights in this book have sparked your interest and you're looking to implement these approaches within your organization, we can help bring this content directly to you. Our tailored training sessions are designed to equip your team with the necessary tools and skills to effectively manage and facilitate change.

By hosting a custom workshop at your company, your team will gain hands-on experience from experts in the field, ensuring that everyone is prepared to tackle upcoming changes with confidence and precision. Whether you're about to embark on a significant transformation or want to improve your ongoing change management processes, our training is customized to meet your specific needs and challenges.

To explore how we can help you and your team excel in change management, please visit us at thechangecheatcode.com and contact us today. We look forward to helping you turn these principles into action and achieve success in your change initiatives!

www.ingramcontent.com/pod-product-compliance
Lightning Source LLC
Chambersburg PA
CBHW071325210326
41597CB00015B/1348